THEORIZING RELATIONS IN INDIGENOUS SOUTH AMERICA

Studies in Social Analysis

Editors: Judith Bovensiepen, *University of Kent*
Martin Holbraad, *University College London*
Hans Steinmüller, *London School of Economics*

Focusing on analysis as a meeting ground of the empirical and the conceptual, this series provides a platform for exploring anthropological approaches to social analysis while seeking to open new avenues of communication between anthropology and the humanities, as well as other social sciences.

Volume 1
Being Godless: Ethnographies of Atheism and Non-Religion
Edited by Ruy Llera Blanes and
Galina Oustinova-Stjepanovic

Volume 2
Emptiness and Fullness: Ethnographies of Lack and Desire in Contemporary China
Edited by Susanne Bregnbæk and
Mikkel Bunkenborg

Volume 3
Straying from the Straight Path: How Senses of Failure Invigorate Lived Religion
Edited by Daan Beekers and
David Kloos

Volume 4
Stategraphy: Toward a Relational Anthropology of the State
Edited by Tatjana Thelen, Larissa Vetters, and Keebet von Benda-Beckmann

Volume 5
Affective States: Entanglements, Suspensions, Suspicions
Edited by Mateusz Laszczkowski and
Madeleine Reeves

Volume 6
Animism beyond the Soul: Ontology, Reflexivity, and the Making of Anthropological Knowledge
Edited by Katherine Swancutt and
Mireille Mazard

Volume 7
Hierarchy and Value: Comparative Perspectives on Moral Order
Edited by Jason Hickel and
Naomi Haynes

Volume 8
Post-Ottoman Topologies: The Presence of the Past in the Era of the Nation-State
Edited by Nicolas Argenti

Volume 9
Multiple Nature-Cultures, Diverse Anthropologies
Edited by Casper Bruun Jensen
and Atsuro Morita

Volume 10
Money Counts: Revisiting Economic Calculation
Edited by Mario Schmidt and
Sandy Ross

Volume 11
States of Imitation: Mimetic Governmentality and Colonial Rule
Edited by Patrice Ladwig and
Ricardo Roque

Volume 12
Matsutake Worlds
Edited by Lieba Faier and Michael J. Hathaway

Volume 13
Theorizing Relations in Indigenous South America
Edited by Marcelo González Gálvez, Piergiorgio Di Giminiani, and Giovanna Bacchiddu

THEORIZING RELATIONS IN INDIGENOUS SOUTH AMERICA

Edited by

Marcelo González Gálvez, Piergiorgio Di Giminiani, and Giovanna Bacchiddu

berghahn
NEW YORK · OXFORD
www.berghahnbooks.com

Published in 2022 by

Berghahn Books

www.berghahnbooks.com

© 2022 Berghahn Books

Originally published as a special issue of *Social Analysis*, volume 63, issue 2.

Library of Congress Cataloging-in-Publication Data

Names: González Gálvez, Marcelo, editor. | Di Giminiani, Piergiorgio,
    editor. | Bacchiddu, Giovanna, editor.
Title: Theorizing relations in indigenous South America / edited by Marcelo
    González Gálvez, Piergiorgio Di Giminiani, and Giovanna Bacchiddu.
Description: New York : Berghahn Books, 2022. | Series: Studies in social
    analysis ; volume 13 | "Originally published as a special issue of
    Social Analysis, volume 63, issue 2." | Includes bibliographical
    references and index.
Identifiers: LCCN 2022007659 (print) | LCCN 2022007660 (ebook) | ISBN
    9781800733299 (hardback) | ISBN 9781800733305 (paperback) | ISBN
    9781800733312 (ebook)
Subjects: LCSH: Indians of South America—Social life and customs. |
    Indians of South America—Kinship. | Ethnology—South America. | South
    America—Social life and customs. | South America—Colonial influence.
Classification: LCC F2229 .T51 2022 (print) | LCC F2229 (ebook) | DDC
    980—dc23/eng/20220310
LC record available at https://lccn.loc.gov/2022007659
LC ebook record available at https://lccn.loc.gov/2022007660

British Library Cataloguing in Publication Data

A catalogue record for this book is available from the British Library

ISBN 978-1-80073-329-9 hardback
ISBN 978-1-80073-330-5 paperback
ISBN 978-1-80073-331-2 ebook
https://doi.org/10.3167/9781800733299

CONTENTS

List of Illustrations   vii

Introduction
Theorizing Relations in Indigenous South America   1
    Marcelo González Gálvez, Piergiorgio Di Giminiani,
    and Giovanna Bacchiddu

Chapter 1
Learning to See in Western Amazonia: How Does Form Reveal Relation?   26
    Els Lagrou

Chapter 2
Looks Like Viscera: Folds, Wraps, and Relations in the Southern Andes   47
    Francisco Pazzarelli

Chapter 3
On People, Sensorial Perception, and Potential Affinity in Southern Chile 68
    Cristóbal Bonelli

Chapter 4
Sorcery, Revenge, and Anti-Revenge: Relational Excess and Individuation
    in the Gran Chaco   83
    Florencia Tola

Chapter 5
The Name of the Relation: Making a Difference in Aweti Onomastics   104
    Marina Vanzolini

Chapter 6
Ritualizing the Everyday: The Dangerous Imperative of Hospitality in
    Apiao, Chiloé   124
    Giovanna Bacchiddu

Afterword
Relations and Relatives   145
    Aparecida Vilaça

Coda
Reflecting Back   153
    Marilyn Strathern

Epilogue
Cemeteries as Metaphors of Who We Are   162
    Claudio Millacura Salas

Index   173

ILLUSTRATIONS

1.1   Baby's carrying bag   31

2.1   *Corral* of guts. Huachichocana, August 2018   48

4.1   Kin relations imbricated in the aforementioned episode   92

INTRODUCTION
Theorizing Relations in Indigenous South America

Marcelo González Gálvez, Piergiorgio Di Giminiani,
and Giovanna Bacchiddu

Whether invented, discovered, implicit, directly addressed, or hiding in plain sight, relations remain the main focus of anthropological inquiry. The centrality of relations to the discipline was recognized early in its history, as soon as society came to be conceptualized as a system of consanguinity and affinity. Later, during the heyday of structural functionalism, the notion of relations was recognized as the main 'object' of anthropological analysis, understood as "association between individual organisms" (Radcliffe-Brown 1965: 189). Relations were relevant because they helped in the establishment of social positions: individuals were more or less equivalent to units of a bigger system (Strathern 2018). Structural functionalism was not alone in maintaining an approach to relations as if they were self-evident. For much of the history of the discipline, the ethnographic categorization of social relations remained a key goal. Yet despite the richness of empirical attention to relations, the notion of relations

Notes for this section begin on page 20.

itself remained largely unproblematized as a device helpful to social analysis. With the advent of structuralism, however, came the first sense of dissatisfaction with the overly empirical nature of relations in anthropological thinking. Lévi-Strauss ([1958] 1987: 301–304) understood relations as operating necessarily upon a distinction between 'reality' and a theoretical model employed to grasp that reality (see also Leach [1954] 1970: 5). The gap between irreducible, constantly fluctuating social phenomena and their theorization was thus made visible, highlighting that relations do not exist as empirically observed practices that can be transposed into self-contained relational systems.

Following this critique, more recent anthropological theorizations of relations have moved away from an emphasis on connectivity between pre-existing units and toward a focus on the constitutive potentials of relations. This shift is part of a broader critique against 'society thinking', the disciplinary tradition of framing human experience as the set of relations connecting society on a large scale with individuals on a small scale (Lebner 2017: 9). By challenging the coherence of social systems as a set of ordered relations, critiques of modern anthropological theory have invited us to reflect on how relations are comprehended, both by anthropologists and by the people with whom anthropologists work. As posited by Strathern (2001), one of the key critical voices against 'society thinking' in the discipline, relations are fundamental articulators of anthropological thinking. To hear a person "call someone a 'relation' tells you there is some other reason for the connection than simply acknowledging it" (ibid.: 73).

Approaches to relations founded not on their empirical discovery but on their abstraction (Holbraad and Pedersen 2017: 131) have relied on the deconstruction of *a priori* distinctions between part and whole (Strathern 1992) and between interior and exterior (Bateson [1972] 2000; Ingold 2011: 69–71). This deconstruction is central, for instance, to Roy Wagner's (1991: 163) idea of the "fractal person," which consists of "an entity with relationship integrally implied." Particularly relevant additions to the conceptual shift in relations from ethnographic data to theoretical notions have included anthropological works in Melanesia (Strathern 1988; Wagner 1991) and lowland South America (Overing 1975; Rivière 1984; Seeger et al. 1979), as well as contemporary analyses of kinship and reproductive technologies (Carsten 2004; Strathern 2005). One important lesson emerging from these apparently unrelated bodies of literature is that once relations have been conceptualized as more than metonyms for sociality, they can make us think about the social by reflecting upon proportions and scales in the connections among entities (Corsín Jiménez 2004: 14).

A movement toward an anthropological theorization of relations is now in full swing. Yet we believe that some space remains within this movement. In fact, most of anthropology's theoretical engagements with relations tend to focus on particular instantiations of them, such as local forms of kinship in specific ethnographic contexts. In this volume, we propose that a way forward in this debate is to engage with a comparative regional theorization of relation notions by addressing different instances of relations analyzed ethnographically. Two analytical strategies are at play here. The first is to draw on the tradition of regional comparative theory in anthropology, taking into account the risks of cultural reductionism implicit in this particular heuristic. The second is to abstract general principles about the condition of existence and the generative potentials of relations through the empirical observation of what emerges as relations from the field. Regional thinking in anthropology has a long, problematic history, given a certain tendency to reduce local complexities by reinforcing key notions as defining cultural traits, such as hierarchy in India or dividuals in Melanesia, which contributes to the reiteration of often unquestioned definitions of cultural areas (Candea 2018: 336). However, despite its origin as an arbitrary artifact of anthropological practice, regional comparison can still be helpful for thinking laterally while keeping in mind the historical production of spatial boundaries for ideas and practices. Regionalism reminds us that notions emerge not only through analytical connections drawn by anthropologists, but also due to deep-rooted connections across multiple, linked places throughout the ethnographic locality (see Englund and Yarrow 2013).

In articulating a comparative analysis of indigenous South America, we are aware that we are bringing together different forms of social belonging and, thus, that we are implicitly contributing to a purification (*sensu* Latour 1993: 11) of indigenous notions and practices, which—observed in everyday life—are often highly hybridized with Western values imposed through colonial rule and/or globalization. Nevertheless, we believe that framing an analysis of concepts of relations in indigenous South America can reveal commonalities across historically connected social contexts, including the Chaco, Amazonia, central Brazil, the Southern Andes, and the Andean highlands, as discussed in the various contributions to this volume. Taken together, these contributions also suggest that rigid boundaries cannot be established between cultural areas in indigenous South America, unlike the customary division between lowland and highland ethnographic literature. Ultimately, a comparative analysis can shed light not simply on what types of relations take place in a given social milieu, but also on how relations could take place as instantiations as well as contradictions of local conceptions of how the world and the self are constituted ontologically. In any ethnographic setting, the abstraction of relations is necessarily produced by an encounter between existing theoretical frameworks and empirical observations that necessarily disturbs both "the expectations of a naive positivism and those of a theoretically omnipotent free play of ideas" (Venkatesan et al. 2012: 45).

In this volume, we ask what a theory of relations might look like by exploring differences and similarities in the ways in which relations are conceptualized across different settings in indigenous South America. The chapters that comprise this collection are diverse in their analytical focus and social settings, but they share a common question: how can relations be conceptualized through ethnographic engagement with empirically observed connections between different peoples and entities in indigenous South America? In answering this question, we engage with native reflections on relations in order to expose some of "the kinds of connections these concepts make possible" (Strathern [1991] 2004: 51). In approaching local understandings of how relations constitute—and are constituted by—different entities, we propose that in indigenous South America the generative power of relations lies at the intersection between a particular ontological configuration of alterity, which we call 'dependence on otherness', and a set of norms and practices, which we refer to as an 'ethics of autonomy'. As argued by Overing (2003: 306), in indigenous South America, autonomy—rather than its impossibility—tends to figure as both the starting point and the product of the social. In this context, autonomy is not linked to individuality, a term that designates a sociological status and ideal whereby subjects are able to carry out separate existences. Rather, autonomy exists within a general asymmetrical social form responsible for shaping groups, formed by "subject[s] who [are] such only according to specific contexts of relations whose conditions (borrowing an expression of Guattari) are never given once and for all" (Lima 2005: 115).

Building on ethnographic insights on the centrality of autonomy as the guiding principle of social relations in the region, we approach the ideal of autonomy as an inherent feature of social and cosmological understandings whereby entities are constituted as the result of relations with others. In light of the constitutive potential in ideas about self and the world, we argue that autonomy, rather than a starting point in the field of social and cosmological relations, consists of an unstable achievement attained in the course of articulating relations with human and non-human others. On the one hand, beings exist as the result of their relational constitution; on the other, relations should be led by different beings in ways so as not to hinder the autonomy of both human and non-human constituents of the relation. The tension between autonomy and dependence on otherness therefore revolves around the recognition that engagement with others is not only a constitutive process for each being, but also an ethical stance toward autonomy, whereby each entity ideally needs to be freed from the control of others.

The contributions to this book ethnographically explore the tension between dependence on otherness and the ethics of autonomy by focusing on one particular process, which we label the 'taming of relations'. We propose this expression in reference to the precarious control over the relational constitution of beings in the quest for preserving the autonomy of each being. A focus on how relations are tamed in indigenous South America provides insight into how relations are understood as constitutive of entities, as well as how these entities struggle to remain themselves while simultaneously being transformed by these relations (see Di Giminiani and González Gálvez 2018). An analysis of the ethics of autonomy, advanced ethnographically in the different contributions to this book, ultimately concentrates on the volatile project of taming relations as a way to ensure the autonomy and/or the stability of most entities inhabiting the cosmos.

This volume is certainly not the first attempt to reveal the entanglement of autonomy and dependence in indigenous South America. Several ethnographic works have already shown how moral principles of autonomy co-exist with conceptualizations of the constitution of beings whereby the constant reproduction of society and the cosmos depends on the incorporation of otherness (e.g., see Bonelli 2014; Course 2011; González Gálvez 2015; Lagrou 2000; Rivière 1984; Surrallés 2009; Vanzolini 2016; Vilaça 2010; Viveiros de Castro 2001; Walker 2013). However, this collection pushes these ethnographic insights further in two ways. First, it aims to situate the relation between autonomy and dependence on otherness not as an overall principle of indigenous South American society, but rather as an open question with multiple possible responses in different social contexts within the region. Its chapters explore this tension by going beyond the classic fields of inquiry (kinship, the body, warfare, and so on), while simultaneously trying to dismantle the geographical frontiers drawn by classical comparative ethnography in the region (i.e., between the Andean highlands and the tropical lowland regions). Second, we argue that the constitutive power of relations in indigenous South America is maintained by the moral and ontological imperative of being related in order to constitute oneself, but only up to the point of not losing oneself in the force of relations (cf. Course 2011). This is what we call the taming of relations—willfully engaging in and withdrawing from relations to take advantage of their force, but avoiding the homogenization of beings that might result from that force through outlining autonomy.

The contributions that make up this collection share an analytical focus on the tension between dependence on otherness and an ethics of autonomy, exemplifying the taming of relations throughout several fields. These fields include aesthetics, which Lagrou explores through a focus on the emergence of forms and patterns in the asymmetrical relations between spirit masters and humans in the context of shamanic practices among the Huni Kuin people (Brazil); pastoralism, the broader human-animal relation in which Pazzarelli situates his analysis of the treatment of animal body parts and herd-marking rituals in the articulation of human-animal relations in the Argentinean Andean highlands; greeting and perceiving, practices fundamental to the establishment of intersubjective relations balancing autonomy and dependence, as Bonelli illustrates in his analysis of the Pehuenche people (Chile); revenge, which Tola explores with particular attention to the unmaking of relations through sorcery in Toba communities of the Argentinean Chaco; naming, a phenomenon that Vanzolini approaches by asking how the endowment and redistribution of names among the Aweti in central Brazil work to pluralize subjectivities rather than stabilize identities; and hospitality, which, as shown by Bacchiddu in the archipelago of Chiloé (Chile), offers a framework for reciprocal sociality that entails obligations exacerbated by unspoken rules of avoidance and silence. While this selection of case studies is not intended as a comprehensive list of relational fields in indigenous South America, it provides us with a comparative framework to examine how specific manifestations of local notions and practices of relations respond to general ontological questions on the nature of relations themselves.

In what follows, we will elaborate further on the idea of the taming of relations by situating this process within existing debates on dependence on otherness and the ethics of autonomy in indigenous South America. We will illustrate how contributions to this collection reflect and expand on existing debates on these two ethnographic phenomena. In concluding this introduction, we will consider the political implications of thinking about concepts of relations in indigenous South America, a social context impacted by the historical effects of colonialism.

Relations and Dependence on Otherness

The highly transformational ontologies found across indigenous South America have been generally described as constituted through ascertaining difference rather than sameness (Viveiros de Castro 2001). Similarity, thus, is a constant endeavor that can be partially achieved through actions that take place within porous boundaries (see Londoño Sulkin 2012; Tola 2012; Vilaça 2002; Viveiros de Castro 2014); identity, therefore, can only ever be a provisional and reversible state (Fausto and Heckenberger 2007: 4). Myths provide one of the most compelling illustrations of the ontological priority of difference over sameness in Amerindian worlds. As first noted by Lévi-Strauss ([1964] 1970), Amerindian myths tend to focus on the process by which all beings, who initially share the condition of humanity, become differentiated. Amerindian myths in fact reveal "an ontological regime ordered by a fluent intensive difference bearing on each of the points of a heterogeneous continuum, where transformation is anterior to form, relations superior to terms, and intervals interior to being" (Viveiros de Castro 2014: 67). In anthropological accounts of Amerindian cosmologies, otherness figures as a generative force in its own right. Otherness, in this case, refers to fluid and uncertain difference, which is framed by particular perspectives emerging from contingent relations. This is the reason why, for instance, beings that are generally considered consubstantial can be treated as potential others in particular contexts. Among many Amerindian groups, death presents a quandary about the nature of loved ones as either entities whose essences continue to be reiterated in their predecessors or others with qualities hardly comparable to those of humans. As argued by Claudio Millacura Salas in his epilogue, the dead remain in the world of the living thanks to multiple processes of intergenerational consubstantialization. While in some indigenous contexts such a reiteration is desired also for its potential to protect indigenous knowledge and memory against colonial assimilation, it might be a source of concern in others. Among some indigenous groups, one of the main objectives of mortuary rituals is to disremember deceased relatives and friends and, in turn, to make them ontologically distinct entities (Taylor 1993: 665), in some cases harvesting their power (see Harris 2000: 27–50). Relations therefore allow the self to recognize any entity as an 'other' embodying the constitutive potential of otherness, essential to the ongoing renewal of both the subject and the cosmos.

Dependence on the other does not imply a mere intersubjective necessity, whereby the other is useful in framing dialogically what or who the subject is. Rather, it implies a predisposition to capture alterity in order to continue in the process of becoming something else, which is unique to each entity. Otherness is thus incorporated through relations, triggering their productive and transformational force. This idea was first advanced by Lévi-Strauss (1995) himself with the theory of 'opening to the other', which asserts that opposition does not result in a dialectical synthesis but rather in a dynamic disequilibrium, a transformational dyad where those related do not become indistinguishable from one another. In Lévi-Strauss's terms, the sustainment of the Amerindian cosmos "depends on this dynamic disequilibrium, for without it this system [of oppositions] would at all times be in danger of falling into a state of inertia" (ibid.: 63).

Anthropological accounts of South American cosmologies have drawn attention to three related principles: first, that humanity is a not a stable condition attached to a discrete category of being (e.g., Lima 1999; Viveiros de Castro 1998); second, that humans share an underlying sameness with non-human others (e.g., Kopenawa and Albert 2013; Lévi-Strauss [1964] 1970); and, third, that human practices are necessarily concerned with both the need for incorporating otherness and the necessity to differ from potential 'sames', such as non-humans (e.g., Ewart 2013; Londoño Sulkin 2012). One of the scenarios in which these three principles appear most noticeably is relations with animals. In many indigenous groups in the regions, animals are endowed with characteristics similar to those found in human social life, such as living in communities and farming. As indicated by Descola (2013: 9), "most of the entities that people the world are interconnected in a vast continuum inspired by unitary principles and governed by an identical regime of sociability" (see also Århem 1996). This precept is pivotal to the definition of animism also advanced by Descola (2013: 129), for whom this phenomenon consists of an ontological regime characterized by an interiority—a field that includes the ability to feel and think, which is potentially shared across all beings—and an exteriority, the body in particular, which is the site of difference for each individual entity.

In anthropology, animism has generally been approached as the basis for Amerindian environmental understandings, especially with regard to many lowland societies for which hunting is the key articulator of interactions with non-human others (Descola 1996; Fausto 2012; Viveiros de Castro 1998). Yet it would certainly be misleading to think of animism as a definitive trait of all Amerindian societies. In some social contexts, for instance, pastoralism emerges as a key articulator for more stable human-animal hierarchies (see Allen 2016). Yet modes of engagement with non-humans that do not fit into common definitions of animism, as is the case in Andean societies, also tend to be characterized by the lack of clear-cut boundaries between humanity and animality, a point made by Pazzarelli in this book. In the Andes, animals and topographical features actively engage in relations of mutuality with humans (Allen 2015: 28–29). Mutual acts of rearing and growing are essential to the co-constitution of humans and non-humans such as plants and domestic animals (Cadena 2015: 103). While modes of engagement with animals, such as animism and pastoralism, could articulate different notions of non-human alterity, in indigenous South America this particular form of relations reflects an overall dependence on otherness, a phenomenon central to the understanding of concepts of relations in this region.

Anthropological observations of the dependence on otherness in indigenous South America not only have considered interactions with non-humans, but also have permeated the analysis of conflictive relations with human others, particularly colonizers and enemies in warfare. In many of the region's indigenous societies, the rationale behind warfare is not annihilation or colonial conquest, but rather incorporation, especially of the enemies' intrinsic power and vitality (see Fausto 2012). As indicated, for instance, in Bacchiddu's chapter, incorporation of hostile others—always a temporary and uncertain solution—can occur only through hospitality, a form of inducement involving offers of food and drink in a domestic context, with the goal of forging alliances. In some indigenous groups, enemies are incorporated more radically, so that customary rituals prescribing the isolation of warriors from society are performed to avoid the dangerous effects of the enemies' blood on the warriors' bodies (Conklin 2001: 142). Shamanism is also understood in terms of both predation and vengeance (Fausto 2012; Whitehead 2002).[1] The idea that the continuity of society depends, among many things, on the consumption of enemies is further reflected in the fact that in some societies, the very term 'enemy' applies both to war captives and hunted animals (Santos-Granero 2009).[2]

Ethnographic accounts of engagement with alterity in indigenous South America have tended to characterize other-becoming as a fluid, transformative process (Gow 1991; Kelly 2011; Vilaça 2010) extending to inter-ethnic relations and colonial politics, highlighting Amerindian societies' ability to cosmologically adopt and incorporate foreign elements regarded as powerful and necessary (Bacchiddu 2017; Hugh-Jones 1992). The theme of other-becoming figures consistently in ethnographic works about lowland societies, which are characterized by highly transformative ontologies. This theme is less present in literature on Andean societies, where subjectivities correspond to more stable categories. While other-becoming in indigenous South America has largely been represented anthropologically through a denial of assimilation logics (see González Gálvez 2016; Gow 2001), irreversible transformation into canonical others is often recognized as a possibility (Course 2013; High 2015). In some cases, engagement with colonial culture appears at once as a means to resist assimilation through the adoption of legal and political strategies and as a source of further assimilation (Di Giminiani 2018).

The ambivalent nature of other-becoming in indigenous South America as a process that can be both open-ended and irreversible, depending on the different contexts where it unfolds, reflects a general concern over the need for otherness. Although it is an ontological imperative for the reproduction of the cosmos, the incorporation of otherness remains a latent threat to the ethics of autonomy observed in the region, as will be shown in the next section. The ethnographic insights offered by this collection suggest that the need for otherness requires an ideal balance between autonomy and dependence on otherness, an effort that we refer to in this volume as the taming of relations. A balance between autonomy and dependence on otherness is built around a dual notion of relations observed in many social contexts across indigenous South America: on the one hand, beings exist as the result of their relational constitution; on the other, relations are performed by different beings in ways so as not to hinder the autonomy of both humans and non-human constituents of the relation. The ethnographic cases offered in this book highlight how the generative power of relations rests on the possibility of their taming, which is necessarily partial given the recognized constitutive power of relations. The taming of relations is ultimately necessary in order to avoid the obliteration of the singularity of each being, given the potential of relations to constantly constitute and reconstitute beings beyond their intentions.

Relations and the Ethics of Autonomy

In anthropological accounts of indigenous South America, autonomy figures as a central theme (see Lima 2005; Overing 2003; Rivière 1984). The relevance given to autonomy in the anthropology of the region has developed as a reaction against communitarian misrepresentation of indigenous societies.

As indicated by Overing and Passes (2000b: 2), the creation of any collectivity requires a moral gaze that is always other-directed, as "the autonomous I is ever implicated within and joined with an intersubjectivity." We have previously seen that relations in Amerindian cosmologies are typically characterized by their constitutive power, which is the motive behind engagement with otherness as an ontological imperative. However, such a power should not be left unrestrained, as it may result in the submission of one of the entities connected to the other. The singularity of each being depends both on the generative potential engagement with otherness and the autonomy carved out in the midst of relational fields through practices aimed at partially removing the individual from these fields and curtailing dependence on otherness. Ethnographically, the taming of relations takes different forms, such as defending personal actions and intentions (Course 2011; Londoño Sulkin 2012), rejecting and avoiding commands and direct instruction (McCallum 1996; Walker 2013), and taking special care when relating to beings beyond the convivial unit of co-resident kin (Gow 1991; Vilaça 2005).

We consider these different attempts to reinforce autonomy as part of an ethics that revolves around human concerns and doubts about the effects that dependence on otherness has on personal autonomy. A focus on autonomy through the lens of ethics means that the taming of relations cannot be reduced to a stable ontological configuration, but rather unfolds as an ongoing ethical context characterized by human uncertainties and indeterminacies (see Di Giminiani and González Gálvez 2018). Highlighted ethnographically by the contributors to this volume, the ethics of autonomy resemble the general features of what Das (2012: 134) has defined as ordinary ethics, namely, a "dimension of everyday life in which we are not aspiring to escape the ordinary but rather to descend into it as a way of becoming moral subjects."

The analysis of the ethics of autonomy necessarily requires a focus on domestic life, a relational context that has been at the core of anthropological research in indigenous South America over the last four decades (see, e.g., Ewart 2013; González Gálvez 2016; McCallum 2001; Overing 1975, 1989, 2003; Tola 2012; Vilaça 2002). Research has shown that the carving out of autonomy unfolds in a general context where human collectivities are fabricated substantially rather than symbolically in the form of group membership. The fabrication of human collectivities depends on actions directed toward the body, which, as first noted by Seeger et al. (1979: 14), constitutes the locus of substance and essence in many indigenous contexts in the region (see also Brightman et al. 2014; Vilaça 2005; Viveiros de Castro 1998). As Rivière (1984: 84) poignantly reminds us, the reproduction of society is not conceptualized in these groups as independent from the bodily reproduction of persons put in motion by multiple forms of relations. Among the different ways in which human collectivities can be momentarily established is conviviality, a morally praised sociability to which cooperative relations are usually ascribed (see Overing and Passes 2000b). Similarly, commensality—the act of sharing food and affect—is endowed with the potential for consubstantialization, the process by which similar substances are shared among different individuals (see Harvey 1998; Viegas 2003; Weismantel 1995).[3] Consubstantialization is particularly relevant to the distinction between affinity and consanguinity. As claimed by Viveiros de Castro (2001: 19), in indigenous South America affinity appears "as the given dimension of the cosmic relational matrix, while consanguinity falls within the scope of human action and intention." Commensality and co-residence are the necessary conditions for affines to turn into consanguineal kin (see Canessa 1999; Gow 1991; McCallum 2001).

The existence of any collectivity depends on social practices through which bodies become similar. Within a general scenario where human collectivities are temporarily constituted through bodily practices among individuals, autonomy consists of an unfinished individual achievement that takes place through an intentional withdrawal from these relations, a process that we have referred to as the taming of relations. The particular ethics of autonomy that can be ethnographically observed in indigenous South America center on a form of contingent engagement with otherness that ideally seeks to preserve the autonomy of oneself and others. The constitution of human collectivities made possible by conviviality, co-residence, and other practices potentially contributing to consubstantiality exemplifies the unstable balance between the need to incorporate otherness and to be transformed by it, both of which are necessary for the ongoing constitution of oneself and the world, on the one hand, and the need to ensure autonomy so that individualities can be partially stabilized, on the other. In the rest of this book, the taming of relations will be represented mostly as a project falling within the realm of human intentionality, particularly those attempts to mediate between a necessary dependence on otherness and the moral need for ensuring autonomy. The chapters following this introduction will reflect and expand on this theme by ethnographically examining practices through which the generative power of relations is tamed and entities are stabilized.

Writing about Relations: The Organization of This Book

The chapters composing this book vary considerably in their regional focus and organization. The six ethnographic cases presented in the following pages offer the readers a comparative overview of how relations can be objectified, represented, and conceptually transformed in indigenous South American contexts. The last three chapters consist of theoretical and reflexive engagements with the potentials of thinking through relations in general as well as specific relations, such as in Millacura's epilogue on death and past, in forging new sensibilities toward representative practices of Western and indigenous alterity in anthropology and beyond. The six ethnographic cases delve into the ethical and ontological tension between the productive potentials of relations and concerns over autonomy. In dealing with uncertainties concerning the representation of this tension, each chapter inevitably tends to lean more toward one pole of the model we have in mind in this book. This is the case for three chapters (those by Tola, Vanzolini, and Bonelli).

Tola's chapter aptly illustrates the configuration of beings as the embodied result of multiple connections. In Qom society, the body is a permeable, porous device that is co-constituted by a multiplicity of beings that come in contact with it, while at the same time co-constituting other porous bodies of other beings. This receptivity and openness toward the other produces a permanent relatedness, a constant movement of expansion and extension that Tola calls a "relational excess." This particular excess leaves subjects vulnerable to the malevolent manipulation of specific bodily components by sorcerers. Persons are constantly forced to create fissures within social networks in order to cut and partially interrupt this relational flow, establishing what the author defines as an "individuation" of the subject, that is, a partial or incomplete restoration of his or her singularity. In Tola's ethnography, the taming of relations finds a rather dramatic solution, as it implies murderous revenge—the only possible tool to disentangle entities from one another when they are connected through deadly acts of sorcery. When a close relative dies, the family may decide to avenge the death through practices performed on the dying body by a specialist in revenge. Yet under specific circumstances, relatives intentionally decide not to take revenge. As shown by Tola, the relation between revenge and anti-revenge is a key aspect of a broader Qom understanding of personhood in which individuation needs to be achieved to avoid the dangers of generalized indifferentiation.

Vanzolini's chapter examines the need for otherness through a focus on the practice of naming among the Aweti of central Brazil. Rather than exclusively acting as labels of identity or as noun substantives, names serve as mechanisms to produce, delineate, and activate relations between different people. As Vanzolini shows, names do not confer a "substantial identity," but rather add qualities to their recipients over the course of their lifetime. Furthermore, they make relations visible while constituting persons, thus embodying counter-identity devices. Their transmission does not fix or determine a person's identity; instead, it allows for the possibility of multiplying what a person is through time and via different name-givers. Others are needed insofar as they trigger the development of personhood for each subject. However, no person's constitution is subdued to the will of others. Hence, the uncontrolled productivity of relations needs to be tamed to guarantee a certain stability—at least within the co-resident group—so as to allow certain degrees of sameness to appear and, through them, differentiation from the non-resident others. Family names connect people to certain kin groups and distinguish them from others, enhancing the intensity and persistence of certain relations to the detriment of others. The acquisition of names and the struggle to develop a unique self reflect a broader tension between the need for otherness and the maintenance of autonomy.

By examining practices of greeting and dying among the Pehuenche of southern Chile, Bonelli's contribution also emphasizes the need for otherness. More specifically, his chapter highlights the relevance of seeing and touching as "key ontological operators for stabilizing the tension between autonomy and dependence on otherness." Building on Viveiros de Castro's (2001) concept of 'potential affinity', Bonelli tackles the notion of perception as an entry point to explore the sensorial constitution of persons in Pehuenche contexts. Greeting and dying are two situations that clearly show the duality of autonomy and dependence on others, insofar as they are respectively linked to the mutual recognition of similarity and to the articulation of an ontological separation between different beings. The possibility that deceased persons might turn into evil spirits that cannot be perceived fully through sight and touch is central to the articulation of relations with deceased others. The analysis of greeting and touching in Pehuenche contexts allows Bonelli to contribute to Amerindian debates on the need for otherness through a specific engagement with speculative ethics and the question of alterity.

The chapters by Lagrou, Pazzarelli, and Bacchiddu place greater attention on the taming of relations through a focus on ethical concerns over autonomy. Based on extended ethnographic research among the Huni Kuin people of Western Amazonia, Lagrou's chapter explores the mythical spirit figure of Yube, to whom people relate through alternating identification and differentiation. To establish a relation with Yube and thus become a shaman, apprentices have to ingest him through a substance, which allows Yube to be part of the individual's body and in turn allows the apprentice "to see through his eyes." However, in order for the apprentice to adopt Yube's power, Yube must be willing to see and devour him or her. This particular form of other-becoming is aesthetically expressed in songs, weaving, and painting. These expressions represent fundamental and indispensable guides for a successful and safe process of other-becoming, leading people through dangerous visionary meanderings in the animal world and the world of the dead. Lagrou outlines a theory of Amerindian relational aesthetics that exposes the self as constantly involved in a process of becoming and always in a state of in-betweenness, which prevents the possibility of independence in any form. Different aesthetic expressions guide the individual in the taming of relations with powerful non-humans in the midst of ceaseless processes of other becomings that lie beyond human control.

Pazzarelli's chapter explores the mutuality of interdependent life forces in the Argentinean Andes by focusing on shepherds, their sheep, and the "folds, wraps, and relations" that are involved between them. In this particular context, relations are organized through analogies, reflections, and correspondences, known as *señas*, which inextricably connect people, animals, forces, and actions and determine knowledge about the past and the future. Butchering an animal and handling its meat and intestines in the correct manner are crucial to ensure fertility, health, and success in herding activities. This is embodied in a vital relational force, *suerte*, which has a material manifestation in the animal's intestines. *Señas* refer to possible correspondences and ontological continuities between the world of the sheep and that of the shepherds. Shepherds may manipulate *señas*—encouraging or deviating from correspondences, fabricating or hiding similarities—to trick predators and avert physical and cosmological losses. The possibility of manipulating relations through physical intervention highlights the significance of taming relations so as to momentarily connect or disconnect specific forces and thus ensure the reproduction of life. The corral works as a sort of fractal structure inasmuch as the redistribution of objects, animals' guts, and human bodies within it reproduces a general continuity of being among different entities. The manipulation of *señas* within a corral, however, never entails an erasure of difference between the human and animal world. While entities are interconnected, they also strive to maintain their personal autonomy, thus making the manipulation of *señas* an uncertain and unpredictable process.

The discussion of the tension between autonomy and dependence on others continues in Bacchiddu's analysis of hospitality in the Chiloé archipelago in southern Chile. Bacchiddu examines how hospitality and the imperative of reciprocity articulate relations in the egalitarian ethics of a remote insular community where the other is first and foremost a guest, one who must be "properly attended to." A strict code, designed to restrain the generative potential of relations, is made evident during the visits people pay one another in their households. Relations play out in dialogic acts of visiting where people alternatively take the role of host or guest, attending or being attended to, offering or receiving, granting or asking favors. This interchangeability of roles, which works to establish asymmetrical relations, weakens the continuous declaration of sameness and equality, and characterizes people's perception of their community. Through the regular alternation of reciprocal roles, asymmetry in relations is controlled. While all individuals are autonomous in choosing whether to consent to or deny such requests, attempts to break free from relational obligations always create serious social and cosmological conflict.

The tension between dependence and autonomy highlighted in the ethnographic cases presented in this volume are tackled in the two commentaries by Aparecida Vilaça and Marilyn Strathern on some of the potential implications of thinking ethnographically about relations as local concepts rather than taken-for-granted heuristics. Vilaça's afterword focuses on kinship as a central mode of relating in indigenous South America. More specifically, it explores the key figure of the brother-in-law as a quintessential articulator of social relations, inasmuch as it contains the extremes of enmity and consanguinity, hostility and kinship. Vilaça shows how the relatively recent acquisition of the Portuguese term *parente*, roughly translatable as 'relative' in English, used by indigenous people in Amazonia only in inter-ethnic contexts to differentiate indigenous from non-indigenous interlocutors, has become a sort of generic 'twisted term', deviating from its original meaning term. *Parente* has become a generic term for 'relation' that excludes real kinspeople and corresponds to what Viveiros de Castro has indicated as the generic term for Amazonian relations: brother-in-law. Central to this reflection is the ambiguity—and richness—offered by the possibility of multiple perspectives on relations included within a single term. Strathern's commentary was initially intended as a contribution to a special issue on Amerindian aesthetics published by Maloca. However, it engages with many of the suggestions about ethnographic concepts put forward by the contributors to this volume. Strathern brings to the fore the general heuristic challenge posed by this collection: to think about relations by reflecting on them from social milieus in a way that anthropologists often do not consider, that is, as links between self-contained units or abstractions. Aesthetic registers are unequivocally part of anthropologists' analytics in their effort to make relations apparent in any context, as they are encountered always under different epistemic and ontological premises.

To think about relations as ethnographic concepts inevitably leads us to reflect back on specific relations that, more than others, highlight the effects and logics of particular forms of relating. Of these relations as phenomena, death holds a central place. Death might appear to involve the erasure of relations. However, as with other non-relations (Strathern 2020: 101), death does not signal the absence of a relational context; rather, it concerns the active construction of new relations through the denial of others. This book ends with an epilogue on death and memory among indigenous people in Chile by Claudio Millacura, based on his intervention in the seminar leading to this volume. Relations with the dead and the past are not simply constitutive of a sense of belonging, even when they contribute to the enduring efforts of indigenous people to preserve inherited knowledge vis-à-vis ongoing processes of colonial assimilation. Relations with the dead are central to a process of consubstantialization that the living do not simply experience, but need to actively engage with as part of today's indigenous struggle to endure. Cemeteries appear as metaphors of a collective 'we', the indigenous people in Chile, to which Millacura belongs, and whose contemporary experience continues to be shaped by violent deaths, both past and present.

Conclusion: Relations as Concepts and Indigenous Struggles against Colonialism

In this introduction, we have engaged with the anthropological examination of relations as both empirical connections and concepts by focusing on one question raised in ethnographic literature on indigenous South America: how can relations be entangled in ways that are constitutive of entities, yet do not obliterate the autonomy of the beings involved in them? An answer to this question lies in particular local manifestations of a process observed throughout the region, that is, the taming of relations, in which ontological and ethical concerns converge. This process appears central to an understanding of one fundamental set of relations—those with colonizers—upon which the continuity of indigenous lived worlds depends. Colonialism is in fact not only a historical factor that has contributed to the obliteration and transformation of many forms of relations and their understandings among indigenous groups in the region. It is also an ongoing structure of domination that indigenous people continuously cope with, among many ways, by reasserting and redefining concepts and practices of relations that sustain autonomous forms of world-making threatened by colonialism. As Millacura invites us to reflect upon in the epilogue, destruction and violence against indigenous people in the past are constitutive of the epistemic erasures in the present, given the active role of the dead in informing present-day senses of belonging among indigenous people. While the ethnographic cases presented in this book do not examine relations between indigenous peoples and colonizers in detail, as noted by Vilaça in her afterword, a focus on relations as concepts in indigenous contexts can help us to reflect further on some of the effects that colonialism and resistance against it hold in today's indigenous societies.

In this book, we understand colonialism as an ongoing historical process that is responsible not only for material forms of dispossession, but also for the attempted erasure of those ontological principles upon which colonized groups experience and understand the world. It is a material process, because colonialism works to rearrange relations between different groups into a "relatively secure or sedimented set of hierarchical social relations that continue to facilitate the *dispossession* of indigenous peoples of their lands and self-determining authority" (Coulthard 2014: 7; emphasis in original). Despite the introduction of multicultural policies aimed at valorizing indigenous heritage and rights over self-determination, dispossession continues to define settler-colonial relations in Latin America (see Rivera Cusicanqui 2016). This is because, from a governmental point of view, indigenous spaces, and in particular natural resources therein, continue to serve as commons necessary for economic growth and development affecting the nation as a whole. With no exception, all of the indigenous groups whose lives are ethnographically represented in this volume are imbricated in colonial relations. Their lived worlds are part of national territories and therefore are impacted by different forms of dispossession, from more visible projects of natural resource extraction to the historical effects of land shortages and confinement in institutionalized territories. Colonialism also concerns the erasure of ontological and ethical principles due to discrimination and assimilation brought about by processes of nation building, including the spiraling effects of the educational fields, evangelization, and inclusion in the market.

The first implication of the analysis of indigenous practices and notions of relations pursued in this book is that such practices and notions inform engagement with colonizers at the same time as they are redefined by colonial relations. As noted by Vilaça in the afterword to this book, most of the chapters of this book engage only tangentially with actual relations with colonizers. This is a key issue of critiques against ethnological tendencies to emphasize the particularity of indigenous worlds and contrast them with the broader social and economic contexts in which they are embedded. The removal of indigenous social worlds from broader colonial relations is, in this case, the result of an analytical abstraction, a model of thinking that is especially concerned with the search for local principles. However, we believe that relations with colonizers are particularly relevant, as they lead to the emergence of political and ethical concerns over what is considered the right way of establishing relations. Colonizers are usually perceived as one of many others with whom one can relate productively. Nonetheless, relations with colonizers entail a severe ontological risk—that of falling victim to domination through complete dependence on powerful others and irreversible transformation into colonial others caused by assimilation pressures (see Course 2013). Rather than assuming a utopian and complete withdrawal from colonial relations, we believe that the taming of relations can serve as a cautionary tale about the search for an ideal balance between refusal and adoption of colonial practices and notions. The taming of colonial relations materializes in the frail balance between capturing what is desirable from colonizers while struggling to remain different from them. The significance of this precarious balance can be found in different settings, including mythical accounts about white people's power (Ireland 1988), trade exchanges (Grotti 2013), and religious and shamanic practices in which features of colonial culture have been resignified (Millán 2019).

The second implication of our focus on the understanding of colonialism in the region concerns the political and analytical possibilities and limitations of articulating dialogically indigenous and settler-colonial models of relations. As shown earlier, one of the key critical issues behind thinking about the political outcomes of developing an indigenous theory of relations concerns the risk of treating indigenous worlds as a 'real model'—as if they occur in isolation from the colonial contexts in which they currently exist. As posited by Hunt (2014), the problem of abstracting indigenous notions from the colonial contexts in which they are found is that non-Western ontologies are reduced to specific nature-culture arrangements and lose their capacity to intervene in their hegemonic counterparts. Therefore, any examination of the ontological possibilities of existence of relations should consider not only how relations of domination are displayed in the scenarios where anthropologists carry out their work, but also how the theorization of these scenarios can contribute to the epistemological and practical superpositions of one reality, in particular that of liberal modernity, over others (Hage 2012: 302). Engaging with local conceptualizations—of relations, for example—can highlight the presence of "ontological disagreement" (Cadena 2015: 280), that is, the recognition of the impossibility of a permanent consensus on the plurality of how the world could be, even in contexts where the supposed imposition of modern coloniality has left little space for indigenous ontologies to thrive, a point most visible in the disparity between academic and indigenous knowledge that Millacura draws attention to in his epilogue.

This edited volume is not intended to be an examination of ethnographic diversity as an end in itself. Rather, by bringing together contributions that highlight the nature of relations as concepts in indigenous South America, it can be read as an invitation to recognize how comparative ethnographic research, despite the inevitable risks of essentialism, can help to illustrate the persistence of locally connected articulations of complex questions—such as what relations are and do—vis-à-vis the homogenizing effects of modern coloniality.

Acknowledgments

We would like to thank the Wenner-Gren Foundation, which made possible the project that resulted in this edited volume, and the Vicerrectoría de Investigación at the Pontificia Universidad Católica de Chile for its additional support. We wish to thank all the workshop participants whose material could not be included in this edited volume, but who contributed enormously to its realization with their insightful works and perspectives: Diego Cagüeñas, Daniela Castellanos, José Isla, José Kelly, Celeste Medrano, Marjorie Murray, Indira Viana Caballero, Rodrigo Villagra, and Marina Weinberg. A special acknowledgment goes to Florencia Tola, who worked on several stages of this overall project. We would like to thank Martin Holbraad and the anonymous reviewers for their insightful comments during the editorial process leading to the first version of this introduction featured in *Social Analysis* as part of a special issue. We are also grateful to Emma August Welter for revising this introduction. We wish to acknowledge the Center for Intercultural and Indigenous Research (CIIR) (CONICYT/ FONDAP/15110006), the National Research

Center for Integrated Natural Disaster Management (CIGIDEN) (CONICYT/ FONDAP/15110017), Anillos project CONICYT PIA SOC180033, FONDECYT Projects No. 11180179 and No. 1191377, Viodemos Center (ANID—Millennium Science Initiative Program—ICS2019_025), and a VRI Inicio grant (No. 11705/2017) from Pontificia Universidad Católica de Chile for their support in the completion of this book. Finally, we would like to thank Maloca, its editorial team, and Marilyn Strathern for granting us permission to reproduce the article "Reflecting Back" in this volume.

Marcelo González Gálvez is an Assistant Professor in Social Anthropology at the Pontificia Universidad Católica de Chile. He is the author of *Los Mapuche y sus Otros: Persona, Alteridad y Sociedad en el sur de Chile* (2016). His research interests include notions of disaster, sports, knowledge and failure, relations, and the theory and epistemology of anthropology.

Piergiorgio Di Giminiani is an Associate Professor of Anthropology at the Pontifica Universidad Católica de Chile. He is the author of *Sentient Lands: Indigeneity, Property, and Political Imagination in Neoliberal Chile* (2018). His research interests encompass political economy and cosmology of land, indigeneity, conservation, statecraft, and neoliberalism.

Giovanna Bacchiddu is an Associate Professor of Anthropology at the Pontificia Universidad Católica de Chile. She has been researching social life in a small, insular community of Chiloé for two decades. She has written on religion, kinship, sociality, and education. She has also conducted research on international adoption.

Notes

1. In the Andes, warfare has customarily taken the form of both uncontrolled violence and ritualized opposition, reflecting a general cosmological principle of dualism that is present in many of the area's indigenous groups (Platt 2010: 317).
2. This point is closely associated with past instances of ritualistic cannibalism, such as the Tupinambá case at the time of European conquest, which constituted the ultimate form of a broader system of warfare vengeance (Viveiros de Castro 2011: 101).
3. The phenomenon of consubstantialization extends also to the constitution of gendered subjectivities. In indigenous South America, gender appears as largely performative, being acquired over time through practices that are always socially defined and constrained (Canessa 2012: 146).

References

Allen, Catherine J. 2015. "The Whole World Is Watching: New Perspectives on Andean Animism." In *The Archaeology of Wak'as: Explorations of the Sacred in the Pre-Columbian Andes*, ed. Tamara L. Bray, 23–46. Boulder: University Press of Colorado.

Allen, Catherine J. 2016. "The Living Ones: Miniatures and Animation in the Andes." *Journal of Anthropological Research* 72 (4): 416–441.

Århem, Kaj. 1996. "The Cosmic Food Web: Human-Nature Relatedness in the Northwest Amazon." In *Nature and Society: Anthropological Perspectives*, ed. Philippe Descola and Gísli Pálsson, 185–204. London: Routledge.

Bacchiddu, Giovanna. 2017. "Updating the Map of Desires: Mobile Phones, Satellite Dishes and Abundance as Facets of Modernity in Apiao, Chiloé, Southern Chile." *Suomen Antropologi* 42 (1): 45–66.

Bateson, Gregory. (1972) 2000. *Steps to an Ecology of Mind*. Chicago: University of Chicago Press.

Bonelli, Cristobal. 2014. "What Pehuenche Blood Does: Hemic Feasting, Intersubjective Participation, and Witchcraft in Southern Chile." *HAU: Journal of Ethnographic Theory* 4 (1): 105–127.

Brightman, Marc, Vanessa E. Grotti, and Olga Ulturgasheva. 2014. *Animism in Rainforest and Tundra: Personhood, Animals, Plants and Things in Contemporary Amazonia and Siberia*. New York: Berghahn Books.

Cadena, Marisol de la. 2015. *Earth Beings: Ecologies of Practice across Andean Worlds*. Durham, NC: Duke University Press.

Candea, Matei. 2018. *Comparison in Anthropology: The Impossible Method*. Cambridge: Cambridge University Press.

Canessa, Andrew. 1999. "Making Persons, Marking Differences: Procreation Beliefs in Highland Bolivia." In *Conceiving Persons: Ethnographies of Procreation, Fertility and Growth*, ed. Peter Loizos and Patrick Heady, 69–87. London: Athlone Press.

Canessa, Andrew. 2012. *Intimate Indigeneities: Race, Sex, and History in the Small Spaces of Andean Life*. Durham, NC: Duke University Press.

Carsten, Janet. 2004. *After Kinship*. Cambridge: Cambridge University Press.

Conklin, Beth A. 2001. *Consuming Grief: Compassionate Cannibalism in an Amazonian Society*. Austin: University of Texas Press.

Corsín Jiménez, Alberto. 2004. "The Form of the Relation, or Anthropology's Enchantment with the Algebraic Imagination." Unpublished manuscript, University of Manchester.

Coulthard, Glen S. 2014. *Red Skin, White Masks: Rejecting the Colonial Politics of Recognition*. Minneapolis: University of Minnesota Press.

Course, Magnus. 2011. *Becoming Mapuche: Person and Ritual in Indigenous Chile*. Urbana: University of Illinois Press.

Course, Magnus. 2013. "The Clown Within: Becoming White and Mapuche Ritual Clowns." *Comparative Studies in Society and History* 55 (4): 771–799.

Das, Veena. 2012. "Ordinary Ethics." In *A Companion to Moral Anthropology*, ed. Didier Fassin, 133–149. London: Wiley-Blackwell.

Descola, Philippe. 1996. *The Spears of Twilight: Life and Death in the Amazon Jungle*. Trans. Janet Lloyd. New York: New Press.

Descola, Philippe. 2013. *Beyond Nature and Culture*. Trans. Janet Lloyd. Chicago: University of Chicago Press.

Di Giminiani, Piergiorgio. 2018. *Sentient Lands: Indigeneity, Property, and Political Imagination in Neoliberal Chile*. Tucson: University of Arizona Press.

Di Giminiani, Piergiorgio, and Marcelo González Gálvez. 2018. "Who Owns the Water? The Relation as Unfinished Objectivation in the Mapuche Lived World." *Anthropological Forum* 28 (3): 199–216.

Englund, Harri, and Thomas Yarrow. 2013. "The Place of Theory: Rights, Networks, and Ethnographic Comparison." *Social Analysis* 57 (3): 132–149.

Ewart, Elizabeth. 2013. *Space and Society in Central Brazil: A Panará Ethnography*. London: Bloomsbury.

Fausto, Carlos. 2012. *Warfare and Shamanism in Amazonia*. Cambridge: Cambridge University Press.

Fausto, Carlos, and Michael Heckenberger. 2007. "Introduction: Indigenous History and the History of the 'Indians.'" In *Time and Memory in Indigenous Amazonia: Anthropological Perspectives*, ed. Carlos Fausto and Michael Heckenberger, 1–42. Tallahassee: University of Florida Press.

González Gálvez, Marcelo. 2015. "The Truth of Experience and Its Communication: Reflections on Mapuche Epistemology." *Anthropological Theory* 15 (2): 141–157.

González Gálvez, Marcelo. 2016. *Los mapuche y sus otros: Persona, alteridad y sociedad en el sur de Chile* [The Mapuche and their others: Person, alterity, and society in southern Chile]. Santiago: Editorial Universitaria.

Gow, Peter. 1991. *Of Mixed Blood: Kinship and History in Peruvian Amazonia*. Oxford: Clarendon Press.

Gow, Peter. 2001. *An Amazonian Myth and Its History*. Oxford: Oxford University Press.

Grotti, Vanessa. 2013. "The Wealth of the Body: Trade Relations, Objects, and Personhood in Northeastern Amazonia." *Journal of Latin American and Caribbean Anthropology* 18 (1): 14–30.

Hage, Ghassan. 2012. "Critical Anthropological Thought and the Radical Political Imaginary Today." *Critique of Anthropology* 32 (3): 285–308.

Harris, Olivia. 2000. *To Make the Earth Bear Fruit: Ethnographic Essays on Fertility, Work and Gender in Highland Bolivia*. London: ILAS.

Harvey, Penny. 1998. "Los 'hechos naturales' de parentesco y género en un contexto andino" [The 'natural events' of kinship and gender in an Andean context]. In *Gente de carne y hueso: Las tramas de parentesco en los Andes* [People of flesh and blood: Kinship patterns in the Andes], ed. Denise Arnold, 69–82. La Paz: ILCA/CIASE.

High, Casey. 2015. "Keep on Changing: Recent Trends in Amazonian Anthropology." *Reviews in Anthropology* 44 (2): 93–117.

Holbraad, Martin, and Morten Axel Pedersen. 2017. *The Ontological Turn: An Anthropological Exposition*. Cambridge: Cambridge University Press.

Hugh-Jones, Stephen. 1992. "Yesterday's Luxuries, Tomorrow's Necessities: Business and Barter in Northwest Amazonia." In *Barter, Exchange and Value: An Anthropological Approach*, ed. Caroline Humphrey and Stephen Hugh-Jones, 42–74. Cambridge: Cambridge University Press.

Hunt, Sarah. 2014. "Ontologies of Indigeneity: The Politics of Embodying a Concept." *Cultural Geographies* 21 (1): 27–32.

Ingold, Tim. 2011. *Being Alive: Essays on Movement, Knowledge and Description*. London: Routledge.

Ireland, Emilienne. 1988. "Cerebral Savage: The Whiteman as Symbol of Cleverness and Savagery in Waurá Myth." In *Rethinking History and Myth: Indigenous South American Perspectives on the Past*, ed. Jonathan D. Hill, 157–173. Urbana: University of Illinois Press.

Kelly, José Antonio. 2011. *State Healthcare and Yanomami Transformations: A Symmetrical Ethnography*. Tucson: Arizona University Press.

Kopenawa, Davi, and Bruce Albert. 2013. *The Falling Sky: Words of a Yanomami Shaman*. Trans. Nicholas Elliott and Alison Dundy. Cambridge, MA: Harvard University Press.

Lagrou, Els. 2000. "Homesickness and the Cashinahua Self: A Reflection on the Embodied Condition of Relatedness." In Overing and Passes 2000a, 151–169.

Latour, Bruno. 1993. *We Have Never Been Modern*. Trans. Catherine Porter. Cambridge, MA: Harvard University Press.

Leach, E. R. (1954) 1970. *Political Systems of Highland Burma: A Study of Kachin Social Structure*. London: Athlone Press.

Lebner, Ashley, ed. 2017. *Redescribing Relations: Strathernian Conversations on Ethnography, Knowledge and Politics*. New York: Berghahn Books.

Lévi-Strauss, Claude. (1958) 1987. *Antropología estructural* [Structural anthropology]. Trans. Eliseo Verón. Buenos Aires: Paidós.

Lévi-Strauss, Claude. (1964) 1970. *The Raw and the Cooked*. Trans. John and Doreen Weightman. London: Jonathan Cape.

Lévi-Strauss, Claude. 1995. *The Story of Lynx*. Trans. Catherine Tihanyi. Chicago: University of Chicago Press.

Lima, Tânia Stolze. 1999. "The Two and Its Many: Reflections on Perspectivism in a Tupi Cosmology." *Ethnos* 64 (1): 107–131.

Lima, Tânia Stolze. 2005. *Um peixe olhou para mim: O povo Yudjá e a perspectiva* [A fish looked at me: The Yudjá people and the perspective]. São Paulo: UNESP.

Londoño Sulkin, Carlos David. 2012. *People of Substance: An Ethnography of Morality in the Colombian Amazon*. Toronto: University of Toronto Press.

McCallum, Cecilia. 1996. "The Body That Knows: From Cashinahua Epistemology to a Medical Anthropology of Lowland South America." *Medical Anthropological Quarterly* (n.s.) 10 (3): 347–372.

McCallum, Cecilia. 2001. *Gender and Sociality in Amazonia: How Real People Are Made*. Oxford: Berg.

Millán, Saúl. 2019. "The Domestication of Souls: A Comparative Approach to Mesoamerican Shamanism." *Social Analysis* 63 (1): 64–82.

Overing, Joanna. 1975. *The Piaroa, a People of the Orinoco Basin: A Study in Kinship and Marriage*. Oxford: Clarendon Press.

Overing, Joanna. 1989. "The Aesthetics of Production: The Sense of Community among the Cubeo and Piaroa." *Dialectical Anthropology* 14 (3): 159–175.

Overing, Joanna. 2003. "In Praise of the Everyday: Trust and the Art of Social Living in an Amazonian Community." *Ethnos* 68 (3): 293–316.

Overing, Joanna, and Alan Passes, eds. 2000a. *The Anthropology of Love and Anger: The Aesthetics of Conviviality in Native Amazonia*. London: Routledge.

Overing, Joanna, and Alan Passes. 2000b. "Introduction: Conviviality and the Opening Up of Amazonian Anthropology." In Overing and Passes 2000a, 1–30.

Platt, Tristan. 2010. "Desde la perspectiva de la isla: Guerra y transformación en un archipielago vertical andino: Macha (Norte de Potosi, Bolivia)" [From the perspective of the island: War and transformation in an Andean vertical archipelago: Macha (North of Potosi, Bolivia)]. *Chungará* 42 (1): 297–324.

Radcliffe-Brown, A. R. 1965. *Structure and Function in Primitive Society: Essays and Addresses*. New York: Free Press.

Rivera Cusicanqui, Silvia. 2016. "Etnicidad estratégica, nación y (neo)colonialismo en América Latina" [Strategic ethnicity, nation, and (neo)colonialism in Latin America]. *Alternativa: Revista de Estudios Rurales* 3 (5): 65–87.

Rivière, Peter. 1984. *Individual and Society in Guiana: A Comparative Study of Amerindian Social Organisation*. Cambridge: Cambridge University Press.

Santos-Granero, Fernando. 2009. "Introduction: Amerindian Constructional Views of the World." In *The Occult Life of Things: Native Amazonian Theories of Materiality and Personhood*, ed. Fernando Santos-Granero, 1–29. Tucson: University of Arizona Press.

Seeger, Anthony, Roberto da Matta, and Eduardo Viveiros de Castro. 1979. "A construção da pessoa nas sociedades indígenas brasileiras" [The construction of the person in Brazilian indigenous societies]. *Boletim do Museu Nacional* 32: 2–19.

Strathern, Marilyn. 1988. *The Gender of the Gift: Problems with Women and Problems with Society in Melanesia*. Berkeley: University of California Press.

Strathern, Marilyn. (1991) 2004. *Partial Connections*. Walnut Creek, CA: Altamira Press.

Strathern, Marilyn. 1992. "Parts and Wholes: Refiguring Relationships in a Postplural world." In *Conceptualizing Society*, ed. Adam Kuper, 75–104. London: Routledge.

Strathern, Marilyn. 2001. "Emergent Properties: New Technologies, New Persons, New Claims." Robert and Maurine Rothschild Distinguished Lecture, Harvard University, 18 April.

Strathern, Marilyn. 2005. *Kinship, Law and the Unexpected: Relatives Are Always a Surprise*. Cambridge: Cambridge University Press.

Strathern, Marilyn. 2018. "Relations." In *Cambridge Encyclopedia of Anthropology*. https://www.anthroencyclopedia.com/entry/relations.

Strathern, Marilyn. 2020. *Relations: An Anthropological Account*. Durham, NC: Duke University Press.

Surrallés, Alexandre. 2009. *En el corazón del sentido: Percepción, afectividad, acción en los candoshi, Alta Amazonía* [In the heart of meaning: Perception, affectivity, action among the Candoshi, Upper Amazon]. Lima: IFEA–IWGIA.

Taylor, Anne-Christine. 1993. "Remembering to Forget: Identity, Mourning and Memory among the Jivaro." *Man* (n.s.) 28 (4): 653–678.

Tola, Florencia. 2012. *Yo no estoy solo en mi cuerpo* [I am not alone in my body]. Buenos Aires: Editorial Biblos.

Vanzolini, Marina. 2016. "Peace and Knowledge Politics in the Upper Xingu." Trans. Julia Sauma. *Common Knowledge* 22 (1): 25–42.

Venkatesan, Soumhya, Matei Candea, Casper Bruun Jensen, Morten Axel Pedersen, James Leach, and Gillian Evans. 2012. "The Task of Anthropology Is to Invent Relations: 2010 Meeting of the Group for Debates in Anthropological Theory." *Critique of Anthropology* 32 (1): 43–86.

Viegas, Susana de Matos. 2003. "Eating with your Favourite Mother: Time and Sociality in a Brazilian Amerindian Community." *Journal of the Royal Anthropological Institute* (n.s.) 9 (1): 21–37.

Vilaça, Aparecida. 2002. "Making Kin Out of Others in Amazonia." *Journal of the Royal Anthropological Institute* (n.s.) 8 (2): 347–365.

Vilaça, Aparecida. 2005. "Chronically Unstable Bodies: Reflections on Amazonian Corporalities." *Journal of the Royal Anthropological Institute* (n.s.) 11 (3): 445–464.

Vilaça, Aparecida. 2010. *Strange Enemies: Indigenous Agency and Scenes of Encounters in Amazonia*. Trans. David Rodgers. Durham, NC: Duke University Press.

Viveiros de Castro, Eduardo. 1998. "Cosmological Deixis and Amerindian Perspectivism." *Journal of the Royal Anthropological Institute* 4 (3): 469–488.

Viveiros de Castro, Eduardo. 2001. "GUT Feelings about Amazonia: Potential Affinity and the Construction of Sociality." In *Beyond the Visible and the Material: The Amerindianization of Society in the Work of Peter Rivière*, ed. Laura M. Rival and Neil L. Whitehead, 19–44. Oxford: Oxford University Press.

Viveiros de Castro, Eduardo. 2011. *The Inconstancy of the Indian Soul: The Encounter of Catholics and Cannibals in 16-Century Brazil.* Trans. Gregory D. Morton. Chicago: Prickly Paradigm Press.

Viveiros de Castro, Eduardo. 2014. *Cannibal Metaphysics.* Ed. and trans. Peter Skafish. Minneapolis: University of Minnesota Press.

Wagner, Roy. 1991. "The Fractal Person." In *Big Men and Great Men: Personifications of Power in Melanesia,* ed. Maurice Godelier and Marilyn Strathern, 159–173. Cambridge: Cambridge University Press.

Walker, Harry. 2013. *Under a Watchful Eye: Self, Power, and Intimacy in Amazonia.* Berkeley: University of California Press.

Weismantel, Mary. 1995. "Making Kin: Kinship Theory and Zumbagua Adoptions." *American Ethnologist* 22 (4): 685–709.

Whitehead, Neil L. 2002. *Dark Shamans: Kanaimà and the Poetics of Violent Death.* Durham, NC: Duke University Press.

Chapter 1

LEARNING TO SEE IN WESTERN AMAZONIA
How Does Form Reveal Relation?

Els Lagrou

My contribution to this book, an attempt at the formulation of a specific Amerindian ontology of relations, is to explore the way in which Huni Kuin[1] ritual songs and design alternately point toward the 'relational constitution of beings' and 'a simultaneous necessity to overcome this condition' (introduction, this volume). A look at how Amerindian people think about images and patterns, as fluid processes of veiling and unveiling form and connectedness, allows us to discover a specific aesthetics,[2] one that I have proposed to call an 'Amerindian relational aesthetics'. This aesthetics emphasizes processes of change and becoming, where selfhood is systematically traversed by otherness, and where images point toward being in-between, as well as to the fact that every entity

Notes for this chapter begin on page 40.

is fractal and can be split in two and in many (Lagrou 2018a, 2018b).[3] In this chapter I show how, through an analysis of the aesthetic battlefield over form that goes on in the ritual songs that guide the experience of the ritual intake of ayahuasca or *huni* (a drink made from the combination of the banisteriopsis caapi vine with the leaves of the psicotria viridis tree), a critical stance can be taken toward the appraisal of asymmetrical relations in Amazonia.

Symmetrical and Asymmetrical Relations in Amazonia

In the 1980s and early 1990s, the theoretical debate in Amazonia turned around the opposition between approaches that privileged the role of predation (the so-called symbolic economy of alterity approach) and those that saw nurturing relations as central to Amerindian sociality (the so-called moral economy of intimacy approach) (see Viveiros de Castro 2002: 334–335; see also the introduction to this book). With the advent of the 'ontological turn' in Amerindian ethnology and the definition of perspectivism and multi-naturalism (or animism) as diametrically opposed to naturalism (Descola 2005; Viveiros de Castro 1998), attention shifted from social relations and kinship studies to human/non-human relations. The mutual implication of nurturing and predatory relations became the ground for an understanding of Amerindian sociality based on predominantly symmetrical relations between kin and strangers, men and women, humans and animals.[4] An emphasis on political independence (through warfare) and interpersonal interdependence can be found in the writings of the founding fathers of Amerindian ethnology, Pierre Clastres ([1974] 1989, [1980] 2010) and Claude Lévi-Strauss (1955), who stress the predominance of egalitarian political systems in lowland South America.

Recently, this relatively unquestioned consensus, as old as the writings of the first chroniclers, has been challenged by a group of archaeologists and ethnologists who are interested in asymmetrical, hierarchical and hereditary relational systems in the Amazon. These systems involve chiefdoms and big agglomerations that are closer to the state formations in Mesoamerica and the Andes than to the egalitarian societies that surround(ed) them (Fausto and Heckenberger 2007; Hill and Santos-Granero 2002). The balance between symmetrical and asymmetrical relations in predominantly egalitarian societies thus became a problem to be examined.[5]

One of the signs of this new turn toward asymmetrical relations is the interest in indigenous concepts of 'masters' or 'owners' of different kinds of collectives and resources. Lima (2005) approaches the asymmetrical aspects of relations among the Yudjá from the point of view of the notion of the master, as the one who engenders and causes others to act. In a similar vein, Costa (2007) explores among the Kanamari the fractal character of the concept of master, or *warah*, a term that encompasses the meanings of chief/body/owner, and can be extended to mean the trunk of a tree and the principal river of a hydrological basin. Among Pano-speaking peoples, the concept for master, *ibu*, translates equally as 'parent' and 'engenderer', someone who stands for a collective.[6] Thus, among the Huni Kuin, *txana ibu*, the master of the oropendola birds, is the name for 'song leader', who, like this bird, is capable of imitating the songs of other birds and beings. *Xanen ibu*, master of the *xane* birds, is the political leader. Like the fluorescent blue bird who gave him his name, he is "the one who goes ahead and is the first to find food," as a young village leader, Edivaldo Yakã, explained to me in the 1990s (see Lagrou 1998, 2007).

Fausto (2008: 330) argues that the relation of masters to their dependents is as central to the comprehension of indigenous socio-cosmologies as the concept of affinity. Other relational modalities, such as marriage and maternity, as well as asymmetric affinity (the relation of father-in-law and son-in-law) or symmetric consanguinity (the relation of siblings), would not have the same salience (ibid.). Building upon his concept of familiarizing predation, Fausto characterizes this relation as a scheme through which predatory relations are converted into asymmetrical relations of control and protection. If the intensive modality of symmetrical affinity (potential affinity) is characterized by enmity, the prototypical relation of asymmetrical consanguinity, represented by the figure of mastery, is that between a master (who can be a father, chief, or patron) and his children-pets (ibid.: 351–352). A vast literature exists on how the terms and techniques of familiarizing pets, war captives, and other strangers (such as anthropologists) converge, all of them consisting in the slow transformation of strangers into kin, of non-humans into humans.

The Amazonian relational universe is too diverse to be captured in a single relational model, but after reading the examples offered by Fausto (2008) to illustrate his master-pet relations, especially in the domain of shamanism, his contention that they would illustrate intrinsically asymmetrical relations of mastery does not seem to result in the perception of a stable figure.[7] The figure keeps moving back and forth between figure and ground, and spirals unfold between encompassing and encompassed, revealing the 'Klein bottle' configuration mentioned by Lévi-Strauss (1985) in *La potière jalouse*, where the interior unfolds into the exterior with no explicit rupture between the two and the figure of fractal relations, of self-similar scaled patterns (Kelly 2001: 95; Lagrou 2018b; Wagner 1991). As Fausto (2008) himself recognizes, a shaman can never be sure to really control as a master the jaguar-being he calls his pet, besides the fact that he himself can enter a process of jaguar-becoming.

In *Vital Enemies*, Santos-Granero (2009) examines the existence of 'slavery' in Amerindian Amazonia. He defines it as the condition of absolute power of the owner/master over the slave, such as in the case of a war captive, who is kept alive as long as his master wants to do so. But even in these extreme cases of subjugation, the possibility of reversal and radical relational transformation is not excluded. We are dealing with relational ontologies that do not conceive of the possibility of the desubjectification or objectification of subjects. All beings are agents who react to the agency of others. Thus, Santos-Granero concludes his study about these eminently asymmetrical relations with the affirmation that "in this region of the world, slavery is … a means of incorporating outsiders—alien enemies—as kin" (ibid.: 226). Even if captives in some cases will never become 'real' kin, the decision to keep them alive would be related to a project of making them similar, of making their body/soul adapt to the new body-collective.

In Huni Kuin language, this process is called *yudawa* (to [re]make the body), and the collective of people living together is called *nukun yuda* (our body). To get used to a new environment means literally to change one's body and its affections. The sharing of food and other substances makes people similar, transforms them into kin. This is due, so it seems, to the intrinsically unstable identity of terms and relations in the Amazon. I illustrate the workings of this specific Amazonian relational dynamics, where it seems to be difficult to fix asymmetrical positions due to a perspectival ontology consisting in the systematic reversal of perspectives, through the examination of the alternating relations of identification and differentiation between a person and Yube.[8] Yube is the spirit owner of the anacondas and the primordial shaman. As we will see, in myth Yube is the one who engendered form and pattern. Being the master of the water world, he brought forth its inhabitants, but also the creative fluids—water, blood, and the visionary vine called *huni* (person) or *nixi pae* (vine of drunkenness).[9] The ritual ingestion of the vine *huni* is the ideal site to see an Amerindian logic of perspectivist inversions and fractal personhood at work. The ontology revealed in *huni* songs is one where the more a person becomes magnified through his identification with Yube, the more he becomes vulnerable to attacks of envious rivals and the doubles of his victims.

Yube: Anaconda-Becoming

For the Huni Kuin, aesthetics is an art of relating with the dead and the world beyond, but also with animals that once were humans and with the other sex. This aesthetics of relating is synthesized in the figure of Yube, an entity that connects, by means of song lines and the lines on its skin, the different spatial domains of existence—heaven, earth, and the waters—as well as different beings who are attracted to each other due to the seduction of the design on their skin. Design marks and makes visible the relations that connect different beings.

This is the idea behind the name that the brothers Sebidua and Txana Xane chose for their longhouse in their newly founded village on the Alto Purus River:

Yubenibu tanani is the name of our university-longhouse. It means 'following the path of those who were transformed into Yube a long time ago'. In our longhouse we started to learn. *Tanani* means to go on learning, in the longhouse. The first ones to teach were *dunu*, the boa, Dua Busen, our ancestor, *uxe*, the moon, and Yubekã, the beetle diviner ... Those who take a lot of *huni* are Yube, all of them together; all this is inside the longhouse of Yube; inside Yube, in his longhouse. The longhouse of Yube taught us: Yube of the moon, the anaconda, the small insect *yube* ... Inside the longhouse one will learn everything. (Sebidua 2014)

Yube is the incestuous ancestor who became the moon and, on his way, traced a rainbow, called the 'path of the dead'. This path connects and separates the living and the dead. The founding relation in this version of the classic Amerindian myth of the origin of the moon, analyzed by Lévi-Strauss (1964–1971) in his *Mythologiques*, is that between brother and sister, who, because of having been too close, are at the origin of celestial temporality, the phases of the moon, and the periodicity of menstruation.[10] The sister of the moon is responsible for having made visible the rules that govern reproduction. Once she marks the face of her nightly visitor with genipap paint, which cannot be washed off, a hidden relation has been revealed and thus been made impossible. Ashamed, Yube decides to die and initiates in this way the reproductive cycle regulated by menstruation. The myth of the moon points toward the omnipresent theme of twins in Amerindian thought—that small differences, in this case between brother and sister, generate great differences, the separation of people living in the sky and on earth (Lévi-Strauss 1991).

Yube is the primordial boa/anaconda, who lives on earth when young and retires underwater when old. The boa is said to engender, and own, all possible patterns on its skin. The use of asymmetric details in a symmetrical weave, where figure and counter-figure alternate without a stable ground, leads to the seamless engendering of new patterns.[11] When, in ancestral times, a couple was making love in a hammock covered with designs and the great deluge covered the earth with water, this ancestral couple became Yube, the boa/anaconda.

Yube is, therefore, an androgynous or double being, an entity composed of two. When painting the body and face of the people with genipap, women produce intricate labyrinth designs that cover the whole surface of the body in a maze. The patterns on the skin are composed of parallel lines that should be kept separate, while following the asymmetrical curves of body and face. As a woman explained to me, these lines are connected to other lines "that should touch ... No lines should be left open." The lines that touch hint at this dual character of Yube, where the angle means the encounter of male and female. The combination of the *xantima* motif with *xamantin*, an important weaving pattern, was described to me on several occasions as referring to sexual intercourse, "to place on the legs, to join." In figure 1, the enveloping motif of the

FIGURE 1.1: Baby's carrying bag. Photograph © Els Lagrou

fabric—with the big path that encompasses the smaller path—is called *xaman-tin*. The fill-in lines of *xantima* refer to the sexual encounter.

Another myth tells us about Dua Busen, the ancestor who went to hunt and saw anaconda woman, covered in labyrinth patterns, come out of the lake and make love to a tapir. Hypnotized, the man comes back the next day and throws genipap fruits into the lake, as he saw the tapir do. When the snake woman appears, he takes her by force, but the woman transforms into a boa constrictor and wraps herself around the man, threatening to devour him. When he agrees to follow her to live as her husband in the lake, she drops the juice of a 'leaf with design' in his eyes so he can see the world of the ana-condas through their eyes, as a human village. It is in this village, living with his new family-in-law, that the man will drink *huni* for the first time. His wife warns him not to partake in the ritual, but he insists. When he starts to feel the effect of the brew, a frightening sensation, his vision changes: he sees his in-laws as anacondas and screams in panic. His wife calls her father to sing for him, but he keeps screaming. The next day nobody wants to talk to him anymore. He has so seriously offended his in-laws that he has to flee in order not to be killed. From his body will grow the vine and the leaves used to make ayahuasca, *huni*.

Many *huni* songs refer to parts of this founding myth. In fact, to take the brew and experience its visions means to live again the experience of the ancestor. The myth explains the complex identity of Yube and the substance of the vine. Called 'the blood of Yube', the vine can be seen as the substance of both instantiations of Yube: the anaconda people and the ancestor who became Yube. The experience of other-becoming is an ancestor-becoming, but it is a becoming ancestor that had already traced the path of other-becoming. Yube is a name that connects several kinds and levels of being(s). Yube is the ancestor who became the moon and connects the sky people with those who stayed on earth. The colored threads that his mother gave him to climb up into the sky became the rainbow. The opening song of *huni* calls the 'women of the vine', who (in primordial times) took the vine of lightness and went up to live in the sky, and asks them to throw the colored threads that connect humans and sky people, making them turn around their mirrors to let the vision come. Yube is the name one uses to address the shaman, a specialist in the *huni* ritual, as well as the ancestor of all anacondas, Yube Xeni, the old huge anaconda, the most powerful of all spirit beings.

To see and to be seen depends on an eminently relational quality that is never given. For Yube, the anaconda spirit, and the people of *huni*, holds what the Yanomami shaman Davi Kopenawa said of his *xapiri* spirit-helpers: to see these image-beings it is necessary to be first seen by them (Kopenawa and Albert 2010). They look at you and thus become visible for you. To see *xapiri* among the Yanomami, one needs to become one of them and see with their eyes. In the same way, to see Yube and his transformational world, you need to see through his eyes. It is therefore not enough to ingest his soul-substance, the visionary vine, the index of his agency inside your body. Yube can decide not to look at you, not to show himself to you, or to show you only 'lies' or simply nothing at all.

The process of anaconda-becoming, a condition for visionary capability, is not evident, besides being a risky enterprise. To be devoured by Yube is at the same time intensely longed for and terribly feared. This is the test that the strong-hearted must pass in their adventure of other-becoming. It is the path to initiation in the art of singing and thus mastering the experience with *huni*, following the path of the ancestor who became Yube. To sing with the power of the vine in your voice, you have to engage in a process of other-becoming, of animal-becoming that only song can trace and undo.

"Yubeb(a)un manikin ee ia ee" means "We yubeb(a)un are playing." "Yube" is we; we are taking the vine in the company of Yube. "Yubeb(a) un" means a lot of them (a multiplicity), we singing. Singing together with Yube, you have to warn Yube to take away the headache; to warn, we sing all the illness we have. I have a lot of illnesses: headache, my knee, my back, fainting. We eat deer, fish, crab, spider monkey, male peccary. All these are names. Yubeb(a)un is us singing. (Leôncio, 2007)

To be swallowed by Yube is necessary in order to be reborn as Yube. Only those who have had the experience of having been eaten and thrown up by Yube have become one with him and have the power to make visions come through song. The vision of Yube arriving is the starting point of all kinds of other processes of transformation involving the person who is having the vision:

> When you see the snake that is going to swallow you, this means he is going to put you in the root of the vine. You are going to be sitting in the root of the vine. The vine transformed itself. Now he has already shown this to you. Actually he is going to show you. This is true as follows. When I took the vine when I was young, I had been transformed, my body had already become vine, but in fact what happened was that he [Yube] had showed me how he became. (Sebidua, 2015)

> From my neck sprouted a vine, which became a big tree. (Txana, 2015)

> I thought I had really become a vine; you will feel it yourself in a vision, but my heart was still beating. (Sebidua, 2015)

The heart still beating, while the 'eye soul' is wrapped up by the agency of other image-beings, points to a process of doubling. The eye soul, which is considered the real soul, realizes that he has not yet died or become totally other because he feels his heart still beating. Lost in a world of image-beings, the eye soul has become trapped, and the song—with a complex enunciator, being we, he, and you—is coming to his rescue. The eye soul himself does not sing. Thus, the one who sings is the interpreter while the other is having the perceptions. This model of two souls—one having the perceptions, the other interpreting them—reminds us of the homunculi model of cognition described by Dennett (1979: 119–122) and cited by Gell (1998: 130–131). The duality between seeing and singing parallels a common phenomenon of double souls in Amazonian theories of personhood. The Huni Kuin consider the existence of a multiplicity of souls that can be gathered around two principal souls: the eye soul, *bedu yuxin*, which is planted in the heart and is responsible for perception, and the body soul, *yuda yuxin*, which is responsible for talk and action (see Kensinger 1995; Lagrou 1998, 2007; McCallum 1996). Huni Kuin ontology, as it unfolds through the analysis of the *huni* ritual, professes a theory of fractal personhood, where every unity is dual and every duality is a movement in-between. The ritual consists in exploring to the limit the lines of flight of this constant process of other-becoming.

When they are killed, game animals have doubles who can take revenge. Thus, a male peccary, when eaten, will cause dizziness (*nisun*) and illness in the hunter by means of his *yuxin*, or double. What exactly the double of the game does to the hunter is discovered during the ingestion of *huni*. Song describes how the *yuxin* of the peccary comes to make love to the hunter's eye soul, wrapping his striped skin around him and inserting his member into the hunter's interior (see Lagrou 2018b). What we see is a succession of relations that invert each other's position: the hunter kills or ingests peccary; the double (*yuxin* or image-being) of the peccary encompasses and penetrates the hunters' *yuxin*; Yube (ancestor, anaconda, and human master of song) depicts and undoes the depicted scene by means of his song. If the sexual predation by the *yuxin* of the male peccary was not counteracted by Yube's song and associated vision, the hunter, now peccary's prey, would become ill and die.

The 'songs to see' thus take seriously the risk of literally becoming what one eats and what one sees (Lagrou 2018a, 2018b). Peccary-becoming, spider-monkey-becoming—these are undesirable virtual destinies that could unfold due to the inversion of the predatory relation if revenge is not averted. Jaguar-becoming and boa-becoming, on the other hand, are actively sought after by initiating shamans. The shamanistic ritual of *huni* is a privileged instance to observe and reveal the logics of an Amerindian ontology in operation. *Huni* is a mimetic, agonistic, and highly aesthetic world in a constant process of animal-becoming, woman-becoming, child-becoming, and even molecular-becoming.[12]

In these songs, the inversions between the positions of predator/prey, consumer/consumed, body/soul, human/animal, male/female, and interior/exterior remind us of Lévi-Strauss's (1991) 'dualism in perpetual disequilibrium'. This dualism implies the possibility of opposed and complementary forms of figure and ground to transform into each other, a characteristic of Huni Kuin patterned design in weaving and painting. The movement of other-becoming and of design is to systematically point toward the in-betweenness of all being that is related to processes of becoming.

That which has been ingested will ingest its 'predator' in turn. That which has been encompassed will encompass and back again. The logic of visualizing pattern in this universe, a pattern in constant and kaleidoscopic movement of metamorphosis, replicates the principle of the Klein bottle (Lévi-Strauss 1985) where—through an alternating inversion between figure and counter-figure and a systematic folding and unfolding of positions—the separation between interior and exterior is suspended.[13]

The same logic that engenders patterned design is found in ritual song. There is a movement of inversion between inside and outside, between what was ingested and what ingests, between the enunciator and that which is said, producing a complex figure of unfolding, multiplication, and other-becoming for the duration of the experience. We find ourselves in the same Amazonian shamanic universe where Michael Taussig (1993: xiii) learned that to see and to know means to partially "become Other," as happens with the optical unconscious and the mimetic capacity analyzed by Walter Benjamin. The idea that the point of view is located in the body implies a "new form of vision, of tactile knowing" (ibid.: 31)—that is, a tactile engagement between seeing and being seen. The eye touches and is encompassed by the surfaces it explores. To know and to see involve a far-reaching process of other-becoming.

The song to call Yube expresses the process and fear of being killed, swallowed, clubbed down, and cut into pieces, as we see in this extract:

mia yuda kuwa eenkiki eenkiki ee	Warming up your body eenkiki eenkiki ee
ikeãtã bani eenkiki eenkiki ee	they almost finished encircling, already
sidikime bainun eenkiki eenkiki ee	it is already coming down;
eenkiki eenkiki ee	
meteseme bainun eenkiki eenkiki ee	coming down in pieces;
xawakame bainun eenkiki eenkiki ee	a liquid is flowing from your body;
pae xawakamenun eenkiki eenkiki ee	the force like a liquid flowing from your body;
xawakame bainun een kiki een kiki	a liquid is flowing from your body;
hawen xawã hinaya eenkiki eenkiki ee	with his macaw tail;
ikeãtã baini een kiki een kiki	they almost finished encircling, already;
pae buakaya eenkiki eenkiki ee	the force has already been taken away;
bua kaya hanuri eenkiki eenkiki ee	taken away over there
eenkiki eenkiki ee	
mia xinan kayawa eenkiki eenkiki ee	making your thought clear
xinan kainkidawen eenkiki eenkiki ee	slowly bringing back your thought
Haa Haa een kiki een kiki	Haa Haa een kiki een kiki
bake yume paein eenkiki eenkiki ee	the grown-up child is drunk
bake yume paein eenkiki eenkiki ee	the grown-up child is drunk
xina kain kidanwen eenkiki eenkiki ee	slowly bringing back your thought
mia paen datea eenkiki eenkiki ee	the force frightened you
paen datebaini eenkiki eenkiki ee	the fear of the force is ebbing away;
ikeãtã baini eenkiki eenkiki ee	they almost finished encircling, already
Haa Haa eenkiki eenkiki ee eenkiki	[onomatopoeia of the voice of the big
eenkiki ee	anaconda Yube calling]
een kiki een kiki ee	

Song master Leôncio explains that the macaw tail refers to seeing blood on the body. Here it is already flowing down. The person will be afraid because he can see himself dying. In vine language, 'grown-up child' is the term for 'person'; it means the person under the pressure of the vine. This song is intended to call forth a very strong force, to call Yube—*hawen pae uinmakin*, to make visible his power, his drunkenness.

The bloody scene of being a victim of Yube is yet another instance of inversion of the position of prey and predator, since one has to swallow Yube's blood, the brew, to become visible for him, to be looked at and thus become a candidate prey. As we saw in the founding myth, the relation between man and woman, with its possible inversions of position between prey and predator, is also central to *huni* visionary experience. In a healing song, the sexual act appears in images of eating and being eaten. When her poor human husband Busen is in a panic because of his first experience with the brew whereby he has a vision of being devoured by his father-in-law, Yube Ainbu (Yube Woman, his wife) sings a song for him: the song of the female snake chewing on the intestines of her lover the tapir. "But this is not reality, this is not what you see in vision. This is vine language to make you feel better," assures song master Leôncio. These are the technical terms in the 'twisted language' (Townsley 1993) of the vine. In vine language you never call the animal spirit or his owner by his everyday name.[14]

Producing design in painting and weaving is a female art, but men need to always evoke design in song. "When you take the vine, you have to stay inside the design," they explained to me. This can be translated as staying inside the perceptive space covered with design in order not to get lost in the spirit world. Pattern functions in this context as a map, guiding the movements of the soul. To *see* properly, one has to *listen*. Song lines and the lines of vision are intrinsically interwoven. This is explained in the following song line taken from a *kaiati* song—a song to help clear one's vision:

Miki pae meka ee ia ee	the vine is playing with you
Huni nama kaiaxun ee ia ee	in the middle of the vine
Hatun nai dewedi ee ia ee	Their song from the sky comes singing
Nai dewe keneya ee ia ee	their song with design
Mane beidaxumen	Singing he brings them

(the vine comes from far away singing for the people to get better)

You see the song as if being drawn; as a consequence the person can see and comes, he hears, this is for the person to feel better. If you hear this song, things will clear up. I who sing feel better, the other who hears also gets better. (Leôncio, 2007)

The song, in other words, traces paths to be followed by the lost eye soul of the suffering person. The eye soul has to follow the design of the song as it unfolds before his eyes to be able to come back, to come close to the body of the one who sings, as well as to come back to his own body. This is the reason why the master of song will lean against the shivering body of the one lost in the world of images and sing—in the plural voice of Yube, anaconda spirit—that we, I, you miss your body.

The vine connects the people by means of the song. It is in you who know, [you] know where he goes, he knows that you know, because he has already swallowed you. [It is he who is singing in you with you.] Goes to the other, it can be that [this one] is afraid. The path of the vine is also to walk between people. If I know how to sing, everybody will feel the way I sing. If the vine is my friend or my wife, I won't feel the effect strongly, but the other will scream. (Sebidua, May 2015)

Patterns as Maps and Traps

Marilyn Strathern (2013) affirms that in Melanesia relations are made manifest through form. Forms such as babies, yams, and artifacts are the outcome of relations. In Western Amazonia, what is shown through patterned form are relations themselves rather than their outcome.[15] Different formal characteristics constitute techniques for the focalization of the gaze, whose kinetic effect of switching between figure and ground causes the opacity of the surface to disappear and produces movement and changing levels of profundity in perceptive space (Lagrou 2011, 2013). The figure thus seems to approach and recede in an alternating rhythm. This visual technique pertains to the highly transformative universe of Amazonian multi-naturalism, being not so much a theory that postulates "a variety of natures" as one that considers "variation *as* nature" (Viveiros de Castro 2014: 74). The engendering of pattern, like a "spider spinning its web" (Ingold 2011) while moving along unfolding lines, follows the logic of variation, of small differences that make every actualization of pattern an act of invention.

Patterns of the Huni Kuin, but also those of the Yudjá, Asurini, and Shipibo, all show a clear resemblance with labyrinth designs (Lagrou 2011, 2013), such as those studied by Gell (1998: 73–95). Gell notes an interesting contradiction in the widespread use of labyrinth design as "defensive screens or obstacles impeding passage. This apotropaic use of patterns seems paradoxical in that the placing of patterns to keep demons at bay seems contrary to the use of patterns in other contexts as means of bringing about attachment between people and artefacts ... Apotropaic patterns are demon-traps, in effect, demonic flying-paper, in which demons become hopelessly stuck, and are thus rendered harmless" (ibid.: 83–84).[16]

As in other parts of the world, labyrinth design in Western Amazonia acts as a screen to connect or to separate the living and the dead, embodied humans and image-beings. The Waiãpi say that a shaman is connected to his auxiliary spirits by means of invisible lines (Gallois 1988). The lines point toward different realms of reality that are normally not visible simultaneously. When the Yudjá are mourning, they never cover their body in design. This is because, although the dead have different perspectives on almost everything, "design means the same to the living and the dead" (Lima 1996: 42). The same holds for the Huni Kuin, who used to cover their body in black when mourning.

The use of design to bring forth the passage between different perspectives, as in the experience with *huni* described above, can be induced or avoided. This is why a sick person should avoid using a hammock woven with labyrinth patterns. Following the lines of the pattern, the eye soul can get lost while the pattern traces for him the path to dead. The agency of design, considered to be the "language of the spirits," as one old lady told me, consists here in capturing the eye soul and making him pass to the other side of perceptive reality, much in the same way that perspectival leaves capture a human's eye soul.[17] It is important to mention that one of the uses of these perspectival leaves is in the context of learning design. Drops are squeezed into the eyes of the apprentice who, as her male companion, longs for a partial boa-becoming. To be able to dream with design and to weave without losing one's way in the labyrinth of lines, an apprentice has to kill a boa and eat its eyes. She will then be able to see as the boa does.

Women avoid revealing the figures hidden in between the lines of the patterns they create. The figure would interrupt the kinetic movement that gives life to the pattern and the surface to which it is applied. Thus, we can also understand why it is not considered advisable to look at the stars. This is so, my adoptive father Augusto Isaka explained to me, because "the line between the stars could draw a circle, and the person who sees this might die." In the same vein, the Yudjá say that "the man who gazes too long at the skin [of a woman] painted with design, trying to follow with his eyes the pairs of lines that inflect and multiply, forming patterns that repeat themselves a multiple number of times and cover the whole body, runs the risk of losing himself on the paths of the surface of reality" (Lima 1996: 42).

To draw patterns can be a risky enterprise. This possibility dawned on me during my last fieldtrip in 2014 when I was observing the desperate attempts of an old lady, a master of design, to trace the path of the extremely complex *xunu kene* motif—a pattern with more turnings than any other pattern known to the Huni Kuin. Each time she got lost, she threw away the paper and started anew, getting more desperate with every attempt that failed. To lose her way in the labyrinth pattern that she herself was tracing prefigured the risk of not finding her way to the village of the dead. The owner of the *xunu* design—the lupuna tree, or tree of Yube—is a living place for *yuxin* beings. This *yuxibu*, master of image-beings, has the power to make it dark for you. When the day suddenly changes into night, this means that a *yuxin* being has made you faint and that you are thus on the path of the dead. To faint and to die are expressed by the same word, *mawa*.

Conclusion

If the subject is defined by one's point of view, how does one 'learn to see' in Amazonia? In this chapter, I examine how song and design teach the Huni

Kuin to see the relational web, hidden behind everyday bodily forms, in which they are enmeshed. We have explored how relations are conceived and how they constitute persons through the study of form and pattern as revealed in the aesthetic battlefield of *huni* engendered by Yube. As we saw, the boa, as one of the avatars of Yube, is the master *par excellence*—a master first devoured who will, in visionary experience, devour the killer in turn so as to enable the neophyte not only to become two, human and Yube simultaneously, but also to multiply, since through their voice, "Yubeb(a)un," a multiplicity of beings will manifest themselves through the terrible sound of the forest. The multiplicity experienced by the person is simultaneously interior and exterior to his being. The fractal logic of Amerindian personhood points toward processes of becoming that are ever-expanding, making the distinction between micro- and macro-cosmos disappear. A complementary process of Yube-becoming consists in the ritual consumption of raw body parts of the boa. The boa is a predator and is never consumed as food. It is considered to be pure soul substance, *yuxin*. Its blood is consumed to produce a consubstantiation—to become like the boa and to have its *yuxin* act in one's favor. The boa, however, maintains its capacity to invert the vector of collaboration; it never becomes its killer's victim or pet but is a voluntary helper who has been convinced or seduced into a relationship.

In this chapter I have argued in favor of a fractal approach to the intricate implication of relations as revealed by form. These relations imply symmetric and asymmetric forms, but the underlying logic, as manifested through the systematic inversion of the positions of prey and predator in *huni* song, is that of a dualism in permanent disequilibrium. In my ethnographic case, the most powerful master, Yube, becomes subject to the same dynamic of inversion between figure and ground and points toward a philosophy of in-betweenness that destabilizes any stable figure of power. Other examples in the Amazonian literature, such as the He complex of the Tukanoan people (C. Hugh-Jones 1979; S. Hugh-Jones 1979), point in the same direction of self-becoming by means of other-becoming, and of infinite spinning between macro- and microcosmos (Reichel-Dolmatoff 1986). To sustain that my ethnographic case is illustrative of the Amazonian universe would require a comparative approach for which we have no space here. However, the transformational logic revealed by the ayahuasca ritual of the Huni Kuin is a strong case to extend our meditation on the mutuality of the gaze beyond the more simple symmetrical perspectival inversions of prey and predator, as described by Viveiros de Castro (1998) in his article on perspectivism, to reveal the workings of processes of other-becoming that spin off and multiply way beyond the encounter between two beings and their power to impose their point of view.

Acknowledgments

I wish to thank the organizers of the workshop "Que és una relación?" that resulted in this book and its participants and commentators for stimulating discussions; the Wenner-Gren Foundation for financing the workshop; the editor of *Social Analysis* and the anonymous reviewers for their insightful comments on previous versions of this chapter; and CAPES and CNPq for the funding of my research. Last but not least, I thank the Huni Kuin on the Alto Purus River for the generosity of their teachings and for welcoming me in their villages during all these years.

Els Lagrou is a Full Professor of Anthropology at the Federal University of Rio de Janeiro and a Researcher at the National Center of Research, Brazil. Her research interests include Amerindian ethnology, its ontological, social, and aesthetic regimes, as well as the anthropology of expressive and agentive forms. She is the author of *A fluidez da forma: Arte, alteridade e agência em uma sociedade amazônica* (2007), *Arte indígena no Brasil* (2009), and *Quimeras em diálogo: Grafismo e figuração na arte indígena* (2013, co-edited with Carlo Severi). In 2016, she curated a show at the National Museum of the Brazilian Indian and was the author of its catalogue, *No caminho da miçanga*.

Notes

1. The Huni Kuin (Real People), as they prefer to be called today, are known in the literature as Cashinahua (Bat People), a name attributed to them by their local enemies, other Panoan-speaking people of the region. The Huni Kuin number more than 12,000 and inhabit both sides of the Brazilian-Peruvian border of the Western Amazonian rainforest. Between 1989 and 1995, I conducted 18 months of fieldwork among them in the villages located on the Brazilian side of the Purus River. Since then, I have continued to work with ritual specialists Leôncio Domingos, Sebidua, and Txana Xane on the translation of shamanistic songs, mostly at my home in Rio de Janeiro or during short visits to their villages. The majority of this material remains unpublished, but see Lagrou (2018a, 2018b).
2. The transcultural applicability of the concept of aesthetics was subject to intense debate in the 1990s (see Gell 1998; Ingold 1996; Overing 1989). For a discussion of the debate, see Lagrou (2007). After the deconstruction of the concept's specific meanings—inherited from eighteenth-century philosophy and the modern Western aesthetical tradition, including its obsession with social distinction and its separation from everyday life—the term has been

reintroduced to stand for the form given to a specific way of perceiving relations in the world (Strathern 2013). I intend to show how this works in the context of an Amerindian ontology.

3. It is important to distinguish the Amerindian relational aesthetics proposed here from the relational aesthetics formulated by Nicolas Bourriaud (1998) to make sense of a movement in the art world of the 1990s in France. The difference between the two derives directly from the relational ontologies they suppose. The relational aesthetics of Bourriaud calls attention to the elicitation of social relations in an urban scenario, while an Amerindian relational aesthetics demonstrates the intrinsic relational quality of all beings, human and non-human. In the first case relations have to be made by individuals who live an isolated urban existence, while in the second case relations are considered to be immanent and constitutive both of the beings and of the collectives they connect. As we intend to show in this chapter, this relational constitution of human and non-human beings has a fractal quality, which implies the relational constitution of all levels of being and supposes a specific Amerindian cosmopolitics.

4. Some authors have questioned the widespread applicability of perspectivism in its so-called strong version, which emphasizes the 'symmetrically inverse' quality of the relations between human and non-human points of view. This difference between reciprocity and non-reciprocity of perspectives is used by Descola (2005) to differentiate his animism from Viveiros de Castro's perspectivism, although the possibility of non-reciprocity or asymmetry of perspectives is not absent from the model proposed by Viveiros de Castro and characterizes Yudjá perspectivism as described by Lima (1996). For a more detailed discussion on this matter, see Lagrou (2018b).

5. See, for example, Overing (1989) on the powerfully productive *ruwang* (shaman and chief) among the Piaroa, whose power does not result in the accumulation of property or in the right to use coercive force. See also Santos-Granero's (1991) exploration of Amuesha chiefs and their 'fatherly love' for the people. For a comparative analysis of Tupi/Guarani prophets and their prestige and power to move people, see Sztutman (2012).

6. For more on this concept, see Lagrou (1998, 2007) for the Huni Kuin, Déléage (2009) for the Sharanahua, and Cesarino (2011) for the Marubo.

7. As is well known, Viveiros de Castro (1998, 2002) has argued for the widespread dominance of (virtual) affinity as the central relational modality in Amerindian cosmopolitical thinking.

8. In a similar vein, Tola in this collection develops an analysis of sorcery-revenge and anti-revenge as being related to processes of individuation and differentiation in a universe where all beings are conceived of as intrinsically interconnected.

9. The similarities between Yube and the He complex of the Tukanoan people are striking and would deserve a comparative approach. For the Desana, see Christine Hugh-Jones (1979) and Stephen Hugh-Jones (1979). For the Cubeo, see Goldman (2004).

10. For an analysis of the complete version of this myth, see Lagrou (1998, 2007). For a comparative study of the myth of the moon in Western Amazonian literature, see Belaunde (2005).

11. This stylistic dynamic of small variations in a motif that engender new patterns can be found in other Amazonian design systems, such as among the Wauja (Barcelos Neto 2008), the Waiãpi (Gallois 2002), and the Sharanhua (Déléage 2007). See also Lagrou (2013). Gonçalves (2009) mobilizes the Lévi-Straussian concept of chromatism in his analysis of the logic of small differences and resemblances in the figuration and distinction of animal species among the Pirahã.

12. The detailed evocation of all these possible processes of becoming of different conditions and affections of being in ritual song brings to life the writings of Deleuze and Guattari (1987) in a concrete and specifically Amerindian way.

13. See Gow (1999) for an account of *yonata* (painting with design) among the Piro people in eastern Peru.

14. See Déléage (2009) for the translation and analysis of Sharanahua ayahuasca songs that display a logic close to, but also interestingly different from, that of the Huni Kuin.

15. There is no place here for an in-depth exploration of the partial connections, similarities, and differences between a relational aesthetics in the Amazon and in Melanesia, which I intend to explore in a forthcoming article. But it should be mentioned that Marilyn Strathern (1988) and Susanne Küchler (2017) point toward the relational character of artifacts and/or patterns in Oceania. Küchler shows how geometric patterns in contemporary patchwork coverlets from the maritime societies of Oceania contain codified information with respect to their complex genealogical system. Referencing Battaglia (1983: 296) on the Sabarl, Strathern (1988: 271–272), gives us "a picture of relationships like joints or elbows, graphically conceived as the angle that an ax blade makes to its shaft ... From the point of view of his/her father's kin, the 'child' is called an 'elbow', the turning point at which valuable objects that have moved away from the village come back again ... The child acts as an agent on their behalf; its shape is an angle encompassing two directions." This example shows that forms can reveal relations in Melanesia as they do in the Amazon, although in general the relational composition of an entity is concealed when the result of the combination of different gendered agencies, such as a child, is revealed. What I wish to show for the generation of pattern in the Amazon is the predominance of relations over the revelation of entities or figures, the outcome of relations (Lagrou 2011, 2013). Huni Kuin women, for example, eschew the revelation of figures when generating pattern. The same phenomenon holds for the Yekuana men and their preference for abstraction when weaving baskets (Guss 1990). Another difference between Melanesian and Amazonian relational aesthetics is that whereas in Melanesia emphasis is placed on kinship and exchange relations between humans, alternating same-sex and cross-sex connections and disconnections, in the Amazon patterning points more to connectedness with non-humans than to different relational patterns among humans. The fractal quality of personhood in Amazonia points

toward a constant process of becoming that implies non-human others, while in Melanesia the fractal quality of a person is first of all genealogical (Strathern 1988; Wagner 1991).

16. In our reading of the labyrinth as a trap, we adopt the point of view suggested by Ingold (2007), that is, of someone who enters the pattern. Ingold thinks that Gell works with a kind of demon's eye perspective that looks at the pattern from the outside. Instead of this, he proposes that "when the demon alights on the surface, it ceases to be a surface at all, and the lines apparently drawn on it become threads that trap the demon as if in a spider's web" (ibid.: 59).

17. The association between trap and design is attested in Cashinahua language (*hantxa kuin*): *kene* translates as design pattern, writing, enclosure (for the reclusion of menarche girls), and trap (see Lagrou 1998, 2007).

References

Barcelos Neto, Aristóteles. 2008. *Apapaatai: Rituais de Máscaras no Alto Xingu* [Apapaatai: Rituals of masks in the Upper Xingu]. São Paulo: FAPESP-EDUSP.

Battaglia, Debbora. 1983. "Projecting Personhood in Melanesia: The Dialectics of Artefact Symbolism on Sabarl Island." *Man* (n.s.) 18 (2): 289–304.

Belaunde, Luisa Elvira. 2005. *El recuerdo de Luna: Género, Sangre y Memoria entre los Pueblos amazónicos* [The memory of Luna: Gender, blood, and memory among the Amazonian peoples]. Lima: Caap.

Bourriaud, Nicolas. 1998. *Esthétique relationnelle* [Relational aesthetics]. Paris: Éd. Presses du réel.

Cesarino, Pedro. 2011. *Oniska: Poética do xamanismo na Amazônia* [Oniska: Poetics of shamanism in the Amazon]. São Paulo: Perspectiva/FAPESP.

Clastres, Pierre. (1974) 1989. *Society against the State: Essays in Political Anthropology*. Trans. Robert Hurley and Abe Stein. New York: Zone Books.

Clastres, Pierre. (1980) 2010. *Archeology of Violence*. Trans. Jeanine Herman. Los Angeles: Semiotext(e).

Costa, Luiz. 2007. "As faces do jaguar: Parentesco, história e mitologia entre os Kanamari da Amazônia Ocidental" [The faces of the jaguar: Kinship, history, and mythology among the Kanamari of the Western Amazon]. PhD diss., Federal University of Rio de Janeiro.

Déléage, Pierre. 2007. "Les répertoires graphiques amazoniens" [The Amazonian graphic directories]. *Journal de la Société des Américanistes* 93 (1): 97–126.

Déléage, Pierre. 2009. *Le chant de l'anaconda: L'apprentissage du chamanisme chez les Sharanahua (Amazonie occidentale)* [The song of the anaconda: Shamanism learning in Sharanahua (Western Amazon)]. Nanterre: Société d'Ethnologie.

Deleuze, Gilles, and Félix Guattari. 1987. *A Thousand Plateaus: Capitalism and Schizophrenia*. Trans. and foreword by Brian Massumi. Minneapolis: University of Minnesota Press.

Dennett, Daniel C. 1979. *Brainstorms: Philosophical Essays on Mind and Psychology*. London: Harvester.

Descola, Philippe. 2005. *Par-delà nature et culture* [Beyond nature and culture]. Paris: Gallimard.

Fausto, Carlos. 2008. "Donos demais: Maestria e domínio na Amazônia" [Too many owners: Mastery and domination in the Amazon]. *Mana* 14 (2): 329–366.

Fausto, Carlos, and Michael Heckenberger, eds. 2007. *Time and Memory in Indigenous Amazonia: Anthropological Perspectives*. Gainesville: University Press of Florida.

Gallois, Dominique Tilkin. 1988. *O movimento na cosmologia Waiãpi: Criação, expansão e transformação do mundo* [The movement in Waiãpi cosmology: Creation, expansion, and transformation of the world]. São Paulo: Universidade de São Paulo.

Gallois, Dominique Tilkin. 2002. *Kusiwa: Pintura corporal e arte gráfica Waiãpi* [Kusiwa: Body painting and Waiãpi graphic art]. Rio de Janeiro: Museu do Índio-FUNAI-CTI (Comissão de Trabalho indigenista), NHI (Núcleo de História Indígena), USP (Universidade de São Paulo).

Gell, Alfred. 1998. *Art and Agency: An Anthropological Theory*. Oxford: Clarendon Press.

Goldman, Irving. 2004. *Cubeo Hehénewa Religious Thought: Metaphysics of a Northwestern Amazonian People*. Ed. Peter J. Wilson. New York: Columbia University Press.

Gonçalves, Marco A. 2009. "Cromatismo: A semelhança e o pensamento cromático ameríndio" [Chromatism: The similarity and the chromatic Amerindian thought]. In *Traduzir o outro: Etnografia e semelhança* [Translate the other: Ethnography and similarity], 113–134. Rio de Janeiro: 7Letras.

Gow, Peter. 1999. "Piro Designs: Painting as Meaningful Action in an Amazonian Lived World." *Journal of the Royal Anthropological Institute* 5 (2): 229–246.

Guss, David M. 1990. *To Weave and Sing: Art, Symbol, and Narrative in the South American Rain Forest*. Oakland: University of California Press.

Hill, Jonathan D., and Fernando Santos-Granero, eds. 2002. *Comparative Arawakan Histories*. Urbana: University of Illinois Press.

Hugh-Jones, Christine. 1979. *From the Milk River: Spatial and Temporal Processes in Northwest Amazonia*. Cambridge: Cambridge University Press.

Hugh-Jones, Stephen. 1979. *The Palm and the Pleiades: Initiation and Cosmology in Northwest Amazonia*. Cambridge: Cambridge University Press.

Ingold, Tim, ed. 1996. *Key Debates in Anthropology*. London: Routledge.

Ingold, Tim. 2007. *Lines: A Brief History*. London: Routledge.

Ingold, Tim. 2011. *Being Alive: Essays on Movement, Knowledge and Description*. London: Routledge.

Kelly, José Antonio. 2001. "Fractalidade e troca de perspectivas" [Fractality and perspective exchange]. *Mana* 7 (2): 95–132.

Kensinger, Kenneth M. 1995. *How Real People Ought to Live: The Cashinahua of Eastern Peru*. Prospect Heights, IL: Waveland Press.

Kopenawa, Davi, and Bruce Albert. 2010. *La chute du ciel: Paroles d'un chaman yanomani* [The fall of the sky: Words of a Yanomami shaman]. Paris: Terre Humaine.

Küchler, Susanne. 2017. "Differential Geometry, the Informational Surface and Oceanic Art: The Role of Pattern in Knowledge Economies." *Theory, Culture & Society* 34 (7–8): 75–97.

Lagrou, Els. 1998. "Cashinahua Cosmovision: A Perspectival Approach to Identity and Alterity." PhD diss., University of St. Andrews.

Lagrou, Els. 2007. *A fluidez da forma: Arte, alteridade e agência em uma sociedade amazônica (Kaxinawa, Acre)* [The fluidity of form: Art, alterity, and agency in an Amazonian society (Kaxinawa, Acre)]. Rio de Janeiro: TopBooks.

Lagrou, Els. 2011. "Le graphisme sur les corps amérindiens: Des chimères abstraites?" [The graphics on Native American bodies: Abstract chimeras?] *Gradhiva* 13: 69–93.

Lagrou, Els. 2013. "Podem os grafismos ameríndios ser considerados quimeras abstratas?" [Can Amerindian graphics be considered abstract chimeras?]. In *Quimeras em diálogo: Grafismo e figuração na arte indígena* [Chimeras in dialogue: Graphics and figuration in indigenous art], ed. Carlo Severi and Els Lagrou, 67–109. Rio de Janeiro: 7letras.

Lagrou, Els. 2018a. "Anaconda-Becoming: Huni Kuin Image-Songs, an Amerindian Relational Aesthetics." *Horizontes Antropológicos* 24 (51): 17–49.

Lagrou, Els. 2018b. "Copernicus in the Amazon: Ontological Turnings from the Perspective of Amerindian Ethnologies." *Sociologia & Antropologia* 8 (1): 133–167.

Lévi-Strauss, Claude. 1955. *Tristes Tropiques*. Paris: Plon.

Lévi-Strauss, Claude. 1964–1971. *Mythologiques*. 4 vols. Paris: Plon.

Lévi-Strauss, Claude. 1985. *La potière jalouse* [The jealous potter]. Paris: Plon.

Lévi-Strauss, Claude. 1991. *Histoire de Lynx* [The story of Lynx]. Paris: Pocket.

Lima, Tânia Stolze. 1996. "O dois e seu múltiplo: Reflexões sobre o perspectivismo em uma cosmologia tupi" [The two and its multiple: Reflections on perspectivism in a Tupi cosmology]. *Mana* 2 (2): 21–47.

Lima, Tânia Stolze. 2005. *Um peixe olhou para mim: O povo Yudjá e a perspectiva* [A fish looked at me: The Yudjá people and the perspective]. São Paulo: UNESP.

McCallum, Cecilia. 1996. "The Body That Knows: From Cashinahua Epistemology to a Medical Anthropology of Lowland South America." *Medical Anthropology Quarterly* (n.s.) 10 (3): 347–372.

Overing, Joanna. 1989. "The Aesthetics of Production: The Sense of Community among the Cubeo and Piaroa." *Dialectical Anthropology* 14 (3): 159–175.

Reichel-Dolmatoff, Gerardo. 1986. *Desana: Simbolismo de los indios tukano del Vaupes* [Desana: Symbolism among the Tukano Indians of Vaupes]. Bogota: Procultura.

Santos-Granero, Fernando. 1991. *The Power of Love: The Moral Use of Knowledge amongst the Amuesha of Central Peru*. London: Athlone Press.

Santos-Granero, Fernando. 2009. *Vital Enemies: Slavery, Predation, and the Amerindian Political Economy of Life*. Austin: University of Texas Press.

Strathern, Marilyn. 1988. *The Gender of the Gift: Problems with Women and Problems with Society in Melanesia*. Berkeley: University of California Press.

Strathern, Marilyn. 2013. *Learning to See in Melanesia: Four Lectures Given in the Department of Social Anthropology, Cambridge University, 1993–2008*. London: Hau Books.

Sztutman, Renato. 2012. *O profeta e o principal* [The prophet and the chief]. São Paulo: EDUSP.

Taussig, Michael. 1993. *Mimesis and Alterity: A Particular History of the Senses*. New York: Routledge.

Townsley, Graham. 1993. "Song Paths: The Ways and Means of Yaminahua Shamanic Knowledge." *L'Homme* 33 (126–128): 449–468.

Viveiros de Castro, Eduardo. 1998. "Cosmological Deixis and Amerindian Perspectivism." *Journal of the Royal Anthropological Institute* 4 (3): 469–488.

Viveiros de Castro, Eduardo. 2002. *A inconstância da alma selvagem e outros ensaios de antropologia* [The inconstancy of the savage soul and other anthropological essays]. São Paulo: Cosac Naify.

Viveiros de Castro, Eduardo. 2014. *Cannibal Metaphysics*. Ed. and trans. Peter Skafish. Minneapolis: University of Minnesota Press.

Wagner, Roy. 1991. "The Fractal Person." In *Big Men and Great Men: Personifications of Power in Melanesia*, ed. Maurice Godelier and Marilyn Strathern, 159–173. Cambridge: Cambridge University Press.

Chapter 2

LOOKS LIKE VISCERA
Folds, Wraps, and Relations in the Southern Andes

Francisco Pazzarelli

La société, nous le savons maintenant, consiste dans un échange de reflets.
—Gabriel Tarde, *Fragment d'histoire future*

Among the Andean shepherds of Huachichocana in northern Argentina, the loops and spiraling shape of the upper colon of sheep and goats are food for thought. The central flexure of the colonic disc defines a transitional segment in the gut, where the centripetal force moving the fecal matter inward becomes centrifugal and drives it toward the rectum, where it is expelled out of the body (fig. 2.1). The people of Huachichocana call this gut a *corral*, using the same Spanish word they use for animal corrals. According to them, there are strong resemblances, or *señas*, between the stone pens where goats and sheep are kept

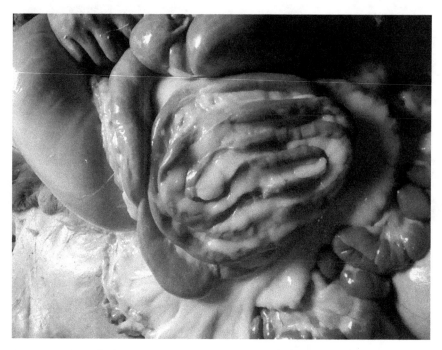

FIGURE 2.1: *Corral* of guts. Huachichocana, August 2018. Photograph © Francisco Pazzarelli

and the loops of the guts that the animals have wrapped in their bodies. "It is a *corral* because it looks like a corral," they argue. This chapter serves as a departure point to explore the nature of forms and forces in the Southern Andes.

English anthropologist Tristan Platt (1986: 255–256; cf. Harris 1986) suggested that contemporary (and probably past) Andean thought privileges square shapes and especially corners to deal with different levels of socio-cosmological dualism and oppositions, approaching a 'logic of forms' (Lévi-Strauss 1966). These relations between forms seem to be everywhere, reflecting each other as mirrors. This "reflection" is described as a "redundant repetition" or "homology" between different levels of thought and social organization, one containing another (Platt 1986: 235, 255). Along with Platt's ideas, Bastien ([1978] 1996: 93) wrote that humans and mountains (and other beings) are related as "infinite reflections of mirrors of different shapes," like a fractal multiplication (see also Bastien 1985: 609n2). In this chapter I will return to this pertinent (and beautiful) insight of 'thinking with forms' to explore the ethnographic material of Huachichocana, a small indigenous community of the Argentinian Andes. However, as suggested by the initial example, rather than lines and squares, I will focus on circular and spiral[1] forms and forces, and on the topological operations of folds and wrappings.

To do so, I will discuss part of my ethnographic work carried out over the last few years, describing the ways in which these relations emerge during the process of animal butchering and in the *señaladas*, the rituals of herd marking. First, I will present some insights on the relational universe associated with corrals that reveal the importance of folding and wrapping operations as conditions for existence. In dialogue with other authors (Arnold and Yapita 2001; Cereceda (1976) 2010; Franquemont et al. 1992), I will discuss how these forms, folds, and wraps could be seen as forces that are replicated in different scales. The resemblances between forms/forces help to reveal connections between different beings and domains of local socio-cosmology. Similar ideas have been described as an expression of an Andean animism (Allen 1982, 2015) and as part of a thought that would develop, at least partially, from different 'correspondences' or 'analogies' (Arnold 1996; Arnold and Yapita 2001; Arnold et al. 1992; Arnold et al. 1996). Second, I will discuss how these resemblances may connect unwanted worlds of relations, especially those enacted from the perspective of predators, such as pumas, that try to attack the shepherd's world of relations. I will argue that folds and wrappings can be manipulated in order to twist these relations and to prevent connections. At this point, it is important to consider the Andean reflections on merographic connections (Arnold and Yapita 2001; Strathern 1999) and on perspectivism (Allen 2015; Arnold and Yapita 2006; Viveiros de Castro 2002) that would allow us to evaluate and describe different types of resemblances. Finally, I will advance some ideas to illustrate that the ways of establishing relations in the mountains are a constant game involving the construction of similarities and differences. In keeping with the comparative spirit of this collection, I will also reflect upon the potential Andean contribution toward a more general discussion about relations in the Amerindian world.

Topologies of Butchering

Huachichocana is a small aboriginal community located in the ravine and pre-Puna region of the Tumbaya department (Jujuy, Argentina), at 3,200–4,000 meters altitude. During my fieldwork, seven families permanently inhabited the place, comprising about 30 to 40 people, including adults and children. This number increases during some rituals or feasts, with the arrival of relatives who have migrated to nearby communities and towns. The *huacheños* have a pastoral agricultural economy, based on the cultivation of different kinds of potatoes, fava beans, maize, and alfalfa (grown to feed livestock) and on the breeding of sheep and goats (the main source of meat, milk, leather, and wool), along with some llamas, cows, pigs, and chickens. Despite this productive diversity, they recognize themselves as shepherds. In fact they are full-time herders, with some families taking care of hundreds of animals and making dozens of kilograms of cheese when milk is plentiful in the summer. Herding thus defines much of their calendars, routines, and circulations through space, within the framework of a rotational system of residence, where some areas are occupied in the wet season and others in the dry season (see Lema 2014). The consumption of animal meat occurs daily as an essential part of meals, and the slaughter of animals is common to all families.

The butchering process starts with shepherds choosing an animal (a goat or sheep). They take it out of the corral, lay it on its left side, and then quickly cut the throat, *pasando el cuchillo* (passing the knife), while holding the head facing east toward the morning sun to ensure future reproduction. When the head is partially separated from the body, the *ánimu* (main spirit of animals and people) also separates and heads eastward. This process must happen quickly to avoid suffering; otherwise, the *ánimu* could take revenge. It could be said that shepherds must fabricate a proper exit and show the way to the *ánimu*, so that it leaves and does not come back. The procedure of disgorging and handling the blood is called *hacer carne* (making meat), because this is when the flesh itself comes into existence. The shepherds repeatedly explained to me that although they choose a large and fat animal, the body can reveal itself as thin and empty inside if they do not perform a proper killing. Therefore, to kill an animal supposes an uncertainty that is resolved when the body is opened and herders verify whether "the meat was made."

This process also allows evaluations of the health of the slaughtered animal and of the past and future of herd reproduction. During the breeding of animals, shepherds seek to form a unit inside the corral: a group of well-behaved animals, usually called *hacienda* or simply *corral*. However, this unit is always fragile because the animals could become *chúcaros* (wild). The relationships with (and within) the *hacienda* depend on the shepherd's efforts to continuously reach an equilibrium—a constant flux of reproduction and the birth of animals, their feeding and growth, and their 'proper deaths'. A group of healthy and fat animals is the visible expression of good herding relations, past and present, and fosters fertile relations that reflect a favorable future for the corral. These resemblances between things or relations are called *señas* and are found throughout most of the Andes. The best known may be those described in the literature as omens: small events or facts (the song of a bird, the fat of a sheep) announcing something (a weather change, a fertile future) that must be decoded so that one can act accordingly (Kessel and Enríquez Salas 2002). However, I prefer to describe the *señas* in a slightly more general way—as effects of a process of co-indexing between forces and forms that partially reflect each other and in which it is possible to intervene. Thus, *señas* are connected with the past and future of the relationships at stake, such as fertility (see also Kohn 2013: 32–33).

I will return now to the butchering sequence. After 'making meat' comes the skinning of the body, involving the opening of the thorax, separation of the legs, evisceration, emptying of the stomach and intestines, and cleaning off the remaining blood. These treatments reveal a very specific topology: to separate things that were together, to join others that were separate, to open, to wrap, to turn, to bend, to unfold. Shepherds emphasize that these processes and treatments must be conducted in the proper way (*doblar bien, envolver bien, voltear bien*). A textile vocabulary better describes these operations and the ontological status of these manipulated parts, because skin and meats are *las ropitas de los animales* (the little clothes of animals). Skinning is associated with an evaluation that is especially concerned with a specific relational force that is still present in fresh and wet meat and bones: *suerte* (luck).

In the Southern Andes, *suerte* is a widespread concept that broadly points to the possibility of carrying out successful activities (Arnold and Yapita 2001; Bugallo 2014; Bugallo and Vilca 2011). People can occasionally be lucky in business, agriculture, or mining, among other pursuits. Luck is not necessarily unlimited, and it may end or be damaged, depending on the relationships established with others. It is neither an abstract concept, since it can be seen, fed, and created, nor an individual one, since it is immanent in the network of relationships of people (Arnold and Yapita 2006: 233–234). In this context, *suerte* is a relational force that sustains the possibility of becoming a shepherd. It is a connection between different kinds of beings that develops from the first years of life when children begin to deal with animals (Arnold and Yapita 2001: 102). All shepherds must have some *suerte*, but it is not an internal property. Shepherds' *suerte* is visible in their connections with herds: not only in the well-behaved, perfect unit of the *haciendas*, but also inside animals, wrapped in their bodies. *Suerte* has material and sensitive forms that are held together by bones, flesh, and viscera—by the guts and gallbladder especially, but also by every wet part (Pazzarelli 2017). It can be seen and touched, since organs are 'relations' (Bastien 1985), but it disappears along with the humidity that evaporates from the meat.

Among the manipulated viscera is the gut *corral*, the upper colon. Other intestines are separated from their adipose tissue, emptied, curled, and twisted like threads to eat. Yet the *corral* is the object of special attention because it is full of *suerte*. Extracted with care and never unfolded, its content is released by making a longitudinal knife cut that, although threatening its integrity, does not affect the disposition of the intestine, the relation between its loops, or its circumference. Thus 'whole', it is roasted and eaten by the shepherds or some other member of the house; it is not shared with guests. If this *corral* is mistreated, the goats' pens, made of stones and wood, would 'unfold' too, affecting the desired unity of animals. Likewise, mistreated animals will not develop viscera with *suerte*. Many domestic punishments and threats are imposed on those who carelessly manipulate the viscera and work against *suerte*.

This special treatment points to relations where viscera and pens are linked by morphological resemblances. Observation of the *corral* practiced during butchering, however, suggests something even more interesting. Its form proposes an original description of how movements of entrance and exit, and the relations between inside and outside, are connected. In the gut *corral*, the centripetal force becomes centrifugal, and both movements, which are in the same direction, are connected in the central flexure. When shepherds affirm that the gut 'looks like a corral'," they do not refer only to the circular analogy; they also refer to these internal forms and forces. They point and follow with the finger the turns of the guts, the flexure, the entrances, and the exits. The *corral* 'looks like a corral' because of these turns too, which are appreciated as a redundancy of the movements and forces that live in stone pens.[2] It could be said that the gut *corral*, wrapped inside the animal body and identified as a *seña* index by the shepherds, at the same time evokes and invokes the corral that is outside, both when it recalls the outer corral as a set of forces of entrance and exits, twisted and folded on itself, and when the shepherds desire it whole and united for the future, and vice versa. Both corrals are *señas*, 'reflections' of the other, and affect and stimulate each other, as the *huacheño* shepherds explain (see also Arnold et al. 1996: 392; Kohn 2013: 32–33). However, as I have suggested, this could go further. When opening an animal body, shepherds not only interpret external forces between corrals; they are also looking for themselves. They open and unfold a body and rummage through the twisted viscera to find and examine a part of the relations that constitute them as herders—the wet *suerte*.

Twists, Folds, and Wraps

In several regions of the Southern Andes, every being is defined by the *ánimu*. All humans, plants, animals, and mountains have some *ánimu*. Considered to be a main spirit (Allen 1982, 2015; Bastien 1985; Bugallo and Vilca 2011), it has sometimes been described as a 'shadow' that accompanies the body, a 'double that animates' (Ricard Lanata 2007; Tylor 2000). In Huachichocana, the *ánimu* is generally described as a part of the person, often invisible, which is inside the body; its loss is always described as an 'exit' (Bugallo and Vilca 2011; Ricard Lanata 2007). This inside-outside relation is never absolute and is best thought of as consecutive wrappings—like those of a textile—between *ánimu* and body, where it is hard to define what is inside of what (Pazzarelli 2017).

The connections between *ánimu* (and other spirits) and a textile topology have been fully investigated in the Southern Andes from different perspectives (see Arnold and Yapita 2006; Arnold et al. 1996; Bugallo 2014; Cereceda (1976) 2010; Dransart 1995; Flores Ochoa 1977). In their ethnography of the Aymara highlands, Arnold and Yapita (2001) show the multiple connections between wool strands and textile wrappings associated with the possibility of existence and life. The first twist begins when the threads of blood and semen cross and fold to form the fetus that will then be wrapped in a woman's womb (Bastien 1985; Platt 2002). Newborns will be progressively wrapped repeatedly by textiles, until they become fully 'bundled' human beings. These "concentric wrappings" (Arnold and Yapita 2001: 35) involved in the constitutions of persons, however, are not just like circles, one inside another (cf. Platt 1986). They are better envisioned as spirals (Dransart 1995) whose loops cannot be easily described as internal to some individual, because some loops are others' wraps (Arnold and Yapita 2006: 112). Beginning with the first turn, the spiral develops turn by turn throughout life, enabling different social relations and making a thicker thread of life thanks to 'envelopes' (such as foods, songs, and chants) provided by others (relatives). At one point, the spiral is twisted together with another (when getting married). However, none of the threads ever stops twisting. It will continue until death, when the thread is unfolded as in an animal-skinning process. This physiological bundle is not just human: animals are bundles, too, and the shepherds' care is one of their wrappings (Arnold and Yapita 2001).

In Huachichocana, the shepherds want animals with good layers of fat because that makes them strong, capable of protecting their vital forces and promoting *suerte*. But here I want to go a step further. On the one hand, I will highlight that folds and wrappings not only reflect each other but can also be fabricated and manipulated to connect, or disconnect, with the generative forces of fertility and *suerte*. On the other hand, some indeterminacy is inherent in the opening of spiral bundles (as in the opening of an animal's body), and this makes the shepherds potential prey for an external agent. To move forward on this, I will return to the topological description of butchering.

To Fold and to Wrap for Others

Once the skinning ends, it is time to dry the meat and the leather. The meat with bones (the still united set of legs, thighs, ribs, spine, and sometimes head) is called *carne fresca* (fresh meat). It is wet, full of luck, and carries some culinary restrictions. It usually cannot be boiled and thus must be put to dry, taking special care to hang it *volteado* (everted), that is, turned inside out with its interior outward, in opposition to how meats wrap the viscera when the animal is alive. Turning fresh meat inside out is important. If it were not done in the proper way, the meat would *parecer viva* (appear to be alive) and attract predators, who would not only steal the meat but, because it is wet, would also steal the luck. When it is dry a day later, the meat loses this status, and the culinary and topological restrictions end. The last process is that of the *cueritos* (little leathers or skin). They must be carefully folded upon themselves, with their legs and head arranged as if the animal were asleep and still alive, then left in some corner of the room. It is necessary to refold the leather *como ellos son, dormiditos* (as the animals are, asleep) at least for a few hours, ideally until the next day. Otherwise, the *ánimu* that was released but still lingers will not become calm and leave this world, with dire consequences for familial luck. It seems that the animal's *ánimu* must 'see' the surroundings and be sure that there is no longer a place for it in this world. The hanging flesh is dead and its 'little clothes' are folded, resembling a live and already wrapped animal, a bundle where it could no longer enter. The next day, when the *ánimu* has left, the leather is put to dry in the sun, turning it inside out like the meat because it is still wet and connected to *suerte* (but no longer with *ánimu*).

Skins should look like living and sleeping animals; meats put to dry should not seem alive. Both situations are connected by the problem of resemblances between things and their effects on external points of view. Resemblances have to be modulated. If the meat is not properly turned inside out, the puma could steal it because it looks like a living animal. If the leather is not properly folded and does not look like a sleeping animal, the *ánimu* could be annoyed and try to take revenge. The aesthetic of the treatment of meats and leathers is linked to the need for others to 'see' it in a specific way: living or dead. It is because of others' views that herders must do things appropriately. Shepherds must be persuasive since they orient others' vision and perceptions.[3] Unfolded, hanging meat in a corner not only makes a relation visible: it also proposes it. The relation is virtually there, but it needs the puma's view to be completed. To wrap is only a part of the process because someone else (puma, *ánimu*) must 'accept' the description being proposed. The meat fold reverses the topology of the living animal and opens the possibility of the existence of meat that is not completely dead for people (because it is wet, with *luck*) but seems to be completely dead to the puma. The folded leather resembles a sleeping live animal for the *ánimu*, although for people it is already an expiring life. The topological adaptation helps to deal with a situation of indeterminacy: the animals were sacrificed, but their meats are still alive, carrying an important and shared relation that could be desired by others. Folding meat and leathers while dehydrating them is an operation of disambiguation, which at the same time enables a 'partial connection': the meat will be dead for the puma, still alive for the *ánimu*.

This is linked to the importance of the gaze as a relational process. In the highlands, where several kilometers can be viewed without encountering any obstacles, the relations between seeing and being seen, showing and hiding, are very important. Family homes are always under gazes that cannot be controlled—neighbors walking on top of a hill, wild animals lurking in the vicinity—and it is therefore necessary to control what is shown, what is left outside the rooms, and the meats and leathers that are manipulated. Showing too much can arouse the envy of others or certain forms of sorcery (the so-called evil eye). The usual recommendation in an encounter with a puma is to stop moving and stare at it so that the animal acknowledges that it is facing a fearless person. In other regions of the Andes, the gaze is also the means *par excellence* to distinguish the specificity of the forms and contours of beings, thus avoiding 'confusions' (Allen 2015; Cereceda 1990). In the previous examples, the life (or lack of life) of meat or leather also depends on external eyes. It could be said that it is the 'work of seeing' of pumas and *ánimus* that makes things appear (Strathern 2013: 78–94). And on these occasions it is necessary to handle the resemblances between things to generate 'confusions' that may be productive (Kohn 2013: 84–85, 100). In the examples discussed, meats and leathers are folded and wrapped to show something that is not there, as if a mirror were made that twists the reflection of what the bodies with the removed viscera would show. The last example that I wish to present involves resemblances fabricated by neither the shepherd nor his animals' bodies.

People's Corrals

During *señaladas* (marking ceremonies),[4] which are held in the summer (although sometimes practiced until Easter), shepherds and their guests perform the marking of animals. These events are loaded with complex details and extend for days, but I will summarize them here, highlighting four phases that show how these rituals are linked to the strength of circular forces and forms.[5] It is all about fabricating corrals, using wool or persons. For each of these phases, it is indispensable to have guests (relatives or friends who are also shepherds) working under the directive of the hosts.

The first phase is defined by the arrival of the guests early in the morning. They will be fed and quickly put to work making the wool flowers that will be sewn and tied to the ears of sheep and goats. From that moment until the end of the ritual, hosts will provide alcohol, coca, and cigars for everyone. The guests sit in a circle around a ring made of crooked colored wool threads, twisted several times. This *corral de lana* (wool *corral*) surrounds the raw materials of the assignment (needles, threads, wool) and defines the limits of the task. Nothing can fall outside the limits of the wool *corral*, or the person responsible will be fined and forced to drink alcohol in excess (*multa*). Transgressing the limits and turns of the corral affects luck.

In a second phase, hosts and guests leave the previous tasks and enter into the pen to start the work of ear marking and flower sewing. This requires much more energy, and a gendered division of labor is performed. Men seek and secure the animals in a row until they are *señalados* (marked) by a man responsible for ear cutting, while women sew the wool flowers in the animals' ears. The task could extend for hours or even days. The animals often try to free themselves; sometimes men and goats duel on the floor, trying to dominate each other. The work ends when the men can no longer secure the animals or cut their ears with precision and painlessly, due to increasing fatigue and drunkenness. During all this time, the hosts make sure that the movements between the inside and outside of the pen are controlled and ritualized. No one can go in or out without drinking some alcohol or wearing a *poncho*. To move without being wrapped in a *poncho* (or something similar) is like being *pelado* (naked or bald)—and nothing naked (not wrapped) can be lucky. To be *pelado* is to appear to others as an ambiguous *seña*, like choosing not to 'resemble' an ongoing ritual that is all about wrappings. Yet carefully attending to all these details ensures the host's luck.

The third phase begins with the departure of people and animals from the pen. Sheep and goats will be pursued by hosts and guests until all of them start walking, almost running, in circles, replicating the corral morphology from inside, like a big, living spiral.[6] Meanwhile, people start to sing *coplas*[7] to encourage animal movements and drink libations of alcohol and maize *chicha*, trying to reach the herds with some drops. After three rounds, the animals are released and then driven to the east, where there is a *mojón* (cairn) wrapped in colored wool, together with flowers, confetti, and alcoholic libations. Again, it is about building another corral on the cairn—this time a miniature one (Bugallo 2014: 341–342)—that evokes and invokes the forces of the corral from which the animals have just emerged. Around the *mojón*, people begin to sing, walking and dancing in circles. From then on, men and animals will separate: the former will remain first in the cairn and then in the house, while the latter will stay on the hill. However, the intimacy gained inside the corral seems to affect the participants (ibid.: 361). Sometimes a game is played in which some men take their hosts or visitors by surprise, knock them down on the floor, and rush to 'mark' them as they do with animals, but with paint. The 'animals' then writhe and fight hard to escape.

In the fourth phase, after singing some more *coplas* in the cairn, the guests are called to the house to continue singing. Once settled in a room, people will form a *ronda* (circle) and sing with their *cajas* (musical instruments made of wood and leather), while dancing non-stop in circles to their right, with slow and wobbly movements. The hosts will offer drinks, coca, and cigars throughout the night. The *ronda* must last at least until dawn; ideally, everyone should sing all night. In the morning, the guests will be released: they can have breakfast and leave. While drunkenness sometimes makes it difficult to finish the work inside the corral, it does allow for beautiful *rondas* during the fourth part of the ritual. After making wool flowers and managing the animals inside the corral, the guests are expected to sing. Mouths and throats sing without stopping throughout the night, while people dance in *rondas* along with the rhythm of the *cajas*. Singing is working: it is part of the expected task of a good guest. At times, drunkenness can cause the singers to slump, or it can unleash fights. None of these situations is appreciated. Sleeping is not an option either, except for older guests. In any case, well-modulated drunkenness can fabricate a highly valued aesthetic expression—that of a perfect circle round of singing, music, and dance, sustained for hours without stopping. A perfect circle round is always a good *seña* of future fertile relations.

When hosts invite guests to such an event and when guests talk about it, the potential joy of the ceremony is described by the possibility of singing in a *ronda*. Going to a marking ceremony is described as *ir a cantar* (going to sing). Consequently, a good ritual is defined by the quality and duration of its *rondas*, of those circles and spirals, as a result of the successful attentions of the hosts: food and drink in appropriate quantities, leaving potential workers-singers neither very sober nor very drunk. When a *ronda de coplas* is solidly constituted through strong voices and dancing bodies, that is when those relations become visible. In that moment, it is evident to everybody involved that the guests have accepted the hosts' attentions and can be described as full guests. Full guests, intoxicated in an acceptable way, are *señas* of well-conducted relations: the herder-hosts know how to do things properly. And the relations are there, in the *ronda*, for all to see.

The task of the shepherd-hosts is to balance the need to attract their animals and the possibility of losing them forever if they do not know how to take care of them. The host-shepherds are busy seducing their guests in the face of the ever-present possibility of losing them forever. The forces that raise/care for animals-guests always act against the inevitable possibility that they will become wild/drunks. In both cases, nurturing relationships (in other words, *suerte*) connect centripetal and centrifugal forces that act against each other. That is why the final evaluation of the ritual is so important. In a *ronda de coplas*, guests lend their bodies to make visible the relations of which the hosts are (or wish to be) made. The shepherd-guests act as obedient animals, helping to fabricate *señas* and to connect the host to the good and fertile nurturing relations that every shepherd desires. Between hosts and guests there will be no envy or competition at the marking ceremony, as there might be in other domestic situations. Everyone knows that the lead perspective of the ritual is that of the host, and nobody can challenge it. The shepherd-hosts watch their guests singing with the same attention that they observe the viscera when butchering animals, trying to recognize themselves in those *señas*.

Fabricating Reflections

As I have pointed out, the gut *corral* is a *seña* that informs shepherds about the general condition of a herd of animals and their present and future fertility.

However, this is not just a morphological analogy or an omen. Instead, we could say that some *señas* refer to events that had already begun to happen in another place. Although they are invisible as such, they can appear and be recognized in other things such as guts. These *señas* do not point to possibilities but to facts with which they have some continuity. For example, the poor condition of a gut *corral* is a reflection of the health of animals that have already begun to fall ill; or a failed round of music is a *seña* of nurturing relations that are no longer working. More than analogies of static morphological relations, *señas* could be described as effects of the same force, enacted in two specific forms. The resemblance should be read in this sense: the shepherds' evaluations of corrals testify that everything is still in place, that they are still connected with the same forces in a healthy way, a reflection partially connected to the classic definition of *señas* (Arnold 1996; Kessel and Enríquez Salas 2002). However, this idea can be further developed.

The *seña* of the gut *corral* is inscribed in a different ontological plane. The inside of the animal body, where the twisted viscera are wrapped, is not part of the same world to which people and the stone pen belong—at least not completely. The difference between inside and outside, however, is not an absolute one; it depends on the thickness of the wrapping, on the quantity of loops. During my fieldwork, the shepherds subtly taught me that observing the viscera allows for a more effective observation of the health of relations, as if avoiding the mediation of so many wrappings. But at the same time, the scarcity of wrappings gives them fragility: if not treated with care, the gut *corral* can be easily ruined or even fall prey to others.

In the daily treatment of animals, shepherds secure these wrappings through practices that are easily recognizable: feeding, keeping away predators, curing, and singing (Arnold and Yapita 2001). These practices deal with *suerte*, although through the mediation of many intermediary twists and wrapping: luck in the stone pen is not visible in such clear and direct ways as in the guts. However, it is there to be seen, experienced, and manipulated. During the marking ceremonies, on the other hand, the shepherds make these breeding relations emerge using the bodies and throats of their guests to fabricate a temporary, almost ephemeral, *corral*. They fabricate the *seña* of which they wish to be a part, so as to stimulate resemblances in other dimensions of their lives. Again, we see the shepherds trying to find themselves in the bodies and affections of others, as when they stir up the viscera of their animals. We are referring to forms that, in the shepherds' eyes, allow the capture and emergence of forces that would otherwise be invisible (Viveiros de Castro 1996: 117): the corrals are similar because they both present and describe a force, twisted in a particular morphology and topology.

Hacer las cosas bien (doing things properly)—making meat, folding, wrapping, feeding, dancing—allows relations to continue to be similar, to resemble each other and then still connect with the same force, like a permanent and ongoing effort for the fabrication of 'sameness' (see the introduction to this book). But these force-forms always demand to be seen in order to be completed. Herding relationships can be evaluated in viscera, and their *señas* can be fabricated and modulated in *rondas* to be seen by shepherds, family members, and guests. In these evaluations, the health of the relationships is secured when it is incorporated in the shepherd's view. It could be said that this 'work of seeing' (Strathern 2013) points to the unambiguous recognition (and sometimes fabrication) of these forces and forms (as *corrales*, pens, and *rondas*), helping these relationships to continue to be replicated everywhere, making them part of a larger generative movement.

Arnold and Yapita (2001) propose that similar arguments regarding growing connections between fertile forces are close to the 'merographic connection' described by Strathern (1992; see also Arnold 1996). The merographic connection refers to the way in which different sets of relationships are connected to others through an act of redescription and are thus included in another context, all associated with a 'procreative model', as suggested by Strathern (1992: 72–87). Strathern states that "the very act of description makes what is being described a part of something else" (ibid.: 204n21), which "rests in the (Western) apperception that persons work to bring into *relationship* with one another whole different *orders* of phenomena, as different ways of knowing the world and as different perspectives on it" (ibid.: 205n22). According to Arnold and Yapita (2001: 200–201), this is similar to some Andean ways of thinking and building relations that try to connect different domains of experience (by creating similarities between pens, one might say) in order to stimulate fertility and luck. This could also be described through reproductive, causative, or stimulus analogies—those that, given specific similarities, provoke certain reactions and seek to connect different dimensions of the world (Arnold 1996: 22; Arnold et al. 1992: 172; Arnold et al. 1996: 392, 406–410). Following this approach, all shepherds and animals grow together within the framework of mutually dependent relations (Arnold and Yapita 2001; see also the introduction to this book). I think this connection between merographic and Andean thinking could be useful in some contexts, as in the *ronda de coplas*, where the guests lend their bodies and voices to join the perspective of the shepherd-host, which prevails over all others. However, the ethnography of butchering is slightly different and does not resemble a merographic connection.

It is important to bear in mind that the animal body is the result of an intense process of mutual constitution with the shepherd. As a result, the butchering process illustrates that, inside animals, shepherds find organs that are, in fact, relations (Bastien 1985). It could be argued that these organs are never objects; they are always parts of other subjects (Strathern 1992).[8] This situation has strong resemblances with the Mesoamerican thought about folds and wrappings analyzed by Pitarch (2013), where the beings constitute an open set of wrapped perspectives. Persons (and other beings) are bundles composed of other parts of persons (and other beings). Pitarch's work proposes a Mesoamerican rereading of Amazonian perspectivism since these folds and wrappings act as perspectives that are not always compatible with each other and must be correctly handled to avoid falling prey to strange beings (ibid.: 118–119; cf. Lima 2002; Viveiros de Castro 1996). This may represent a case of topological perspectivism: the connections between different beings and perspectives depend on the correct execution of the operations of wrapping and unwrapping. By alternately showing and hiding, these operations orient the development of alien gazes.[9]

Similarly, in Huachichocana the topological operations at times have to deal with the gazes of other beings, and the worlds enacted by these relations cannot be easily incorporated in other perspectives without danger. The folding and wrapping of meat and leather take care of modulating the connections with other beings, assuming the ambiguous position that the moist parts of animals possess. To topologically manage this ambiguity is to assume that animal sacrifice and butchering connect different sides of the world, different beings (since part of the shepherd is retained in the moist animal meat), and that this connection will persist until the dehydration process ends. This is when pumas and *ánimus* could dangerously pounce into shepherds' relations. The human relational world is always being challenged by external points of view and can sometimes be seduced into seeing some things and not others—an 'art of seduction' as an aesthetic modulation of perspectives (Lagrou 2007: 137–155). In these situations, the topological adjustments try to modulate and lead the puma and the *ánimu*'s gaze so that it develops in a direction that does not affect the shepherd's world of relations. The process of wrapping and everting meats and leathers introduces a difference and prevents a connection. As Strathern (1999: 247–249) argues, in the merographic connection "each perspective in including another viewpoint as a part of itself must exclude the other *as a perspective,*" while "[in perspectivism] the point at which the viewer was conscious that he or she had a perspective on things would be the point at which he or she would meet (so to speak) the reciprocal perspectives of other life forms. Each would thus include the other's perspective *as a perspective.*"

This point of view could be useful in thinking about those fabricated *señas* in Huachichocana that attempt to keep worlds apart. After exploring analogical and merographic thought in the Andes, a more recent book by Arnold and Yapita (2006: 272–274) poses some similar arguments about the constitution of the self in relation to the other. They argue that in certain situations the logics of ontological predation are expressed in a similar way to how they are defined for lowland perspectivism—as a vital process of incorporation of the other (as a subject) into the self (Viveiros de Castro 1996). In some contexts, *suerte* would also be the result of a similar process: "'Luck' designates an aspect of the fertilizing forces incarnate in the captured enemy that has to be released. In releasing this 'luck', the captured thoughts in the head of the other are thereby transformed for one's own benefit" (Arnold and Yapita 2006: 233; see also 274). This Andean modulation of perspectivism (Allen 2015), as well as the Mesoamerican one (Pitarch 2013), has descriptive potential to further utilize our ethnographic data. Arnold and Yapita's (2006) interpretation of *suerte* rests on descriptions of warlike situations involving the capture of enemies and is more or less literal, depending on the case. In our example, the relation is between non-coincident human and non-human perspectives that challenge one another and can occasionally be described as enmity, especially between pumas and shepherds fighting for sheep and goats.

The question that emerges, then, is, why would a folded meat that 'looks dead' not be interesting from the puma's perspective? In this sense, a folded 'dead' meat is pure object, and because of this the puma will not want to wrap itself with it (as in a merographic connection when things-as objects are incorporated into one's perspective). Instead, as the shepherds with whom I worked maintain, the puma is interested in the 'lucky' meat, the 'still alive' meat, with a 'shepherd' inside. The puma wants that meat because of its perspectival quality and not despite it (see Strathern 2013: 388–391). Using the forces of topological relations to seduce others' vision, as in the case developed by Pitarch, the *huacheño* shepherds disguise and hide their *suerte* retained by the moist meat. We are in the presence of almost simultaneous relations that express the existence of two non-coincident perspectives about the same thing (see also Arnold and Yapita 2006: 100). This is perhaps what the shepherds tried to teach me: when the puma looks at the hanging meat, it does not see what we see. It sees what the shepherd sees as only a part of reality, but upon seeing it, that 'part' becomes a 'whole' for the puma (Lima 2002). Only in this way does the puma move away from the houses disregarding the 'dead' meat. Here, the reflection capacity of *señas* is twisted to reflect just a part of the animal-shepherd bundle, like a skewed mirror. And that could approximate a perspective definition of *seña*.

Closing Remarks

In this text I have attempted to describe and analyze the forces that in the Southern Andes exist in connection with others—forces that reflect each other mutually yet never identically. They are redundant relations of similarity (Platt 1986), vital for life and fertility, which nonetheless always emerge in specific forms, differentiating each being or set of relations. I have developed this analysis through the idea of *seña*, understood as a resemblance or co-indexing process between beings or parts of beings, and through specific examples involving the *corral* and its capability to promote *suerte*. *Corral* and *suerte* are presented as coincident forces/forms that are potentially present in viscera, material structures, objects (wool), body movements, and dances. In line with the introduction to this book, these resemblances point toward an idea of mutual dependence between beings (Arnold and Yapita 2001; Bugallo 2014; Lema 2014). Each being or context connects with the same *corral* (the same topological force of the circle and the spiral) and the same luck, although *corral* and luck are always expressed as something different for each of them. Similar arguments are found in other regions of the Andes (Allen 2015; Arnold 1996; Arnold et al. 1992; Franquemont et al. 1992). From these points of view, connecting different dimensions of life would imply incorporating *corral* and *suerte* into a larger generative movement, activating stimulus analogies or merographic connections in their Andean modulation.

But the ontological status of the topological relations in Huachichocana supposes other interesting movements, because relations can sometimes be evaluated, manipulated, and fabricated to avoid connections rather than activate them. Resemblances are not always encouraged; not all topological operations seek unambiguous relationships, nor do they attempt to intensify connections between forces and forms. All this is made explicit in the butchering process. When shepherds kill and open an animal, they find not just the traces of an external 'individual' or object capable of being incorporated as part of other things (as in a merographic connection). They also find a trace of a person, a trace of themselves wrapped in their animals that could be potential prey for others. When folding meats and leathers, shepherds try to prevent their world from resembling the world of the pumas by making it unattractive to them. These operations that disguise the subjects wrapped in animal bodies are intended to keep things separate, to reinforce difference. The analysis in this chapter advances these concepts, proposing some ideas to think about relationships as forces/forms that can (and sometimes must) be twisted.

I have argued that the perspectival quality of these Andean relations resembles both the Amazonian (Allen 2015; Arnold and Yapita 2001, 2006) and the Mesoamerican (Pitarch 2013) models. But before attempting to find perspectivism in the Andes, we can use the descriptive and analytical potential of these concepts to better describe our contexts (as also pointed out by Allen 2015). Resorting to the discussion on perspectivism allows us to emphasize that not all topological relations, or *señas*, linked to *suerte* can be described as analogical. Analogies and merographic connections are only a part of the story. To fully comprehend the shepherds' world of relations, it is necessary to introduce the topological Andean version of the difference of perspectives. In the examples provided in this chapter, these differences are expressed in terms of predatory relations (*ánimu*-shepherd, puma-shepherd). In the literature, these dangerous or destructive relations have often been treated as counterparts of fertility, as if, in a process of taming, the shepherds incorporate danger or destruction in their lives as fuel to boost fertility. But in this dual balance, the weight of fertility is always greater.

This type of merographic connection, which subsumes danger (as an object) under fertility, can be useful to analyze some cases, as in the rounds of *coplas*, when current enmities between shepherds are suspended to join the perspective of the host. But other contexts simply do not operate like that. When shepherds fold leathers and meats, they look for a different type of connection; they are attentive to the gaze of the pumas, who seem to have little interest in fertility. It is not a perspective added to another here. It is two points of view that cannot be simultaneous: one challenges the other. Shepherds defend themselves by twisting relations, folding meats and leathers so that the world 'looks like' something else.

At this point, the ethnography of Huachichocana can perhaps provide elements to think about an Amerindian theory of relations that needs no totalizing models. Drawing comparisons with the lowlands and Mesoamerica (even with Melanesia) can be helpful to explore continuities between ways of fabricating relations that overcome the so-called ontological barriers. The viscera of the *huacheños* may be useful to illustrate that many almost simultaneous worlds exist between fertility and predation.

Acknowledgments

I am very grateful to Giovanna Bacchiddu, Florencia Tola, Piero Di Giminiani, and Marcelo González Galvez for organizing the fascinating workshop "What Is a Relation?" Special thanks go to Els Lagrou, Marcelo González Galvez, and José Antonio Kelly for their challenging comments. Luisa Elvira Belaúnde, Denise Arnold, Verónica Lema, José María Miranda, and Indira Caballero also provided illuminating readings. Finally, I am grateful to the anonymous readers and to Martin Holbraad, the editor of *Social Analysis*, for their inspiring comments. This chapter draws on the project "Cosmopolitics of Cooking," financed by the Faculty of Philosophy and Humanities, National University of Córdoba, Argentina, from 2016–2018.

Francisco Pazzarelli holds a degree in History and a PhD in Anthropological Sciences from the Universidad Nacional de Córdoba, Argentina. Currently, he is a Professor in the Department of Anthropology at the same university and Adjunct Researcher at CONICET. Since 2006 he has carried out research in the Argentine Northwest, both from an archaeological and an ethnographical approach. His research interests are focused on food transformation techniques and their consequences on native theories of the body and the person, and on human-animal relationships

Notes

1. Harris (1986: 279n16) suggests that the notion about circular forms could even precede that about squares and corners characteristic of the Inca period.
2. On the generative force of forms, see Arnold and Yapita (2001) and Franquemont et al. (1992).
3. I use the verb 'orient' in connection with Strathern's (1992: 57) commentary on Munn's work in Melanesia: "The very process of making something visible is a social act that orients the entity (person, vessel) outwards towards those in whose eyes it appears."
4. The word *señalada* derives from the Spanish words *señal* and *señales*, in reference to the ceremonial cuts made in the ears of animals; but it has no relation, far as I know, to the word *seña*.
5. Full descriptions of similar events can be found in Arnold and Yapita (2001), Bugallo (2014), and Dransart (1991).
6. Dransart (1995: 236) makes a similar observation about the Isluga community in northern Chile: "The dance movements inside the corral, during the earlier part of the ceremony, more closely reflect the stages involved in spinning and plying yarn."
7. The *copla*, a poetic musical genre of mixed origin (pre-Hispanic and Spanish), generally employs four thematically linked verses.
8. Drawing on Wagner (1977), Strathern (1992: 79) explains this in more detail: "When a Melanesian looks inside a person (a relation), he or she finds other persons (relations). But such a relative is thereby composed of other relatives only insofar as the person takes on the task of attending to them. A flow of substance may be perceived as a reason for a counter-flow of gifts, thus producing a social relationship that contains the flow ... The Melanesian person thereby sustains the image of flowing substance through the wealth that is returned in the opposite direction, even as his or her descendants may return the flow (the substance) to him or her."
9. References to 'topological' mirrors and reflections are also present in Mesoamerica. As Pitarch (2013: 24) puts it: "The mirror does not reflect: it unwraps, it unfolds."

References

Allen, Catherine. 1982. "Body and Soul in Quechua Thought." *Journal of Latin American Lore* 8 (2): 179–196.

Allen, Catherine. 2015. "The Whole World Is Watching: New Perspectives on Andean Animism." In *The Archaeology of Wak'as: Explorations of the Sacred in the Pre-Columbian Andes*, ed. Tamara L. Bray, 23–46. Boulder: University Press of Colorado.

Arnold, Denise Y. 1996. "Introducción." In Arnold and Yapita 1996, 1–28.

Arnold, Denise Y., Domingo Jiménez, and Juan de Dios Yapita, eds. 1992. *Hacia un orden andino de las cosas: Tres pistas de los Andes meridionales* [Toward an Andean order of things: Three tracks of the Southern Andes]. La Paz: ILCA.

Arnold, Denise Y., and Juan de Dios Yapita, eds. 1996. *Madre melliza y sus crías: Ispall mama wawampi, antología de la papa* [Twin Mother and her babies: Ispall Mama Wawampi, anthology of the potato]. La Paz: Hisbol and ILCA.

Arnold, Denise Y., and Juan de Dios Yapita. 2001. *River of Fleece, River of Song: Singing to the Animals, an Andean Poetics of Creation*. Bonn: BAS and ILCA.

Arnold, Denise Y., and Juan de Dios Yapita. 2006. *The Metamorphosis of Heads: Textual Struggles, Education, and Land in the Andes*. Pittsburgh, PA: University of Pittsburgh Press.

Arnold, Denise Y., Juan de Dios Yapita, and Cipriana Apaza M. 1996. "Qipa Mama wawampi: Analogías de la producción de la papa en los textiles de Chukiñapi, Bolivia" [Qipa Mama wawampi: Analogies of potato production in the textiles of Chukiñapi, Bolivia]. In Arnold and Yapita 1996, 373–411.

Bastien, Joseph W. (1978) 1996. *La montaña del cóndor: Metáfora y ritual en un ayllu andino* [The mountain of the condor: Metaphor and ritual in an Andean ayllu]. La Paz: Hisbol.

Bastien, Joseph W. 1985. "Qollahuaya-Andean Body Concepts: A Topographical-Hydraulic Model of Physiology." *American Anthropologist* (n.s.) 87 (3): 595–611.

Bugallo, Lucila. 2014. "Flores para el ganado: Una concepción puneña del multi-plico (puna de Jujuy, Argentina)" [Flowers for cattle: A *puneña* conception of *multiplico* (puna de Jujuy, Argentina)]. In *Comprender los rituales ganaderos en los Andes y más allá: Etnografía de lidias, herranzas y arrierías* [Understanding livestock rituals in the Andes and beyond: Ethnography of wrestlers, *herrenzas*, and *arrierías*] ed. Juan Javier Rivera Andía, 311–363. Aachen: Shaker Verglag.

Bugallo, Lucila, and Mario Vilca. 2011. "Cuidando el ánimu: Salud y enfermedad en el mundo andino (puna y quebrada de Jujuy, Argentina)" [Caring for the animus: Health and disease in the Andean world (puna and quebrada de Jujuy, Argentina)]. Nuevo Mundo. http://nuevomundo.revues.org/61781.

Cereceda, Verónica. (1976) 2010. "Semiología de los textiles andinos: Las *talegas* de Isluga" [Semiology of Andean textiles: The *talegas* of Isluga]. *Chungará* 42 (1): 181–198.

Cereceda, Verónica. 1990. "A partir de los colores de un pájaro" [From the colors of a bird]. *Boletín del Museo Chileno de Arte Precolombino* 4: 57–104.

Dransart, Penny. 1991. "Fibre to Fabric: The Role of Fibre in Camelid Economies in Prehispanic and Contemporary Chile." PhD diss., University of Oxford.

Dransart, Penny. 1995. "Inner Worlds and the Event of a Thread in Isluga, Northern Chile." In *Andean Art: Visual Expression and Its Relation to Andean Beliefs and Values*, ed. Penny Dransart, 228–242. Aldershot: Avebury.

Flores Ochoa, Jorge. 1977. "Aspectos mágicos del pastoreo: Enqa, enqychu, illa y khuya rumi" [Magical aspects of grazing: *Enqa, enqychu, illa, and khuya rumi*]. In *Pastores de puna: Uywamichiq punarunakuna* [Pastors of puna: *Uywamichiq punarunakuna*], ed. Jorge Flores Ochoa, 211–237. Lima: Instituto de Estudios Peruanos.

Franquemont, Edward M., Christine Franquemont, and Billie Jean Isbell. 1992. "Awaq ñawin: El ojo del tejedor, la práctica de la cultura en el tejido" [*Awaq ñawin*: Weaver's eye, the practice of fabric culture]. *Revista Andina* 10 (1): 47–80.

Harris, Olivia. 1986. "From Asymmetry to Triangle: Symbolic Transformations in Northern Potosi." In Murra et al. 1986, 260–279.

Kessel, Juan van, and Porfirio Enríquez Salas. 2002. *Señas y señaleros de la Santa Tierra: Agronomía andina* [Signs and signalers of the Holy Land: Andean Agronomy]. Quito: Abya Yala/IECTA.

Kohn, Eduardo. 2013. *How Forests Think: Toward an Anthropology Beyond the Human*. Berkeley: University of California Press.

Lagrou, Els. 2007. *A fluidez da forma: Arte, alteridade e agência em uma sociedade amazônica (Kaxinawa, Acre)* [The fluidity of form: Art, alterity, and agency in an Amazonian society (Kaxinawa, Acre)]. Rio de Janeiro: TopBooks.

Lema, Verónica. 2014. "Criar y ser criados por las plantas y sus espacios en los Andes septentrionales de Argentina" [Raise and being raised by plants and their spaces in the northern Andes of Argentina]. In *Espacialidades Altoandinas* [High Andean spaces], ed. Alejandro Benedetti and Jorge Tomasi, 301–338. Buenos Aires: FFyL-UBA.

Lévi-Strauss, Claude. 1966. *Mythologiques*. Vol. 2: *Du miel auz cendres* [From honey to ashes]. Paris: Plon.

Lima, Tânia S. 2002. "O que é um corpo?" [What is a body?]. *Religião & Sociedade* 22 (1): 9–20.

Murra, John V., Nathan Wachtel, and Jacques Revel, eds. 1986. *Anthropological History of Andean Polities*. Cambridge: Cambridge University Press. Originally published in French in 1978.

Pazzarelli, Francisco. 2017. "A *sorte* da carne: Topologia animal nos Andes meridionais" [The luck of the flesh: Animal topology in the southern Andes]. *Horizontes Antropológicos* 23 (48): 129–149.

Pitarch, Pedro. 2013. *La cara oculta del pliegue: Antropología indígena* [The hidden side of the fold: Indigenous anthropology]. Mexico City: Artes de México.

Platt, Tristan. 1986. "Mirrors and Maize: The Concept of *Yanantin* among the Macha of Bolivia." In Murra et al. 1986, 228–259.

Platt, Tristan. 2002. "El feto agresivo: Parto, formación de la persona y mito-historia en los Andes" [The aggressive fetus: Childbirth, formation of the person, and myth-history in the Andes]. *Estudios Atacameños* 22: 127–155.

Ricard Lanata, Xavier. 2007. *Ladrones de sombra: El universo religioso de los pastores del Ausangate (Andes surperuanos)* [The thieves of shadows: The religious universe of the shepherds of the Ausangate (South Peruvian Andes)]. Lima: Instituto Francés de Estudios Andinos/Centro Bartolomé de las Casas.

Strathern, Marilyn. 1992. *After Nature: English Kinship in the Late Twentieth Century.* Cambridge: Cambridge University Press.

Strathern, Marilyn. 1999. "The Ethnographic Effect II." In *Property, Substance and Effect: Anthropological Essays on Persons and Things*, ed. Marilyn Strathern, 229–261. London: Athlone Press.

Strathern, Marilyn. 2013. *Learning to See in Melanesia: Four Lectures Given in the Department of Social Anthropology, Cambridge University, 1993–2008.* London: HAU Books.

Tylor, Gérald. 2000. *Camac, camay y camasca y otros ensayos sobre Huarochirí y Yauyos* [Camac, camay and camasca and other essays on Huarochirí and Yauyos]. Cuzco: IFEA-CBC.

Viveiros de Castro, Eduardo. 1996. "Os pronomes cosmológicos e o perspectivismo ameríndio" [The cosmological pronouns and Amerindian perspectivism]. *Mana* 2 (2): 115–144.

Viveiros de Castro, Eduardo. 2002. *A inconstância da alma selvagem e outros ensaios de antropologia* [The inconstancy of the savage soul and other anthropological essays]. São Paulo: Cosac Naify.

Wagner, Roy. 1977. "Analogic Kinship: A Daribi Example." *American Ethnologist* 4 (4): 623–642.

Chapter 3

ON PEOPLE, SENSORIAL PERCEPTION, AND POTENTIAL AFFINITY IN SOUTHERN CHILE

Cristóbal Bonelli

Almost two decades ago, Viveiros de Castro (2001) proposed affinity as the generic mode or relational principle of relatedness in South America. Inspired by Rivière's (1984, 1999) work on the Amerindian notion of kinship and, more importantly, by Lévi-Strauss's (1943) account regarding the model of affinity and relations with strangers in South America, Viveiros de Castro (2001) has shown how in Amazonia affinity prevails over consanguinity. In other words, his argument is that while affinity as the "dimension of the cosmic relational matrix" (ibid.: 19) is a given, consanguinity needs to be constructed through human action and intention. In order to go beyond the conceptualization of affinity as kinship ties, Viveiros de Castro introduced the concept of 'potential affinity' as a given generic relational value—a virtual dimension in which "kinship is the process of actualization" (ibid.: 22). This generic relational value had already been described by Lévi-Strauss (2000) through the analogy of a 'hinge' (Fr. *charnière*) between two ubiquitous opposites: affinity, as a hinge, (dis)connects human and divine, friend and enemy, kin and outsider, and so on. Thus, the conceptualization of the hinge of potential affinity indexes a relational domain that exceeds interspecies borders and involves intensive and transformative relations between humans and animals, plants, and spirits. In this way, it captures the tension at the core of this book. As a principle of relationality, potential affinity entails a continuous tension between a cosmological dependence on otherness and the necessity to maintain a certain kind of differentiating autonomy between self and the other.

Building upon ethnographic insights based on 18 months of fieldwork carried out in the district of Alto Bío Bío in Southern Chile, where more than 80 percent of the population are Pehuenche-Mapuche people residing in the mountains, in this chapter I would like to suggest that potential affinity, as a principle of relationality, demands a conceptualization of sensorial perception as inherently social and an understanding of sociality as radically perceptual. More specifically, I will explore how, among the Pehuenche, seeing and touching are key ontological operators for stabilizing the tension between autonomy and dependence on otherness in everyday life, as highlighted in this book.[1]

I begin this chapter with a discussion about how a relational dual scheme in Southern Chile, predicated upon the existence of invisible doubles, strongly permeates sensorial experience and the very constitution of 'real people' or *che*. Then, by focusing on greeting practices, I analyze how seeing and touching are key ontological operators at stake in enacting *che* through the mutual sensorial perception of real people who do not precede such encounters. The following section examines what occurs when the relational dual scheme is radically fractured in funerary practices as well as the existence of a particular evil spirit known as *witranalwe*. In concluding this chapter, I establish how relations between real people do not precede mutual sensorial perception but can be seen as the result of such perceptions, thus shedding light on the persisting conceptual continuities between Pehuenche and Amerindian kinship.[2]

Pehuenche Doubles and Sensorial Perception

In order to shed light on how the tension between autonomy and dependence on otherness is expressed in Pehuenche daily life, I would like to start by exploring the ways in which Pehuenche people conceptualize—and enact in practice—what it means to be a person. At the risk of being judged for providing univocal definitions, I have elsewhere written about Pehuenche personhood being a particular composition of various capacities (Bonelli 2012). Most of the Pehuenche whom I met during fieldwork conceptualize themselves as having two 'spirits'. I had the opportunity to discuss this idea with Francisco, a Pehuenche friend in his sixties, who told me: "People *have* two spirits: one that is capable of going away, the little crazy one called *am* or *ina mongen:* one's spirit, their *ina* that walks a little bit behind them, that comes behind. Their *mongen* is what is alive, too, but is invisible. That's their *ina mongen.* And the other spirit which always stays close to people and which is a spirit of life: the *püllü.*"

A Pehuenche person can be envisaged as a composition of different capacities or elements, namely, an *am*, a *püllü*, and a corporeal support sometimes called *kalül.*[3] The *am*, or the invisible double of the person, is always in the company of a *püllü*, a word that is polysemic and often refers to the spirit of the earth, which does not belong to the person since it pre-dates and post-dates people's lives. Every person is in co-existence with a particular *püllü* that, under normal conditions, is a part of their personal composition. I once naively asked my friends if I had a *püllü* too. Making fun of such an odd question, they replied that if I did not have a *püllü*, I could not be alive. Thus, in Alto Bío Bío, a person seems to be a multiply constructed composition: the person, or *che*, is a convergent personal space consisting of an *am*, a *püllü*, and a corporeal support.

Descriptions of this personal composition seemed to me, at least at the very beginning of my fieldwork, to be contradictory. My thinking was probably shaped by particular ideas about the self and the body that could be associated with liberal premises embedded in the arguments proposed by, for instance, John Locke, the English philosopher regarded as one of the most influential thinkers of the Enlightenment and considered to be the founder of classical liberalism. For Locke ([1694] 1975: 335), a person is a "thinking intelligent being, that has reason and reflection, and can consider itself as itself, the same thinking thing, in different times and places."[4] In contrast to this, I found myself puzzled by the fact that the *ina mongen* was part of the self, but not totally. The *ina mongen* was described to me as the invisible 'image' of the visible person. How could I envision an image that was not visible? How could I conceptualize this personal composition and be faithful to this complex ontological configuration without having to remain trapped within a logical, liberal Lockean paradox for which, simply put, similarity precedes difference?

Francisco's statements strongly resonated with ethnographies of other South American indigenous understandings of beings and their doubles, characterized by a metaphysical affirmation of the two rather than the negation of one (see Clastres 1974; Lima 1999). To put it in terms of the tension this volume is concerned with, autonomy (and in this case personal autonomy) was not predicated on identity, but on difference and duality. In fact, some of my Pehuenche friends often greeted me with a phrase that clearly reflects this principle: "You have already arrived, you were already here!" The image of myself reproduced in this sentence referred to my "little crazy" *am*, or *ina mongen*, as Francisco called it. My *ina mongen* could be seen in one place when my physical body was in another. Over time I realized that the sensorial perception of myself at stake in my ethnographic relation to the Pehuenche was not simply located where my physical body seemed to be. Instead, it entailed a kind of double perception.

This duality was expressed in different ways in Alto Bío Bío. For example, it can be revealing to recall the way in which Pehuenche people refer to their cognitive experience of thinking, called *rakiduam*, which is generally translated as 'thought' (see also González Gálvez 2016). If we consider that during the day the *ina mongen* always "walks a little bit behind," as stated by Francisco, it should not be surprising that singular utterances with the verb 'to think' that refer to the speaker's center (e.g., "I think") are not used. Rather, a passive form ("I was told by my thought") is the usual way of referring to one's thoughts. It is not necessary to speak Chedungun, the Pehuenche language, to realize the importance of this grammatical form, since even when speaking Spanish, Pehuenche people refer to thoughts as slightly separated from the speaker, rarely articulating sentences such as "I think." Their *rakiduam* appears separated from themselves, and this duality is illustrated in utterances such as "I do not know what is my thought" or "What does your thought think about this?"

During fieldwork, it took me some time to realize that this duality pervaded sensorial experiences in different ways and that in daily life, and under normal conditions, what a person is capable of seeing is not the indexical (invisible) *am* of another person, but rather their visible corporeal support (Ch. *kalül*). Moreover, after a few months living in Alto Bío Bío, I came to understand that the relational dual scheme underlying the people's composition refers not only to real people, but also to a generic relational scheme shared by different beings: even if the *am* is always explicitly defined as the invisible part of a person, animals are also often described as having an *am*. Put differently, animals, like people, are the result of the assemblage of different components. Every time someone who is awake sees the image of another person or animal, they refer to it as an *am*—an invisible double that manifests itself as a fleeting visible appearance, able to be seen but not touched. The relation between the person or animal and the *am* is not stable. My host Pedro and some of his friends once saw a little calf near the river while they were looking for their cow, which was eating grass somewhere in the area. After having found their cow, they came back to the place where the calf had been. They could not find it, and there were no visible traces of the animal at all. On another occasion, in that same place, they heard the loud roaring of a bull. When they looked for the bull, ready to catch it with a rope, there was no sign of it anywhere. Pedro told me that these animals that appear and disappear are called "enchanted animals" (Sp. *animales encantados*), also referred to as an animal's *am* (Ch. *am kullin*). What I wish to highlight here with regard to sensorial perception is the fact that doubles are able to be seen, but always unable to be touched.

This relational duality involving corporeal supports and doubles goes beyond people and animals and can be thought of as part of a wider Pehuenche relational scheme in Southern Chile. Generally speaking, trees, rivers, mountains, stars, the moon and the sun, all have/are their invisible double, which is known as *ngen* and generally translated as 'owner'. Some examples include the *ngen* of the sun (Ch. *ngenantu*), the moon (Ch. *ngenkullen*), the stars (Ch. *ngenwalen*), the araucaria tree (Ch. *ngendegi*), and so on. Each time someone enters an uninhabited place, or whenever someone needs to pick medicinal plants from the mountains, it is necessary to approach the place's or plant's *ngen* and ask its permission. My friend Bernardita told me she had discovered years ago that "the mountain was really alive" when the *ngen* of the mountain (Ch. *ngenmawida*) punished her and her sister Silvia because they were walking through forbidden places. The *ngenmawida* caused them to be disoriented so that they no longer knew where they were.

In a general sense, and in order to foreground how the tension between autonomy and dependence on otherness in Southern Chile is also an expression of this wider relational dual scheme, my aim here is to examine the relational similarities between *am* and *ngen*. A preliminary way to think about these is to conceive of the differences as being merely perspectival: the Pehuenche see themselves as being and having an *am*, while at the same time acknowledging the existence of other subjectivities or *ngen*. In the same way, the *ngen* might see themselves as being and having an *am*, even as they acknowledge the existence of other perspectives that could possibly be called *ngen*. While *ngen* are not able to be seen under normal conditions and live their lives within determined places, keeping some distance from the Pehuenche, animals and people co-exist within the same plane of visibility. In the same way an owner (Ch. *ngen*) inhabits a house (Ch. *ruka*), which is called *ngenruka*, I suggest that doubles inhabit and take care of their corresponding corporeal supports, a relation framed by the same caring relational scheme as *am-kalül*. The *am* and its corporeal support and the *ngen* and its corporeal support are dual aspects of a same singular composition. This relation is not necessarily one of mutual constitution between corporeal supports and their doubles, however, as a double can live without its mortal corporeal support, whereas a corporeal support cannot do so without its immortal double.[5]

What I am interested in highlighting here is the centrality that doubles have in configuring sensorial perception in Alto Bío Bío, which is also expressed through Pehuenche understandings of sleeping (see Bonelli 2012). In fact, any illusion of a personal unity that exists during waking hours is dispelled during the night. While a person is sleeping, her *ina mongen* goes away, entailing heavy risks for the sleeper. I was always told that when someone was having a nightmare, it was imperative to immediately wake that person up, as she could be the victim of evil spirits' attacks. It was only through sensorial perception involving being seen and touched by another real person that *che* could be fully enacted: an *am* in relation to its corporeal support needs another *am* in relation to its corporeal support in order for a person to be enacted as a real person. I heard many stories in Alto Bío Bío about people who had actually been killed by evil spirits while sleeping because they were not awakened it time by other real people. However, I could not gain a better understanding of what was at stake in these statements until I began to realize the very relevance of greeting practices. Indeed, as I will show in the next section, waking up someone else while sleeping strongly resonates with what occurs in greeting practices—a moment in which sensorial perception by personal compositions makes possible the emergence of real people who do not precede such encounters.

Greetings, Mutual Sensorial Perception, and People

The extreme importance people confer on greetings in Alto Bío Bío is an ethnographic fact that anyone spending a few days living in a Pehuenche community would easily notice. During my first weeks in the field, every time I explicitly declared my intention to live within a Pehuenche community, I was strongly advised to learn how to greet people properly as a prerequisite before doing so. This recommendation was surprising to me and pushed me to begin thinking that the act of greeting was not conceived of as spontaneous speech, instrumental only in starting a conversation, but rather as a key ontological social transaction. In this sense, and as Course (2011) has argued, I quickly realized that, among the Mapuche, to refuse a greeting is to refuse the existence of social relations and to refute the prerequisite to such relations—that is, shared personhood. However, as far as greetings are concerned, the relation between sensorial perception, in general, and seeing and touching, in particular, have been completely left out of anthropological analyses and obscured by the focus placed on spoken communication (Course 2007, 2011; Quidel Lincoleo 2001). In this chapter I would like to emphasize the relevance of sensorial perception over language transactions. This is key for my argument as it brings to the fore the relevance of sensorial perception as preceding the very emergence of people.

Once, when attending the funeral of a young Pehuenche woman, the excitement and darkness of the occasion distracted me from noticing the presence of a good friend with whom I had spent the whole day. When we met at work the following day (we were building a house together), he was extremely offended because I had not seen him and greeted him at the funeral. In a very sad tone of voice, he asked me: "Am I not a person?" (Ch. *Chengelan iñche?*). What is important to stress regarding his statement is that it clearly points out one of the central arguments of this chapter: without mutual sensorial perception, a person cannot be fully enacted, resulting in the non-establishment of proper kinship ties. In other words, a real person or *che* can only be fully activated through the eyes of others, a common idea among ethnographers of Amazonia.

As the Mapuche linguist Jaqueline Caniguan (2005) has argued, greetings are a social norm that can be expressed in more or less formal interactions. It is interesting to consider in depth Caniguan's analysis of greetings and her particular focus on a specific word used to refer to the act of greeting. This word is *pentukun*, which has usually been translated with reference to the more structured conversational transaction two people have when meeting each other. However, what is striking for my argument is that the word *pentukun* itself is a semantic composition made of different actions or verbs: the verb 'to see' (Ch. *pen*) and the verb 'to touch' (Ch. *tuku*). Semantically speaking, the word itself makes no reference to acts of speech as such, but rather refers to sensorial experiences preceding language that render social relations possible. What is even more interesting is that Caniguan conceives of seeing as a collective action that can also be translated as an 'encounter', as confirmed by Augusta's ([1916] 1991) Mapuche-Spanish dictionary. Within my argument, this very act of encountering necessarily entails not only physical contact between people by shaking hands or hugging, but also the visual recognition of the participants. What I am interested in foregrounding here are the clear associations of continuity—if not fully apparent ones—between the actions of seeing and touching and the capacities of the double-*am* and its corporeal support. Put simply, a person needs to be seen and touched by another person in order to emerge as a real person, the very operator of this recognition being the sensorial perception concerning seeing and touching. Put another way, if we consider persons as objectified relations in the eyes of others, made up of a spiritual capacity and a corporeal support, it is not surprising that the very act of greeting involves actions concerning capacities of the double-*am* (seeing) and the corporeal support or *kalül* (touching).

Mutual sensorial perception between real people thus implies the very presence of singular assemblages between *am* and corporeal supports. In other words, in Alto Bío Bío sensorial perception always entails a duality or a dual relational scheme that precedes the autonomy of individual persons. Indeed, what I want to suggest is that the very possibility of real people activation is predicated upon sensorial perception in the first place. Following from this, it becomes relevant to explore what occurs when the duality *am*-corporeal support is radically fractured. Funerary practices and a particular evil spirit known as *witranalwe* are paradigmatic examples for analyzing this fracture.

From *Am* to *Witranalwe* and the Unmaking of Mutual Sensorial Perception

Now that I have discussed how a relational dual scheme in Southern Chile predicated upon the existence of invisible doubles strongly permeates sensorial experience and the very constitution of real people or *che*, and how greeting practices entail seeing and touching as key ontological operators at stake in enacting *che* through mutual sensorial perception, I can now concentrate on how the existence of a wicked spirit known as *witranalwe* (the verb *witran* can mean 'to visit', whereas *alwe* is generally translated as 'soul') disrupts and challenges the normal functioning of sensorial perception among Pehuenche. My aim here is to be able to understand better the relation that exists between the *am* and the corporeal support (Ch. *kalül*) and to render explicit that, for the Pehuenche, invisible doubles should not be thought of in opposition to what is material; instead, they can be considered as a necessary precondition for sensorial experience.

According to Bacigalupo (2007), a *witranalwe* is a personification of a Spanish man on a horse who exploits Mapuche men and rapes their wives. Citarella (2000) and Course (2011) explain how witches create *witranalwe* from femurs recovered from abandoned cemeteries. The bones are attached together and brought to life in a secret ceremony, and the *witranalwe* is then sold to a customer. Course states that *witranalwe* "serve their owners as guardians of the sheep and cattle that make up the owner's wealth. During the day they live in a small jar inside the house, and only at night do they emerge and take on their full size" (ibid.: 34).

In my ethnography, however, the uniqueness of the *witranalwe*, and what renders it different from other evil spirits, lies in the fact that it corresponds to the *am* or *ina mongen* of a person who has died (see also Citarella 2000) and has stayed, strolling 'somewhere around', rather than reaching the *wenu mapu*, the place that the living double inhabits after a person's death. In more specific terms, I was told that a *witranalwe* corresponds to an ex-*am* of a person who was not a good person during his or her lifetime—a person who was a *weya am* (roughly translatable as 'bad person' or 'bad human intentionality'). *Weya am* are a favorite resource of witches; the *witranalwe* is an *am* that has been 'fixed' by witches. In the words of my host Pedro: "And they, witches, take out spirits from the deceased, the *am*, the spirit, evil spirits that are *fixed* by those witches. There are good *am* and evil *am*. The *am* is the spirit … *Weya am*, those are bad, those are around with witches, with the devil. The witches [Ch. *kalku*] say that they are interested in having evil spirits [Ch. *kalku*] so they can harm other people."

In a very general sense, as Course (2011) has described, the *witranalwe* can be seen as 'a human non-person'. However, I suggest that it is more precise to say that a *witranalwe* is a former-person without corporeal support—a former *am*, in a certain sense depersonalized, given its existence as an eternal outsider to the corporeal support of the *che*. My objective here is not to analyze death,[6] but rather Pehuenche people's sensorial capacities for seeing and touching in relation to this collection's main concern, that is, the tension between autonomy and dependence on otherness. Nonetheless, it is important to mention some aspects of the death of a Pehuenche person in order to shed light on how dying entails the fading out of a person's autonomy. In general, and as other anthropologists have already demonstrated (Bloch 1988; Mosko 1983; Strathern 1988, 1992), the moment of death is crucial in understanding a person's composition. It is interesting here to consider some aspects of the funerary practices that are conducted in cemeteries. Even if burial could be described as a 'simple affair' inside ritual practices (Course 2007), I view it as necessary to comprehend the Pehuenche person's decomposition at the moment of death. Here I seek to shed light on how dying entails the risk of 'untamed relationality', understood as an ontological imbalance between autonomy and dependence on otherness.

In all the burials that I witnessed, near the end of the ceremony it was of great importance for each person to throw one or two handfuls of soil over the coffin, which had been placed in a hole in the ground. In Alto Bío Bío, this act, known as 'the last service' (Sp. *el último servicio*), is intended to fully cover the corpse with soil so people can make sure that the dead person is not going to become visible again. A typical mealtime joke among my herbalist friend's family, referring with jocularity to the moment of the last service, was to say: "We should take advantage of being able to eat, because later on we will just be eating soil." Most importantly, in Alto Bío Bío the last service is crucial because people fear that witches with bad intentions (Ch. *weya rakiduam*) can use and abuse the *am* outside of the personal composition. However, it is also possible that people fear the possible transformation of the *am* into *witranalwe* without any intervention of witches, but simply as a result of the deceased's immoral behavior while alive.

When an old *ngendumu*[7] of the community died, I noticed that my host Pedro was particularly concerned. His worries had begun at the house of the deceased (Sp. *finao*) during the wake (Ch. *umatun*), when he noticed that the casket was smaller than the corpse. "He was one of the big ones," Pedro told me, "and if no one changes the casket, the deceased won't leave peacefully." Despite his great concern, no one did anything to remedy the situation. Pedro's distress increased when, once in the cemetery, he noticed that the hole that had been dug for the coffin was not sufficiently wide or deep. "That hole is too small," he remarked. "The deceased will not leave satisfied." That night, remembering the life of the departed, Pedro's worries had not abated. Days later, another friend explained to me that Pedro's concern was due to the fear of actually seeing the deceased, or *finao*, as an *am* again, outside of the singular co-existence: "If the deceased did not leave calmly, he is not going to rest in peace, so he will reappear in his house. Somebody might see him as an *am* flying around his house."

When someone dies, the *am* continues to exist even as the corporeal support progressively decomposes.[8] In fact, the *am* must be aided in leaving the corpse by people who are alive, as it is still dependent on others. What is at stake here, I think, is that the *am* lacks visible corporeal support—a residence—from where it can be activated as a *che* through mutual perception. This fact also makes it incapable of communicating its departure to its fellows. The night after a wake, a friend dreamt that he was attending his own funeral, and he was actually able to see the proceedings from above. The great problem in this dream was that he was unable to tell the people at the funeral that he was well. "I dreamt my *am*," he told me. The impossibility of communicating affects the *am* in death, leaving it as an outsider to its own singular co-existence. Consequently, the deceased person is left in a position of anti-social vulnerability that might enable it to be captured by witches' powers. Thus, the *am*, far away from the corporeal support, appears to be extremely dependent on the assistance of the community, or more specifically on the last service.

What I would like to suggest is that the last service is a moral service of reciprocity: the *am* is helped so that it can leave successfully, but at the same time the community is protected against the *am*'s possible reappearance. Moreover, for the Pehuenche, the main problem the former-person entails, especially when considered from the perspective of victims of nocturnal attacks (see Bonelli 2012, 2014), is that the ex-*am witranalwe* is a being that can be neither physically recognized nor touched, and a visitor who cannot be greeted is a person who cannot be fully activated. In other words, ex-*am witranalwe* visitations reveal, in a negative form, what Course (2011: 161) conceptualizes as the central ontological dilemma of Mapuche life: the idea that "to be a person one must enter into social relations, and it is through the perspective of the 'Other' that one is attributed the status of *che*." But the perspective of this other called *witranalwe* is the perspective of a former *am* without a residence—without corporeal support—that has been exiled for eternity from the relations between kin, which are determined in part by the similarity of constructed corporeal supports. In part, I think that this evil spirit can be thought of as a social capacity turned into an immoral one, since the lack of its corporeal support makes mutual sensorial perception between real people impossible. In fact, and this is the main point of this chapter, in order to engage in relations with real Pehuenche people, it is necessary to be able to see and touch one another. That is why greetings among the Pehuenche are ontologically relevant: they are the paradigmatic performances in which real people are fully activated by mutual seeing and touching.

Conclusions

In this chapter I have tried to establish that, among the Pehuenche, perception is social as much as sociality is perceptual. Following and experimenting with the framing of this book, I have considered how the tension between dependence on otherness and autonomy is expressed through the mundane relevance people give to sensorial perception in general and to seeing and touching in particular. Indeed, all the materials I have mobilized in this chapter show how the minimal unit of analysis of sensorial perception in Pehuenche life is not one of separated unities, but an assemblage of multiple capacities involving visible and invisible relational entities.

I would like to finish this chapter by proposing that the tension between autonomy and dependence on otherness might be considered as a conceptual outcome mostly afforded by the ethnographic persistence of potential affinity as a hinge between dual ubiquitous opposites. I have aimed to show how potential affinity in Southern Chile, understood as a 'sensorial hinge', not only (dis)connects human and divine, friend and enemy, kin and outsider, but also affords the very constitution of real people. In this sense, the redescription of potential affinity through an ethnographic account of Pehuenche mutual sensorial perception might be a way to open up—and perhaps dilute—the analytical separation and predefined abstractions at stake in the considerations of autonomy as a moral condition and of dependence on otherness as an ontological destiny. Viewing autonomy and dependence on otherness as two sides of the same 'sensorial hinge coin', so to speak, what I have attempted to demonstrate in this chapter is not only that *che* in Southern Chile can be seen as the sum of visible physicality plus the capacity for productive sociality (see Course 2011), but also that real people can be fully enacted only through mutual sensorial perception strongly predicated upon a relational dual scheme entailing doubles plus corporeal supports. I suggest that it is through mutual sensorial perception among real people that all these relations are objectified as persons.

Acknowledgments

I would like to thank the editors of this book for their comments on preliminary versions of this chapter. I also extend thanks to the anonymous reviewers and Martin Holbraad for their generous and insightful suggestions. Research for this paper was supported by the Center for Indigenous and Intercultural Research (CIIR) (CONICYT/FONDAP/15110006), the Center for Integrated Disaster Risk Management (CIGIDEN) (CONICYT/FONDAP/15110017), and FONDECYT Projects No. 11180179 and No. 1191377. I also thank Emma Welter for having corrected my English.

Cristóbal Bonelli is an Associate Professor in the Department of Anthropology at the University of Amsterdam. He currently is the Principal Investigator of the ERC project "Worlds of Lithium," which aims to anthropologically understand planetary decarbonization strategies based upon lithium-ion batteries in three countries: Chile (lithium extraction), China (battery production), and Norway (lithium recycling). He also collaborates with the Center for Integrated Disaster Risk Management (Conicyt/Fondap/15110017) and the Indigenous and Intercultural Research Center (CIIR) (CONICYT/FONDAP/15110006).

Notes

1. Following Taylor (1993) and Surrallés (2003), Ewart (2008) has already shown how vision may be a key sensory dimension in distinguishing the human from the non-human within Amerindian cosmologies.
2. Recent scholarship on Mapuche people has demonstrated the partial correspondence of Mapuche kinship notions and practices from general principles observed elsewhere in indigenous South America (see Bonelli 2014; Course 2011; González Gálvez 2016). By analyzing the Mapuche concept of the true person (Ch. *che*), understood as the non-essentialistic construction of different types of socialities, Course (2011) has argued that Mapuche people, when considered through traditional understandings of kinship, are confined within consanguineal kin, and that the relative values of consanguinity and affinity found elsewhere in South America have been inverted to a certain extent by both forced settlement on reservations and the imposition of a system of patrilineal inheritance by the Chilean state.
3. I will use the idiom 'corporeal support' rather than 'body', given that the latter has clear and distinct uses in different traditions, for example, the perspectivist tradition in anthropology and the biomedical tradition in the sciences. By 'corporeal support' I suggest the material structure that supports the other capacities entailed in the composition of people.

4. Fausto (2008), from whom I took inspiration, has already analyzed this statement in relation to Amerindian notions of ownership.

5. Leaving aside the many complexities of the different uses of the word *ngen*, it is evident and undeniable that the word always refers to the existence of one thing in relation to another: *ngen* is the evocation of a relation. The common translation of *ngen* as 'owner' (Sp. *dueño*) makes apparent its relational nature. However, this translation is equivocal, since *ngen* does not imply a relation of possession as the English term 'ownership' does (Course 2012; Di Giminiani 2018; Fausto 2008).

6. For a detailed analysis of Mapuche death, considered as a process of synthesis carried out in ritual practices through the dead person's biography, see Course (2007). For an analysis of cognitive aspects of mourning among the Jivaro, see Taylor (1993). For other seminal work on death among Amerindian peoples, see Carneiro da Cunha (1978), Overing (1993), and Viveiros de Castro (1996).

7. *Ngendumu* is the name given to one of the most important organizers of the fertility ritual (Ch. *nguillatun*).

8. In this regard, Bonning (1995: 112) points out that the decomposition of a corpse is a sign of the estrangement of the *am*, stating that "the form of the body, the phenotype of the human body depends on the presence of the *am*." Bonning comes to the conclusion that the *am* is "a 'formative principle' that allows each thing (and not only human beings) to end up being exactly what it is" (ibid.: 114).

References

Augusta, Félix. (1916) 1991. *Diccionario araucano* [Araucanian dictionary]. Temuco: Editorial Kushe.

Bacigalupo, Ana Mariella. 2007. *Shamans of the Foye Tree: Gender, Power, and Healing among Chilean Mapuche*. Austin: University of Texas Press.

Bloch, Maurice. 1988. "Introduction: Death and the Concept of a Person." In *On the Meaning of Death: Essays on Mortuary Rituals and Eschatological Beliefs*, ed. Sven Cederroth, Claes Corlin, and Jan Lindström, 11–30. Uppsala: Almqvist & Wiksell.

Bonelli, Cristóbal. 2012. "Ontological Disorders: Nightmares, Psychotropic Drugs and Evil Spirits in Southern Chile." *Anthropological Theory* 12 (4): 407–426.

Bonelli, Cristóbal. 2014. "What Pehuenche Blood Does: Hemic Feasting, Intersubjective Participation, and Witchcraft in Southern Chile." *HAU: Journal of Ethnographic Theory* 4 (1): 105–127.

Bonning, Ewald. 1995. *El concepto de pillán entre los mapuches* [The concept of *pillán* among the Mapuches]. Buenos Aires: Centro Argentino de Etnología Americana.

Caniguan, Jaqueline. 2005. "Apuntes sobre el Pentukun: Mari mari lamngen" [Notes on the Pentukun: Mari mari lamngen]. *Azkintuwe* (February–March):

15–16. https://www.mapuche-nation.org/espanol/html/nacion_m/cultura/ nm-art-03.htm.

Carneiro da Cunha, Manuela. 1978. *Mortos e os outros* [Death and others]. São Paulo: Hucitec.

Citarella, Luca, ed. 2000. *Medicinas y culturas en la Araucanía* [Medicines and cultures in Araucanía]. 2nd ed. Santiago: Editorial Sudamericana.

Clastres, Pierre. 1974. *La société contre l'état* [Society against the state]. Paris: Minuit.

Course, Magnus. 2007. "Death, Biography, and the Mapuche Person." *Ethnos* 72 (1): 77–101.

Course, Magnus. 2011. *Becoming Mapuche: Person and Ritual in Indigenous Chile.* Urbana: University of Illinois Press.

Course, Magnus. 2012. "The Birth of the Word: Language, Force, and Mapuche Ritual Authority." *HAU: Journal of Ethnographic Theory* 2 (1): 1–26.

Di Giminiani, Piergiorgio. 2018. *Sentient Lands: Indigeneity, Property, and Political Imagination in Neoliberal Chile.* Tucson: University of Arizona Press.

Ewart, Elizabeth. 2008. "Seeing, Hearing and Speaking: Morality and Sense among the Panará in Central Brazil." *Ethnos* 73 (4): 505–522.

Fausto, Carlos. 2008. "Donos demais: Maestria e domínio na Amazônia" [Too many owners: Mastery and domination in the Amazon]. *Mana* 14 (2): 329–366.

González Gálvez, Marcelo. 2016. *Los mapuche y sus otros: Persona, alteridad y sociedad en el sur de Chile* [The Mapuche and their others: Person, alterity, and society in southern Chile]. Santiago: Editorial Universitaria.

Lévi-Strauss, Claude. 1943. "The Social Use of Kinship Terms among Brazilian Indians." *American Anthropologist* (n.s.) 45 (3): 398–409.

Lévi-Strauss, Claude. 2000. "Postface." *L'Homme* 154–155: 713–720.

Lima, Tânia Stolze. 1999. "The Two and Its Many: Reflections on Perspectivism in a Tupi Cosmology." *Ethnos* 64 (1): 107–131.

Locke, John. (1694) 1975. *An Essay Concerning Human Understanding.* Ed. Peter H. Nidditch. Oxford: Clarendon Press.

Mosko, Mark S. 1983. "Conception, De-conception and Social Structure in Bush Mekeo Culture." *Mankind* 14 (1): 24–32.

Overing, Joanna. 1993. "Death and the Loss of Civilized Predation among the Piaroa of the Orinoco Basin." *L'Homme* 126–128: 191–211.

Quidel Lincoleo, José. 2001. *Cosmovisión Mapuche y etiología Mapuche de la Salud, en Makewe-Pelale: Un estudio de caso en la complementariedad en Salud* [Mapuche worldview and Mapuche health etiology in Makewe-Pelale: A case study on complementarity in health]. Washington, DC: Pan American Health Organization.

Rivière, Peter. 1984. *Individual and Society in Guiana: A Comparative Study of Amerindian Social Organisation.* Cambridge: Cambridge University Press.

Rivière, Peter. 1999. "Shamanism and the Unconfined Soul." In *From Soul to Self*, ed. M. James C. Crabbe, 70–88. London: Routledge.

Strathern, Marilyn. 1988. *The Gender of the Gift: Problems with Women and Problems with Society in Melanesia.* Berkeley: University of California Press.

Strathern, Marilyn. 1992. *Reproducing the Future: Essays on Anthropology, Kinship and the New Reproductive Technologies*. Manchester: Manchester University Press.

Surrallés, Alexandre. 2003. "Face to Face: Meaning, Feeling and Perception in Amazonian Welcoming Ceremonies." *Journal of the Royal Anthropological Institute* 9 (4): 775–791.

Taylor, Anne-Christine. 1993. "Remembering to Forget: Identity, Mourning and Memory among the Jivaro." *Man* (n.s.) 28 (4): 653–678.

Viveiros de Castro, Eduardo. 1996. "Le meurtrier et son double chez les Araweté: Un exemple de fusion rituelle" [The murderer and his double among the Araweté: An example of ritual fusion]. Trans. Estela dos Santos Abreu. *Systèmes de pensée en Afrique noire* 14: 77–104.

Viveiros de Castro, Eduardo. 2001. "GUT Feelings about Amazonia: Potential Affinity and the Construction of Sociality." In *Beyond the Visible and the Material: The Amerindianization of Society in the Work of Peter Rivière*, ed. Laura M. Rival and Neil L. Whitehead, 19–44. Oxford: Oxford University Press.

Chapter 4

SORCERY, REVENGE, AND ANTI-REVENGE
Relational Excess and Individuation in the Gran Chaco

Florencia Tola

> Without one there cannot be many
> and without many it is not possible to refer to one.
> Therefore one and many arise dependently
> and such phenomena do not have the sign of inherent existence.
>
> —Nagarjuna, *Las setenta estrofas de la vaciedad*[1]

On 5 October 2008, I received a phone call in Buenos Aires with the news that Qom leader Timoteo Francia had passed away that morning in the hospital in Formosa, the northernmost city of the Argentinean Chaco. The medical diagnosis was tuberculosis, but the social diagnosis that would come later indicated sorcery. I took the first flight to Formosa and went to the church where the wake was being held. Timoteo's father Zenón, an evangelical pastor, hugged me and

Notes for this chapter begin on page 99.

said: "He's gone, my sister. He's already gone." As a consolation, he whispered to me: "His sister saw in dreams that he was bewitched. [The shaman aggressor] sent one [invisible arrow] to his stomach and one to his head. She saw it. We already know who the aggressor was, sister, but since we are evangelicals, what can we do?"

The Qom people, customarily known as Toba according to Guaraní identification, are the largest indigenous group in the Argentinean Chaco.[2] They belong to the Guaycurú linguistic family. While most of the Qom population lives in urban and rural areas around northern Argentina, communities are also located in Paraguay and Bolivia across the Gran Chaco of South America. Guaycurú groups, constituted through the union of extended families, are historically characterized by a social organization shaped by nomadism and hunter-gatherer economies (see Braunstein and Miller 1999; Cordeu and de los Ríos 1982). Colonization processes, however, imposed sedentary land use among the Qom.

In Qom society, death is generally considered a murder that can be consequently avenged—as the Qom people say, *la contra* (the counter-attack) has to ensue. The person responsible for the murder must be found. This could be a shaman, a sorcerer, or any individual with an avenging motive. Like most deaths among the Qom, Timoteo's was considered the result of a murder. The wake, which lasted several days, was particularly tense. Close family members kept talking about avenging Timoteo's death. Hypotheses were considered in relation to several questions, such as who had come to visit Timoteo, who his wife's lovers could be, and what possible grudges his abandoned ex-wife might hold. Other political leaders' envy was thoroughly analyzed and interpreted amid feelings of anger and sadness on the part of Timoteo's parents, siblings, uncles, aunts, nephews, and nieces.

Qom reflections on death as the result of sorcery attacks (*daño*) and on revenge (*contra*) lie within a theory about relations, persons, and bodies. In the Qom "metaphysics of the relation" (Viveiros de Castro 2013: 53), the person is a device that condenses a multiplicity of relations with human and non-human beings, and these relations are expressed through corporeal effects (emotions, physical or behavioral features, illness, affects). Rather than being circumscribed to the limits of her/his body, the Qom person expands toward other beings with porous bodies and is made up of bodily extensions (fluids, substances, parts) and components (souls, shadows, names) that are attached or detached according to the type of relation and the entities that are being related to (Tola 2009, 2012). All entities considered as persons are potentially interwoven with(in) each other. *Shiȳaxaua* is the Qom lexeme that I translate as 'person'. According to some Qom interlocutors, this term could also be translated as 'to go with/to be accompanied'. This native interpretation agrees with several assertions recorded during my fieldwork, such as the expression "I am not alone/only [*solo*] in my body," uttered by Seferino, a young shaman, while explaining that his body was composed of spiritual components, substances, fluids, and emotions coming from other human and non-human entities with which he interacted. Through this expression, Seferino also implied that he existed even outside his 'own' body (Tola 2012).

The composite and relational character of the Toba person may lead, under some circumstances, to what I call a 'relational excess'. In this Amerindian context (the Gran Chaco region), all entities are understood as capable of communicating with, permeating, and being affected by others. Persons expand toward other porous persons, producing a permanent relatedness: fluids, emotions, names, bodily parts circulate among people, generating interconnectedness and relationality. Babies receive from their parents the *lqui'i*, which is the capacity to feel/think, and the corporeal aspect. Corporal fluids circulate between generations, transmitting knowledge and emotions. Due to this interconnectedness, people's actions deeply and inevitably affect other people.

In this chapter, I explore the idea that Qom social life alternates between this relational excess and the search for fissures that are needed to sever—or at least to pause—this excessive relatedness. This search for fissures is dictated by the fact that relational excess makes the individual vulnerable to malevolent manipulation by others, whose attacks target specific elements of the individual, given that the Qom person is generally understood as composed by detachable features (hair, skin, names, substances, etc.). Among the Qom, persons are considered a vortex of relations or, in Marilyn Strathern's (1996) terms, a 'network'. Strathern refers to network as "a concept which works indigenously as a metaphor for the endless extension and intermeshing of phenomena" (ibid.: 522). Can this network be "'stopped' from further extension" (ibid.: 523), as the author expresses it? Is there some mechanism by which the one can be separated from the many? Is there a moment at which the Toba network can be cut?

To answer these questions, I will look at practices of sorcery, revenge, and anti-revenge among the Qom people. Ethnographic analyses enable us to think about these practices and ideas as mechanisms for intentionally creating, fissuring, expanding, and retracting the network that Qom individuals embody. I will highlight the existence of degrees in the relational excess produced by sorcery and revenge and examine individuation and anti-revenge practices that are intended to block the network. I understand individuation as the process by which individuals are made such through their unfinished and partial removal from the networks they embody. Several cases recorded during my fieldwork show that the cycle of attack and revenge does not repeat *ad infinitum*. In some circumstances, relatives of the victims of sorcery and revenge decide to cut the network—that is, to separate the one and the many—and not to take vengeance. A focus on practices and ideas of sorcery, revenge, and anti-revenge can shed light on how processes of individuation unfold in ways that a person—composed by others—becomes singular.

In this chapter, I argue that in Qom society the individuation of persons made up of components as disparate as fluids, names, shadows, and emotions—components capable of crossing porous bodily borders—requires practices directed at differentiating each individual from others who are constituted within the same broader process put in motion by the circulation of the same components. Some of these practices are associated with revenge and anti-revenge, aimed at momentarily removing the individual from the network of relations that constitute her or him, since, as we have seen, the Qom person is understood as one possible outcome of multiple shared relations. As suggested by Gonzalez, Di Giminiani, and Bacchiddu in the introduction to this book, the constitutive power of relations in indigenous South America is maintained by the need to balance a dependence on otherness with the autonomy of beings. In the ethnographic context presented in this chapter, the tension between dependence and autonomy is expressed through fissures—such as those associated with practices of revenge and anti-revenge—that are intended to curtail the relational excess that characterizes and defines the Qom persons.

To examine the relationship between individuation and revenge, I will begin with a general account of Qom practices of sorcery that lead to murder (*daño*) and revenge (*contra*). I will then present some aspects of the Qom kinship system, highlighting how relatives are produced by processes of consubstantiality through regular physical intimacy and shared corporeal fluids and food (Overing and Passes 2002; Vilaça 1992, 2002, 2005). It is within the consubstantial kindred group that sorcery and revenge occur, especially toward a spouse, in marriages that are considered incestuous. I will point out that kin are made and unmade through consubstantiality, marriage, incest, and sorcery. Finally, I will turn to episodes in which revenge does not occur—events that produce what I call 'anti-revenge'. I seek to understand the reasons for anti-revenge decisions, considered as attempts to cut the relational excess produced by kinship norms, among other factors.

Qom ethnographies show the centrality of consubstantiality in line with ethnographies of the Gran Chaco area (Otaegui 2013, 2019; Tola 2012), together with sorcery and revenge—themes that have been abundantly portrayed in lowland South American societies. Over the last three decades, Amerindian ethnography has developed concepts of great theoretical productivity to analyze the relations between identity and alterity. Debates on predation and relations with enemies concern the relationship between victim, aggressor, and avenger at the core of contemporary shamanic sorcery and revenge practices discussed in this chapter. Among the most frequently discussed concepts, we can find 'predation' (Descola 1996; Erikson 1987; Fausto 1997, 2001; Rivière 2001; Taylor 2001; Vilaça 2002, 2005; Viveiros de Castro 1986) and 'enemy', especially concerning the relationship between victim and warrior (Carneiro da Cunha and Viveiros de Castro 1985; Conklin 1993; Lima 2005; Sterpin 1993; Taylor 2001; Vilaça 1992; Viveiros de Castro 2002). Ontological predation refers to the idea that the self and the *socius* require the appropriation of the other for their own existence and reproduction—an alter that is familiarized and transformed into a constitutive part of the self. At the heart of this Amerindian philosophy of predation is the notion of the enemy. The self requires for its very existence the passage through alterity; the other is usually the enemy. Murderers attach to their bodies symbolic resources from the enemy (souls, trophies, names, scalps, songs, etc.) obtained after war incursions (Viveiros de Castro 2002: 290). What is incorporated keeps traces of alterity. It is not a total identification between the one and the other. The other remains other and, as such, provides a different point of view about the self. What is incorporated is, more precisely, a relation (ibid.).

Significantly, these practices resemble those observed historically in the context of inter-ethnic wars and the capture of scalps, a phenomenon recorded by travelers, missionaries, and ethnographers of the Gran Chaco (Karsten 1926, 1932; Lozano 1941; Métraux 1937; Nordenskiöld 1912; Palavecino 1933). Wars between pairs of ethnic enemies were often motivated by revenge, understood less as a circle that closes at some point than as an interminable social phenomenon (Sterpin 1993: 58n12). The so-called Chaco war, similarly to Jibaro wars and the Tupinamba revenge system (Clastres 1974; Sztutman 2007), would have had neither a beginning nor an end (Sterpin 1993), since there would always be a death to avenge if we think of any death as a murder. This debate resonates with the sorcery and revenge practices discussed in this chapter—practices that indeed resemble a never-ending chain of death and revenge throughout different generations.

Sorcery and Revenge

Since beginning my research in Qom rural communities in 1997, I have continually heard stories about killings by sorcerers and shamanic attacks.[3] *Pi'oxonaq* (shamans) are "experts in sucking": through suction, blowing, and prayer, they cure the victims of other shamans' attacks. The very act of curing implies an attack on the aggressor. On the other hand, *conaxanaxae* (sorcerers) are usually women who "get hold of" bodily extensions or other detachable components of the victim (fluids, shadows, names, etc.) in order to merge them with harmful devices (toads, frogs, vipers, bones of the dead) and cause their death. Expressions I heard in multiple contexts—such as "White people kill each other with weapons, we kill in a well-hidden way," "There's always an enemy lurking," or "There's an invisible war going on …; people are envious, relatives kill each other"—expose the centrality of sorcery and shamanic attacks in Qom social life, as well as the tensions inherent at the very core of kinship relations.

Envy is usually recognized as the main cause of shamanic and sorcery attacks. Pettiness (refusing to share) and ostentation (attempts to mark social differentiation) are morally condemned since they both produce envy, which in turn motivates the attacks (see also Gordillo 2006: 142–145). Even if conviviality within communities and residential units implies daily practices in which substances, fluids, dreams, and lives are shared, according to my interlocutors, pettiness, ostentation, envy, and revenge are also intrinsic features of Qom sociability. People often made statements—"We must make war against sorcerers," "Let's remedy," "Let's do the *contra* [counter-attack]," "Let's cure the dead"—that introduced me to the concept of revenge as a duty, a social obligation, rather than an option. When a co-resident relative dies, the living can turn to a *contra* specialist, an *'enaxanaxaic* (avenger), who is usually a man. 'Doing the *contra*', that is, performing a counter-attack on the sorcerers, is vital because, among the Qom and other Amerindian peoples, death is experienced as a gradual murder. As Anne-Christine Taylor (1998: 333) has suggested, "the inherent feature of humans is to finish the killing, not to die." As I have argued previously (Tola 2009), illness and death are often considered processes derived from intentional human or non-human actions (cf. Allard and Taylor 2016). The *'enaxanaxaic* manipulates the moribund body and, after some time, his actions will cause the death of the aggressor. This practice, which the Qom call 'curing the dead', consists of acting on the body of someone at the point of death who has been the victim of sorcery leading to murder. It usually involves performing violent acts on this body, such as breaking bones (arms, legs), cutting body parts, introducing objects into it, or force-feeding it, with the objective of having the sorcery rebound on the initial attackers, causing their death and thereby achieving the revenge. For it to be effective, the 'cure of the dead' requires that the body be warm, since the heat indicates that the aggressor (his *nqui'i* or non-human partners) is still inside the victim.

The term 'cure' is rather misleading because this practice does not involve healing but rather the opposite. Whereas the healer cures the ill to prevent their death, the avenger maneuvers the moribund bodies to 'cure' them in order to cause the death of others: the actions performed on the body are meant to produce a reaction on the culprits, causing their death. The culprits' physical reaction to the *contra* will reveal their identity and, consequently, their guilt. The expression 'cure the dead' shows that the persons upon whom painful actions are exercised are perceived and treated as if they were dead—they are already dead while still alive.

Two examples can clarify this point. During fieldwork I was told that a witch took a child's leftover food and used the saliva contained in the food to perform an attack on her. The child died as a consequence of the witch's actions. Upon the request of the child's parents', the *'enaxanaxaic* hanged the sick child just before her impending death. This action was intended to reveal the witch's identity and cause her death. A few weeks later, a neighbor died as the result of a sudden asphyxiation. Since she had died in a similar manner to the sick child, the parents were assured that she was in fact their child's murderer. Another story regards a young man who became ill and began to feel excessive heat in his throat, a phenomenon that his family immediately associated with a witch's manipulation of his food. Just before the young man's death, the *'enaxanaxaic* force-fed him, despite his excruciating throat pain, in an attempt to 'cure the dead' and attack the witch responsible. Later, an old lady, apparently not related to the youth, quickly lost weight and eventually died subsequent to the action performed by the avenger on the dying youth, an event that proved a connection between the two deaths, similarly to the child's case. Both stories revolve around the transference of the avenger's actions on the victim to the (putative) attacker.

As previously indicated, the Qom person is understood as a porous entity constituted by several relations that connect people to one another. Those who are more intimately connected are close family members who share the same substance. They are more vulnerable to one another since they can easily hurt each other, due to what I have described as relational excess. In this sense, kinship is directly involved in all instances of sorcery, revenge, and death. Only consubstantial relatives (or non-related co-resident neighbors) can access the victims, manipulate their body parts and substances, and cause their death. Those who are closely related can easily kill one another or be killed. In other words, consubstantiality and death are inextricably linked.

A Qom friend explained to me that the witches who intend to murder someone try to contact a relative, asking him or her to steal an object belonging to the victim, or some material that could contain the victim's bodily substance, in order to perform the murderous attack:

> Let's say that you're a relative of the *conaxanaxae* [sorcerer]. She tells you, "Go find a pair of that person's shoes and bring them to me." You take them and give them to her without knowing what she will do. Then that person dies and something happens to you: your hand melts or you die. The sorcerer does not go herself, but sends a relative. She takes care of herself in case they make war against her, because when a person [a victim] dies he can have his eyes burnt or a dagger stuck in his belly or his nose covered with something …, his bones broken before he dies. Only then the effect is produced on whoever grabbed the things, first, and on the *conaxanaxae* later, if the revenge works … If they don't do [curing the dead], the person dies, is buried, and the *conaxanaxae* remains alive.

These words show how the sorcerer proceeds and the revenge is conceived. The sorcerer sends a relative to grab the bodily extension of the person she wants to kill, knowing that revenge enacted on the victim's body will first take effect on that relative. The relative could be a child, who would unknowingly contribute to a murder, or it could be someone the witch managed to persuade by bad-mouthing the victim. The victim could also be someone considered responsible for previous deaths, so in this case his or her murder would seem justified to prevent further deaths in the community.

The above story also reveals the extreme permeability of relations among sorcerers, victims, and intermediaries. If a victim is avenged through 'curing the dead', the manipulation of the victim's moribund body directly affects the bodies of the intermediary and the sorcerer. This point is consistent with the 'logic of contagion' that sorcery sets in motion. The sorcerer boils the object containing substances of the victim with other items that are considered extremely dangerous, such as toads, snakes, and bones found in forests and cemeteries.[4] The mixing of these substances will affect the victim: whatever happens to the substances will also happen to the victim (see also Miller 1979; Palavecino 1935).

Interestingly, my interlocutors consider revenge as a response in the context of a war. The succession of witchcraft attacks and revenge are generally referred to as actions carried out within a slow yet unceasing war, a point that I will return to later.

As seen so far, the succession of attack and revenge is predicated upon a general ontological principle that highlights the permeability of bodies in Qom society. Let us now move to an analysis of the conceptual pairing of relational excess and individuation. Relational excess can be observed in the ways Qom people make and unmake kin, as well as through the association between incest and sorcery. In particular, Qom matrimonial practices are consistent with the spiraling effects of sorcery and revenge.

Relational Excess: Making and Unmaking Relatives

Qom marriages tend to be oriented toward the margins of consubstantial cognatic kindred in which, due to genealogical amnesia and geographical distance, consanguineous relatives become blurred and thus many consan-guineous unions are not considered as such. Sons-in-law and brothers-in-law are integrated into the family through uxorilocal rules, leading to a process of consubstantialization through which difference is diluted and consanguinity is extended to affines. This matrimonial system combines a blurring of dif-ferences engendered by an increasing conviviality among non-consanguines. The reaffirmation of such differences in subsequent generations makes mar-riage possible within a consanguineous network that is not always perceived as such. This implies that the potential for incest is always present.

Sharing bodily fluids, human substances, animals and plants, affections, experiences, and dreams transforms a man and a woman into spouses (*l'hua*), affines into family (*familia*, as the Qom say in Spanish), and non-consanguines into consanguines. They gradually become relatives through the circulation of different substances and the transformations of their related bodies. Sorcery and revenge are generated among close relatives with whom consubstantiality has been gradually achieved. Both practices aspire to produce a gradual disjunction within the cognatic kindred. Sorcery attacks and revenge succeed each other until close people become dissociated, contributing to the unmaking of relations between consanguineous people, including affines who have been consanguinized. Those attacked and avenged are usually close relatives (Tola 2009, 2012; Wright 2008).

Attackers and avengers living in the same residential unit kill one another when motivated by rumors, envy, jealousy, or spite. Only close relatives are harmed or avenged, since it is between them that a 'mutuality of being' (Sahlins 2013) has been instituted. If a couple separates, people often resort to sorcery to break the consubstantiality that had been created between them. On the other hand, if one of the partners wishes the other to come back, the consubstantiality itself will facilitate the return. Consubstantial ties are considered so strong that shamans can act on them to reconstitute separated couples. As a shaman who specializes in love affairs explained: "It is easy to make estranged husbands return, because they shared the bed with their children. If fathers and children embrace each other a lot, it's easy to get those fathers back, by treating the children, moistening their head with plants, and usually the father returns." Fathers and children who regularly sleep together, embracing each other, are understood as intimately connected; thus, acting on the children is believed to influence the estranged fathers, making them return. While consubstantiality may help reconstitute a separated couple, it certainly facilitates murder and revenge. The following account, related by a Qom friend, shows an instance of multiple sorcery-revenge that involves close relatives.

Before dying, a little boy [1 in fig. 4.1] said that his aunt [2 in fig. 4.1] collected his breadcrumbs. A shaman put remedies inside the boy ['cured the dead']. A month later, the aunt died in her sleep. It [the revenge] was accomplished. The aunt's daughter [3 in fig. 4.1] went to [the town of] Laishi for two years, and during those two years the father [4 in fig. 4.1] of the [dead and avenged] boy was sick with bites [due to sorcery actions performed by the woman who went to Laishi]. The man died. Before he died, he said he saw the niece who left. "I don't know why I see her, and she even laughs—take her out of the door," he said. The man died and the shaman 'cured' him by feeding him with paper. Two months after he died, [the niece] came back, and they say that she had a fever at night, that she saw the [dead] uncle who was bothering her at night. Something burst inside her and she died. Family members are killing one another ... The man who died said that he was killed by his sock [which the woman who went to Laishi had stolen].

Aggressors and victims are thus aunt–nephew and uncle–niece, and both pairs are part of a single family composed of a married couple, a sister, a sister-in-law, and two first cousins (see fig. 4.1). In the sequence, attacks by sorcerers and counter-attacks by avengers alternate as follows: 2 practices sorcery on 1 → 1 dies and is avenged → 2 dies as a direct effect of the revenge done to 1 → 3 bewitches 4 → 4 has a vision of his aggressor (3) and dies → 4 is avenged → 3 has a vision of 4 avenged and dies.

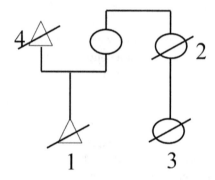

FIGURE 4.1: Kin relations imbricated in the aforementioned episode

This narrative also highlights the centrality of visions that often reveal attackers to the dying victims. When this happens, they utter the attackers' names, prompting their families to proceed with a *contra*. When a victim does not name an attacker, the avenger 'cures the dead', hoping that his actions will affect the attacker. We will later see how visions also occur to attackers, who can be stalked by the spirits of their victims.

As I witnessed throughout my long-term research among the Qom, the destruction of entire families due to sorcery and revenge is more frequent if the spouses are close kin. Although such unions—considered incestuous—are forbidden, in fact a large number of marriages occur among consanguineous relatives.[5] The Qom kinship system generates a network of close relatives within which people must find a marriageable partner. Inevitably, the rules imply an excess of proximity between persons, producing a permanent risk of incestuous unions. Qom people deal with this excess by cutting the related network, linking incest to sorcery and transforming the excess into enmity. I will return to this point later.

When a man and a woman marry despite being closely related, this is referred to as *denanaxa'n*. This term expresses simultaneously the actions of creating and cutting the network. According to the context, it is translated as 'announcing/harming with shamanism/sorcery'. A possible interpretation could be that incestuous unions announce misfortune that will occur within the consanguineous kindred where the incest was committed. The announced misfortune coincides with the beginning of sorcery and revenge between ex-spouses, whose separation could put the entire family at risk. The matrimonial connections or relinkings between persons belonging to the same two groups (i.e., affinal connections between two consanguine families that continue throughout generations), articulate relations between groups of kindred that—precisely due to the relinkings—are strictly bound to each other. This makes a Qom community an extensive network of close-knit relatives, with consanguine relatives married to each other or individuals married to the consanguines of their consanguines' affines. Thus, the separation of a consanguine couple and the beginning of sorcery and revenge practices among former partners could lead to the fission of the community. People often relate how entire communities dissolved and others were formed due to the separation of a consanguine couple, originating attacks and counter-attacks between close family members. As unions between persons with excessive proximity, incestuous marriages may have devastating effects, resulting in strong internal divisions among residential units.

In addition to 'announcing' a tragedy, the above-mentioned term *denanaxa'n* encompasses the possibility of sorcery having taken place. It is noteworthy that a single lexeme in Qom designates what in Spanish or English is indicated by two: incest and sorcery. According to the Qom, incest-sorcery is the same phenomenon containing two facets: excessive proximity between spouses and the rupture of this excess through sorcery between a close-kin couple. In other words, the concept of incest-sorcery contains the idea of both making and unmaking relatives. This is even more evident if we consider that both incest and sorcery indicate an excess of relatedness. If incest is a repetition of identity over identity, an excess of proximity implies sorcery. Sorcery contains the 'relief valve'[6] to this excessive proximity, that is, incest. In a single term, Qom people express both the problem and the solution: for them, incest and sorcery effectively coincide.

Having discussed the making and unmaking of relations through sorcery and incest, let us now turn to an ethnographic analysis of situations seeking to cut the relational excess in which revenge killing does *not* occur. In these cases, the chain of deaths is interrupted with the intention of avoiding rather than perpetuating revenge and further deaths. As José Kelly (pers. comm.) observed, an ethnography from the point of view of the dead would show that revenge is analogous to marriage in the sense that revenge produces death in the same way that marriage produces life. If relinked marriages redouble living persons, revenge redoubles dead persons.

Individuation: The Anti-revenge Process

When sorcery and revenge occur in sequence in the same community and within the same group of families, relations become extremely tense. Accusations of pettiness and envy and the fear of attacks are exacerbated. People often reminded me that one must be alert because "there is always an enemy nearby, stalking." Tension increases, and the escalation seems endless. What can be done to break the revenge chain and alleviate the tension?

First and foremost, physical and emotional distancing between members of families involved in sorcery-revenge is pivotal to fracturing relational excess. As argued so far, relational excess is the necessary condition for sorcery and revenge since the individuals involved are permanently linked through the circulation of substances, fluids, dreams, and forced kin relations. However, the decision not to avenge the dead leads to breaks in relational excess and is also a way of dissolving the bonds between the living and the dead. This excess continues even after death, since the actions of the living affect the actions of the dead, as I will explain below.

In these cases, "the war is cut off," as the Qom say, in pursuit of what I refer to as 'anti-revenge'. Intentionally not performing revenge is an attempt to break the chain of potential deaths, to create discontinuity with the murderer and between the living and the dead. Let us examine two cases in which consanguineous relatives may decide not to take vengeance.

The first case occurs when an individual shows symptoms of '*alaxaic* (death madness) before death. This term indicates the actions of someone who became insane, yet Qom people differentiate the '*alaxaic* state from other states of madness. People who suffer from '*alaxaic* see and name some spirits; they complain about them and clearly suffer due to these visions. Such alterations in their behavior lead their relatives to conclude that the spirits appearing in these visions belong to people who have been murdered by the '*alaxaic* person. From then on, an '*alaxaic* person is considered a murderous sorcerer. Acknowledging this state of 'death madness' seems to be a prelude to the sorcerers' death process, because the immediate consequence is that those thought to be sorcerers are removed from all networks of relations: their relatives suddenly decide to cut their connection with them. This implies that the suspected sorcerers are forced to live apart, eat alone, and so forth. In one such case, a woman, noticing that her elderly mother was '*alaxaic*, asked her children to take their grandmother underneath a tree, 50 meters away from their household. The old lady was left there, deprived of food and water, and she died shortly afterward. Relatedness, conviviality, and consubstantiality are disrupted and cut.

At first, I was surprised that nobody spoke of dead relatives with affection. Throughout 20 years of fieldwork in the same Qom communities, I found that most of the deceased elders had been accused of suffering from '*alaxaic* and were thus deemed to be sorcerers. As in most Amazonian societies, for the Qom some moribund or dead people become 'others'—enemies or predators (Allard and Taylor 2016; Tola 2006)—and are hence extremely dangerous. The dead are feared because they can return to the world of the living and take with them those relatives who suffer and cry for their absence. Furthermore, a dead husband may return and kill his widow if she has not respected the mourning prohibitions. That is another reason why no one dares to avenge '*alaxaic* people when they die. Their relatives decide not to continue a war that would end up killing them: in these cases, instead of war there is a firm decision to pursue anti-revenge. Not performing revenge aims at breaking the chain of potential deaths: with the non-revenge of the sorcerer, nobody is killed, and others who have died are prevented from being avenged. In this way, relatives of '*alaxaic* people do not risk deadly revenge. By means of anti-revenge, relatives produce discontinuity with the sorcerer, breaking all expression of relatedness with her. Also, anti-revenge enhances continuities with other families, especially those of the victims of the no-longer-relative-sorcerer, since everyone finds out that the victim has not been avenged.

Another anti-revenge situation occurs when someone is indirectly revealed to be a murderous sorcerer. Sometimes the victim sees the attacker just before dying and names him or her. Seeing the spirits of the dead and being named by someone who is dying are irrefutable proofs of the sorcerer's guilt. Unmasked sorcerers are then disconnected from their kindred, individualized, condemned to loneliness and to their progressive transformation into 'another'.

Both situations of becoming other, of which I witnessed a great number of cases, appear to be on the same side of a Möbius strip. At one point in the strip, there is the victim of the sorcery attacks, who sees and names the aggressor, and at another point there is the aggressor, who, in a state of madness, sees and names the victims. The victim names those who caused his or her death, and the person who becomes '*alaxaic* names not his or her murderers, but the people whom he or she killed. Depending on the perspective, victims and aggressors are two alternating facets of a single indissoluble relationship. This Qom Möbius strip expresses that in the process of making kin, the reverse is always implicit. At some point in the process (e.g., when marriage is undone), the bonds between ex-spouses and their kindred are read from the other side of the strip, with ex-spouses and their relatives now seen and treated as potential attackers. A person is both the victim of a sorcerer (when he/she is about to die) *and* the sorcerer's enemy (being fusioned with the attacker and becoming dangerous for the living), since the body of the victim contains the aggressor. In other instances, a person is a body altered by the maneuvers of the avenger. Due to all these actions, a person can be the aggressor toward his/her own murderer: the victims' spirits torture the sorcerers (*'alaxaic*) through visions, making them crazy and causing them to be cut off from all networks.

What Is a Relation? Amerindian Perspectives on Sociality and War

Throughout this chapter I have highlighted the existence of a relational network that links humans to one another and to non-human beings. As argued in the introduction to this book, "beings exist as the result of their relational constitution." In the initial moment of sorcery and murderous aggression, there is an enhanced state of fusion between the victim, the attacker, and the non-human entities. Parallels and differences can be drawn between my analysis of Qom sorcery, revenge, and anti-revenge and the predatory model developed from the killer-enemy relationship in contexts of Amerindian war.

In the same way that through a deadly attack the warrior and the Chaco enemies merge and consubstantialize in different stages,[7] in a murderous attack Qom sorcerers introduce a detachable part of themselves into their victims, fusing parts of the victim with non-human entities. The composite and relational character of the person is the necessary condition for the relational excess that enables the circulation and manipulation of fluids and bodily substances (blood, semen, saliva, hair), movable and detachable parts of the person (shadow, soul, name), and objects that were in intimate contact with him or her (clothing and ornaments). In this relational network, which exists by default in Qom ontology, aggressors and victims are intertwined. This is the precondition for the potential entanglement between them, as well as between themselves and animals, plants, and non-humans.

Following the relational excess, a second, important point is that taking revenge on the body of the dying person is possible because the victim is considered to contain the enemy. As explained earlier, victim and murderer are fused in the body of the victim. This fusion is what allows the revenge, since acting on the dying person produces repercussions on the attacker. As the murderer is inside the victim, the gradual fusion between the two represents a lethal risk for the living. As shown by Viveiros de Castro (2002: 279) in the Araweté case, the risk lies with the dead person's relatives. The victim may wish to take revenge on the murderer, but as the victim is a constituent part of the aggressor, eventually the attacks fall on the aggressor's relatives. In the Nivacle case, the warrior must tame the spirit of the victim until he can incorporate it as a part of himself (Sterpin 1993). However, there is always the risk that the victim will become a predator and incorporate the warrior into his own enemy group. In contemporary Qom revenge practices, the words addressed to the dying person suggest that revenge affects the aggressor. The spirit of the dead, considered a potential predator of the living, is asked to leave them and take his murderers with it. Due to the relational excess, the family must distance itself from the victim. Only in this way will the spirit of the dead depart with his or her enemy (a relative), leaving other close relatives behind.

A third observation is that the *'alaxaic,* the sorcerer who enters a state of madness and begins to be seen by his close relatives as an 'other', is left to die alone. Like the Chaco and Tupi warrior,[8] conditions of insanity or semi-consciousness are due to the images of victims tormenting the aggressors at the end of their lives. Eventually, victims will return to torture and gradually kill their aggressors. In the Araweté case, the death of the killer after his deadly attack suggests, as Viveiros de Castro (2002: 285) explains, an "alienation," since "the image of the victim" captures the aggressor. We have seen that in the Qom case the images of victims also alienate their murderers in the final moments of their lives.

Practices linking sorcerer-shamans, victims, and avengers, on the one hand, and warriors and enemies, on the other, express a basic ontological instability conjugated with predatory actions that are never unidirectional, but reversible. The "most ritually elaborated and ideologically dense moments," says Viveiros de Castro (2002: 291), have as protagonists this *"two-headed unit between killer and victim that mirror each other and reverberate to infinity."* My analysis accounts for the way in which the sorcerer-victim unit is never an exclusively mono-directional unit with fixed identity positions. On the contrary, both positions are mirrored or, as shown before, ceaselessly follow one another along a Qom Möbius strip. In fact, more than being a cycle of revenge that begins and ends, these mechanisms activated in contemporary contexts would seem to be the "sociological operator" (Sterpin 1993: 39) in the production of sociality through the alternation between the production of relational excess and individuation.

At present, and unlike the classic Amerindian schema in which the killer contains part of his victim, it is the Qom victim who contains his or her aggressor. The killer's point of view gives way to the enemy's point of view, and now it is the victims who contain within themselves their aggressors and where the practices that will mirror the tensions and rivalries *ad infinitum* are structured—at least until an *'alaxaic* appears and the point of view is assumed by the aggressors, who are tortured by their own victims.

This chapter has illustrated the potential alternation between relational excess and individuation in a particular Amerindian context—that of Qom society. Sorcery attacks and revenge and anti-revenge procedures facilitate this alternation. Sorcery and shamanic attacks between close relatives break the consubstantial network and promote the beginning of an individuation process. In turn, revenge performed on the body of a moribund close relative re-establishes the relational excess because it enhances the fusion between victims and enemies, as well as between the dead and the living. Anti-revenge practices reinforce fissures in the network as well as processes of individuation, breaking the fusion between sorcerers and their relatives and between them and their potential victims. By performing revenge upon some and not others and by marking distance from sorcerers through anti-revenge, Qom people carry forward their relations with excesses and fissures, consubstantiality and temporary distancing. In Qom sociality, the relational network exists by default, and the process of differentiation is produced through procedures that break the relational excess.

Epilogue

"They're close relatives," my friend Pedro told the shaman who had offered to avenge his 50-year-old son, recently deceased. In this case, the medical diagnosis was diabetes, but the shaman's diagnosis was sorcery. Pedro, his daughter-in-law, and his grandchildren accepted the shaman's offer: that night, after the wake, the *contra* would be done. "You will be with me in the room, but you must not cry," the avenger told Pedro, and he accepted. Locked inside with his only son and the *'enaxanaxaic* (avenger) amid words, shouts, and gestures, Pedro listened attentively to the avenger as he introduced a white liquid into the deceased's mouth:[9] "Remember the color of this bottle. Take it all." After advising his daughter-in-law and grandchildren of the care that should be taken during the years of mourning, Pedro warned them: "Five people, four of them close female relatives and one male, were the ones who caused the death of my son." Five very close people would soon fall under the effect of the *contra*. The first, Pedro told me, was his own sister-in-law, who later spat white foam from her mouth in agony. At that moment, Pedro recalled the words of the avenger.

Pedro relayed this story to me when he visited me in Buenos Aires as I was finishing the writing of this text. It displays the nuances of revenge and the *contra*, exposing the signs that, in total discretion, are read by relatives, enemies, and shamans to interpret the behavior and intentions of others. After narrating the details of the *contra* performed upon his son, he told me that, so far, four of his son's murderers had died, and one of them had been taken directly from the hospital to the morgue. Significantly for the logic of anti-revenge, Pedro knew that if the deceased went to the morgue, he would not be avenged. The mother of the deceased had already realized that her son was in an *'alaxaic* state and had heard him pronounce the name of his victim, Pedro's son. For this reason, the supposed culprit was transported directly to the morgue. "The war will be cut off," Pedro told me.

Acknowledgments

I am grateful to all the participants of the workshop "What Is a Relation? Ethnographic Perspectives from Indigenous South America" held in Santiago de Chile in 2017, in particular Daniela Castellanos and Diego Cagüeñas for their comments. I would also like to thank Marina Vanzolini, José Antonio Kelly, and Antonela dos Santos for their enlightening observations, and all the members of the Núcleo de Etnografía Amerindia (NuEtAm) for their generous reading. I am grateful to the journal's editor and the two anonymous reviewers for their very valuable comments. Lastly, I wish to express my gratitude to the Qom families and communities with whom I have been working for more than 20 years.

Florencia Tola has a PhD in Social Anthropology and Ethnography from the Ecole des Hautes Etudes in Social Sciences of Paris and from the University of Buenos Aires. She is a Professor at the University of Buenos Aires and at the National University of San Martín (Argentina). Since 2005 she has been a Researcher at the National Council of Scientific and Technological Research (Argentina), and she is also an Associate Researcher at the Centre EREA (Enseignement et Recherche en Ethnologie Amérindienne) of the CNRS (France). Starting in 1998, she has conducted ethnographic fieldwork among the Toba People of the Argentinean Chaco.

Notes

1. Taken from Fernando Tola and Carmen Dragonetti, *Nihilismo budista: La doctrina de la vaciedad* (Mexico City: Primeá, 1990). Unless otherwise indicated, all translations are my own.
2. Throughout this chapter I will use the terms Qom and Toba interchangeably.
3. Since 1998, I have conducted fieldwork among Qom residents of a peri-urban neighborhood in Formosa as well as in the rural communities of San Carlos, Riacho de Oro, Kilómetro 503, and Santo Domingo in the province of Formosa. Ethnographic insights are based on research experiences in these localities, whose communities comprise approximately 300 individuals.
4. Toads, worms, serpents, and other creatures living near or underneath the ground are deemed disgusting and believed to be connected with witchcraft. Bones found in cemeteries are considered still vital and containing part of the defunct soul. If these elements are mixed with extensions of a living person, her life could be in extreme danger.
5. Marriages between members of a bilateral extended family are considered incestuous. An individual cannot marry any siblings (real or classificatory) or

the sibling (real or classificatory) of a relative from any genealogical level, as long as there is memory of the genealogical chain that unites them or memory of the classificatory relation of their ancestors. The use of kinship terminology operates as a central factor in the rule prohibiting incest. The only forbidden affines are the spouse of a parent (deceased or not) and the spouse of a son or daughter (deceased or not). A relationship with the spouse of a sibling is also considered incestuous as long as the sibling is married.

6. I thank one of my reviewers for this expression.

7. Both in the Chaco (Nivacle, Toba-Pilagá) and among the Tupi (Araweté) groups, the relationship between killer and victim is one of enormous ontological instability. The spirit of the murdered or scalped enemy and of the killer are fused. After a deadly attack, the Araweté killer, for example, enters a state of semi-consciousness in which he becomes other by possessing within himself the spirit of his victim (Viveiros de Castro 2002). The initial relationship of "deadly alterity" is transformed into a relationship of "fusional identity" (ibid.: 273) and, with the death of the murderer, the victim becomes an "appendix" of the murderer (ibid.: 274). In the Nivacle (Gran Chaco) case, the spirit of the enemy continues to manifest in the vicinity of his headless body and must be tamed by the warrior. After this process, the victim becomes part of the murderer (Sterpin 1993: 44).

8. In both the Chaco and Tupi cases, there is a risk that the victim will become the predator and perform lethal actions against his murderer. Among the Araweté people, the killer's state of semi-consciousness is due to the fact that his soul, fused with the victim's, moves away from him and he goes through a process of "becoming a corpse" (Viveiros de Castro 2002: 272). Among the Nivacle people, the warrior may fall into a state of unconsciousness because of possession by his victim's spirit; he may live with his enemies as if he were one of them (Sterpin 1993: 44).

9. Although at this point the victim is dead, his body still being warm is considered proof that the attacker is still present and that the *contra* can be successfully performed.

References

Allard, Olivier, and Anne-Christine Taylor. 2016. "Traitement des cadavres et mémoire des personnes en Amazonie" [The treatment of corpses and the memory of people in the Amazon]. In *Qu'est-ce qu'une sépulture: Humanités et système funéraires de la Préhistoire à nos jours* [What is a burial? Humanities and funerary systems from Prehistory to the present day], ed. Michel Lauwers and Aurélie Zemour, 141–154. Antibes: APDCA.

Braunstein, José, and Elmer S. Miller. 1999. "Ethnohistorical Introduction." In *Peoples of the Gran Chaco*, ed. Elmer S. Miller, 1–22. Westport, CT: Bergin & Garvey.

Carneiro da Cunha, Manuela, and Eduardo Viveiros de Castro. 1985. "Vingança e temporalidade: Os Tupinambás" [Revenge and temporality: The Tupinamba]. *Journal de la Société des Americanistes* 71: 191–208.

Clastres, Pierre. 1974. *La société contre l'état* [Society against the state]. Paris: Minuit.

Conklin, Beth A. 1993. "Hunting the Ancestors: Death and Alliance in Wari' Cannibalism." *Latin American Anthropology Review* 5 (2): 65–70.

Cordeu, Edgardo, and Miguel de los Ríos. 1982. "Un enfoque estructural de las variaciones socioculturales de los cazadores recolectores del Gran Chaco" [A structural approach to socio-cultural variations of hunter-gatherers of the Gran Chaco]. *Suplemento Antropológico* 17 (1): 147–160.

Descola, Philippe. 1996. "Constructing Natures: Symbolic Ecology and Social Practice." In *Nature and Society: Anthropological Perspectives*, ed. Philippe Descola and Gísli Pálsson, 82–102. London: Routledge.

Erikson, Philippe. 1987. "De l'apprivoisement à l'approvisionnement: Chasse, alliance et familiarisation en Amazonie amérindienne" [From taming to supply: Hunting, alliance, and familiarization in the Amerindian Amazon]. *Techniques & Culture* 9: 105–140.

Fausto, Carlos. 1997. "A dialética da predação e familiarização entre os Parakanã da Amazonia Oriental: Por uma teoria da guerra ameríndia" [The dialectics of predation and familiarization among the Parakanã of Eastern Amazonia: Toward a theory of Amerindian war]. PhD diss., Federal University of Rio de Janeiro.

Fausto, Carlos. 2001. *Inimigos fiéis: História, guerra e xamanismo na Amazonia* [Faithful enemies: History, war, and shamanism in the Amazon]. São Paulo: EDUSP.

Gordillo, Gastón. 2006. *En el Gran Chaco: Antropologías e historias* [In the Gran Chaco: Anthropologies and stories]. Buenos Aires: Prometeo.

Karsten, Raphael. 1926. *The Civilization of the South American Indians*. London: Kegan Paul, Trench, Trubner.

Karsten, Raphael. 1932. "Indian Tribes of the Argentine and Bolivian Chaco: Ethnological Studies." *Societas Scientiarum Fennica* 4 (1): 10–236.

Lima, Tânia S. 2005. *Um peixe olhou para mim: O povo Yudjá e a perspectiva* [A fish looked at me: The Yudjá people and the perspective]. São Paulo: UNESP.

Lozano, Pedro. 1941. *Descripción corográfica del Gran Chaco Gualamba* [Corographical description of the Gran Chaco Gualamba]. Tucumán: Universidad Nacional de Tucumán.

Métraux, Alfred. 1937. "Études d'ethnographie Toba-Pilagá (Gran Chaco)" [Toba-Pilagá ethnographic studies (Grand Chaco)]. *Anthropos* 32: 171–194, 378–401.

Miller, Elmer S. 1979. *Los tobas argentinos: Armonía y disonancia en una sociedad* [The Argentine tufas: Harmony and dissonance in a society]. Mexico City: Siglo XXI.

Nordenskiöld, Erland. 1912. *La vie des Indiens dans le Chaco (Amérique du Sud)* [Indian life in Chaco (South America)]. Trans. Henri Beuchat. Paris: Delagrave.

Otaegui, Alfonso. 2013. "Los nuestros que están lejos, los otros que están cerca: El afecto, la comida y los clanes en la cotidianeidad de los ayoreos del Chaco boreal" [Ours that are far away, the others that are close: The affection, the food, and the clans in the daily life of the Ayoreo of the northern Chaco]. In *Gran Chaco: Ontologías, poder y afectividad* [Gran Chaco: Ontologies, Power, and Affectivity], ed. Florencia Tola, Celeste Medrano, and Lorena Cardin, 161–185. Buenos Aires: IGWIA/RUMBO SUR.

Otaegui, Alfonso. 2019. "'I'm Crying for the Beautiful Skin of the Jaguar': Laments, Non-humans and Conviviality among the Ayoreo of the Northern Chaco." In *Non-Humans in Amerindian South America: Ethnographies of Indigenous Cosmologies, Rituals and Songs*, ed. Juan Javier Rivera Andía, 224–251. New York: Berghahn Books.

Overing, Joanna, and Alan Passes, eds. 2000. *The Anthropology of Love and Anger: The Aesthetics of Conviviality in Native Amazonia*. London: Routledge.

Palavecino, Enrique. 1933. *Los indios pilagá del Río Pilcomayo* [The Pilagá Indians of the Pilcomayo River]. Buenos Aires: Imprenta de la Universidad.

Palavecino, Enrique. 1935. "Notas sobre la religión de los indios del Chaco" [Notes on the religion of the Chaco Indians]. *Revista Geográfica Americana* 3 (21): 373–380.

Rivière, Peter. 2001. "A predaçao, a reciprocidade e o caso das Guianas" [Predation, reciprocity, and the case of the Guianas]. *Mana* 7 (1): 31–53.

Sahlins, Marshall. 2013. *What Kinship Is ... and Is Not*. Chicago: University of Chicago Press.

Sterpin, Adriana. 1993. "La chasse aux scalps chez les Nivakle du Gran Chaco" [Scalp hunting at the Nivakle of Gran Chaco]. *Journal de la Société des Américanistes* 79: 33–66.

Strathern, Marilyn. 1996. "Cutting the Network." *Journal of the Royal Anthropological Institute* 2 (3): 517–535.

Sztutman, Renato. 2007. "Cauim pepica: Notas sobre os antigos festivais antropofágicos" [Cauim pepica: Notes on ancient anthropophagic festivals]. *Campos* 8 (1): 45–70.

Taylor, Anne-Christine. 1998. "Corps immortels, devoirs d'oubli: Formes humaines et trajectoires de vie chez les Achuars" [Immortal bodies, duties of oblivion: Human forms and trajectories of life among the Achuar]. In *La production du corps: Approches anthropologiques et historiques* [The production of the body: Anthropological and historical approaches], ed. Maurice Godelier and Michel Panoff, 317–338. Amsterdam: Éditions des Archives Contemporaines.

Taylor, Anne-Christine. 2001. "Wives, Pets, and Affines: Marriage among the Jivaro." In *Beyond the Visible and the Material: The Amerindianizaton of Society in the Work of Peter Rivière*, ed. Laura M. Rival and Neil L. Whitehead, 45–56. Oxford: Oxford University Press.

Tola, Florencia. 2006. "'Después de muerto hay que disfrutar, en la tierra o en el mundo celestial': Concepciones de la muerte entre los tobas (*qom*) del Chaco argentino" ['After death you have to enjoy yourself, on earth or in the heavenly world': Conceptions of death among the Toba (*qom*) of the Argentine Chaco]. *Alteridades* 16 (32): 153–164.

Tola, Florencia. 2009. *Les conceptions du corps et de la personne dans un contexte amérindien: Indiens Toba du Gran Chaco sudaméricain* [Conceptions of the body and the person in an Amerindian context: Toba Indians of South American Gran Chaco]. Paris: L'Harmattan.

Tola, Florencia. 2012. *Yo no estoy solo en mi cuerpo: Cuerpos-personas múltiples entre los tobas del Chaco argentino* [I am not alone in my body: Multiple bodies-persons among the tuffs of the Argentine Chaco]. Buenos Aires: Biblos/Culturalia.

Vilaça, Aparecida. 1992. *Comendo como gente: Formas do canibalismo Wari'* [Eating like people: Forms of Wari' cannibalism]. Rio de Janeiro: Editora da UFRJ.

Vilaça, Aparecida. 2002. "Making Kin Out of Others in Amazonia." *Journal of the Royal Anthropological Institute* (n.s.) 8 (2): 347–365.

Vilaça, Aparecida. 2005. "Chronically Unstable Bodies: Reflections on Amazonian Corporalities." *Journal of the Royal Anthropological Institute* (n.s.) 11 (3): 445–464.

Viveiros de Castro, Eduardo. 1986. *Araweté: Os deuses canibais* [Araweté: The cannibal gods]. Rio de Janeiro: Jorge Zahar/Anpocs.

Viveiros de Castro, Eduardo. 2002. *A inconstância da alma selvagem e outros ensaios de antropologia* [The inconstancy of the savage soul and other anthropological essays]. São Paulo: Cosac Naify.

Viveiros de Castro, Eduardo. 2013. *La mirada del jaguar: Introducción al perspectivismo amerindio* [The look of the jaguar: Introduction to Amerindian perspectivism]. Buenos Aires: Tinta Limón Ediciones.

Wright, Pablo. 2008. *Ser-en-el-sueño: Crónicas de historia y vida toba* [Being-in-the-dream: Chronicles of Toba's history and life]. Buenos Aires: Biblos/Culturalia.

Chapter 5

THE NAME OF THE RELATION
Making a Difference in Aweti Onomastics

Marina Vanzolini

The starting point of this reflection is a trivial incident that took place while I was living with the Aweti, a Tupi-speaking group inhabiting the region of the headwaters of the Xingu River in central Brazil: the fact that one day I received from a friend in the village the name of a mythical character, which, as far as I know, is not among the names usually adopted by the Aweti to name themselves. Understanding personal names to be intrinsically relational, I propose to ask here what they can reveal about an indigenous concept of relation.

As Marilyn Strathern (1995) has observed, relations happen between anthropologists and her/his interlocutors on several scales. In the field, anthropologists learn about the form and content of relations in their subjects' worlds, drawing logical relations between them. In a series of articles analyzing the history of the term 'relation' in the English language, Strathern (2013, 2014, 2016) points out how the emergence of a generic concept encompassing both epistemological and social relations is the product of a transformation that took place throughout the seventeenth and eighteenth centuries. As argued by Strathern, the process by which the epistemological notion of relation as a

Notes for this chapter begin on page 119.

means for knowledge (via classification, comparison, etc.) is extended to imply a person's connections to other people, including kin and non-kin, has some implications for the values we attribute to this generic notion today. First, there is the idea of the relation as something abstract that happens between concrete people—that is, something that can be traced through/as knowledge—which therefore excludes the alternative understanding that relations, especially kin ties, can be integral to people, as concrete as they are. Second, relations are generally understood as something that connects through similarities, thus eclipsing all forms of connection through difference. A third implication is the general evaluation of relation(s) as good.[1]

It might be asked, then, what happens when the generic term is absent—as is the case with the Aweti language, which has no name designating 'the relation', only names describing particular forms of connection, such as friend (*to'o tat'yp*), mother (*-ty*), and so forth. I take this as an indication that, for the Aweti, relations can only be recognized (or are only of interest) for their particular effects. Thus, and taking personal names as a possible entry to the issue, the ontological question, what is a relation?, must build itself here into a much more restrictive formulation: what is the form of relation established by the Aweti through names? I will follow this lead by approaching my own relation with the Aweti as mediated by a name.

The notion that names are relational devices is not new in anthropological theory.[2] In exploring this idea, I propose that Aweti personal names should not be viewed primarily as being related to a question of individual or group identity, as Western common sense would take it, even if the act of naming always implies some degree of identity stabilization of name-receivers (and their groups). Rather, Aweti personal names also work as counter-identity devices. Considered in their combining effects, they can be understood as mediators between continuity, marking the identity and mutual dependency between kin who share names (as shall be seen), and differentiation, produced by the effects specific names can have on people. The vivid interest that the Aweti display toward personal names and their efforts to select the right names for their children ultimately exemplify the 'taming of relations' (see the introduction, this volume) as an entry point for understanding the effects of relations in the constitution of the world in indigenous South America.

The debate on indigenous onomastics in lowland South America has been highly informed by the contrast, proposed in the 1980s by Viveiros de Castro, between societies with the internal transfer of names, as is the case in the Upper Xingu, northwest Amazon, and central Brazilian Ge peoples, and those in which names come from outside of the *socius*, for example, ancient Tupi's acquisition of names from dead enemies (Hugh-Jones 2006; Viveiros de Castro 1992). As pointed out by Viveiros de Castro (1992), these different ways of naming people imply different conceptions of the person and the social.

Thus, the adoption of names of one's enemies, animal names, or even names of mythical beings, common among several Tupi-Guarani peoples, should be understood as "a true *heteronomy* (contrasting with the homonymy among the Ge), a function of the fundamental *heteronomy* of their cosmology" (ibid.: 155). To be named after the other is to partially turn into the other and thus perceive oneself as someone's other, an ontological principle expressed in different levels of the life of these peoples.[3] In accordance with Viveiros de Castro's presentation of these two logics of naming as poles of a continuum, later readings of this contrast allow viewing them as complementary aspects present in the same onomastic practices (see Hugh-Jones 2006). Following this lead, I propose that, although bestowed by familial transmission, Aweti personal names have an effect on the receivers comparable to that of names acquired outside of the social world in other Amazonian societies.

This has important consequences for an understanding of the Aweti political system and, I would venture to say, of the political practices of their Upper Xinguano neighbors. The region known in the ethnological literature as the Upper Xingu is inhabited by speakers of Arawak, Carib, and Tupi languages, as well as Trumai, a language isolate. These groups come together for ritual and matrimonial exchanges in a culturally fairly homogeneous multi-lingual community, making it difficult to avoid overarching pan-Upper Xinguano generalizations inspired by ethnographic studies produced in each village or language group. When the Aweti talk about their regional identity, as opposed to other indigenous peoples, they often refer to their staple diet (manioc sprinkles and fish),[4] their particular body ornamentation, and their rituals, the most representative of which is a funeral celebration motivated by the death of a village chief that ideally brings all the people inhabiting the region to the host village.[5] Indeed, chiefdom is a major topic in publications about Upper Xinguano groups. It is associated with what has been described in anthropological literature as a regional aristocracy characterized by a sort of hereditary transfer of status, aspects that stand out in contrast to the egalitarian political organization common to most Amazonian peoples (Clastres [1974] 2003; Overing and Passes 2000; Sztutman 2013). But how do Upper Xinguanos themselves talk about the relation referred to as heredity in the ethnological literature? In Aweti speech, names play a central role in the recognition of chiefdom as an inherited status. Building on this, I suggest that we approach name-giving as a native theory of descent.

The recognition of the inadequacy of some classical anthropological concepts to describe Amazonian indigenous societies is a well-known turning point of the anthropology of that area starting in the mid-1970s, when ethnographic knowledge about the region began to increase significantly (Overing Kaplan 1977; Seeger et al. 1979). The notion of descent and its conceptual associates—lineages and corporate groups—are central to this discussion, which arose from the urge to develop new and positive categories to describe

Amazonian groups that otherwise appeared as amorphous and acephalous in comparison to African descent-based societies. In a brief review of the ethnological literature inspired by that movement, Peter Rivière (1993) noticed, however, that for many Amazonian cases a critical engagement with anthropological theory did not imply a full rejection of the concept of descent, leading instead to an 'Amerindianization' of that notion. The alteration of analytical concepts is a consequence of what Viveiros de Castro (2004) later advocated as anthropology's major task, that is, to pay close attention to the 'equivocations' involved in the process of translating indigenous ideas into anthropological terms. With regard to kinship theories, this might imply overcoming the dichotomy between nature and culture as the implicit background of a concept like descent, classically thought of as a jural (cultural) connection as opposed to a biological (natural) filiation (Viveiros de Castro 2009). In fact, as we shall see, the transmission of familiar names among the Aweti shortcuts the nature-culture opposition, producing not groups of rights and duties, but persons constituted of moral and physical characteristics alike. By labeling Aweti's ideas about this transmission as a native theory of descent, I mean that names can be mobilized by the Aweti in a way that is analogous to how the notion of descent was classically used—as an explanation for positions of status, for instance. But of course descent would then mean something totally different from anthropology's classical notion.

What can we learn about Aweti's ideas about relations through this investigation? As mentioned earlier, Strathern's analysis of the English (or perhaps we should say Western) notion of relation is especially valuable for making explicit that, despite the fact that modern Euro-Americans obviously recognize many possible forms of relation (epistemological and social), this generic concept carries some very specific values that tend to appear as its prototypical form. The prototypical form of relations for Amazonian indigenous philosophies has long been a subject of Eduardo Viveiros de Castro's (2002, 2004) work, as influenced by Lévi-Strauss's interpretation ([1956] 2008, 1993) of Amerindian dualisms. Viveiros de Castro (2004: 16) argues that the brother-in-law relationship, a relation between entities differently related to and through the same term (a woman), plays in Amerindian thought a role comparable to that played by the notion of brotherhood for Euro-Americans: "The common word for the relation, in Amazonian worlds, is the term translated by 'brother-in-law' or 'cross-cousin'. This is the term we call people we do not know what to call, those with whom we wish to establish a generic relation. In sum, 'cousin/brother-in-law' is the term that creates a relation where none existed. It is the form through which the unknown is made known."

I believe the following analysis presents a particular instantiation of relations based on difference, not on similarity. Surprisingly, it does so in the domain of descent, which is classically associated with ideas of similarity and continuity.

My Names

When I began my research with them in 2004, the Aweti,[6] an Upper Xinguano Tupi-speaking group, unlike their neighbors in the region, did not have much experience with anthropologists, other than brief contact with a few researchers whose focus had been the collection of linguistic materials. Since the beginning of our relationship, and probably based on these previous encounters, they had clear expectations about what I would be working on: I was there to record stories. Under the guidance of my hosts, the conditions were soon settled for working on narratives with the two most well-known narrators of the village. Since one of them refused to let me record his stories until I could understand their language, I first had to rely on the simultaneous translation offered by his eldest son. The storytelling sessions were usually accompanied by family members who were at home, always interested in hearing the stories that he "carried in his eyes," as he explained to me one day, in contrast to my way of keeping them on paper. One day, a few years later, when I could now understand his stories by myself, one of the wives of this man gave me the following name: Ehezu.

Ehezu is the name of the youngest wife of Tati'a, the Bat, a marginal character in one of the stories about the origins of the world as known today that I had been listening to. Interestingly, the second wife of the same narrator soon added that my partner, who was with me in the village during that period, could be called Mawutsini, a creator hero whom Xinguanos usually associate with God (when the question of cosmological translation comes up). In the story, Mawutsini is the son of Ehezu, but this apparently did not pose a problem for my friends. What seemed to be even more puzzling to me, however, was the fact that we were associated with such mythological characters.

The names did not really 'catch on'. Some people in the village, jokingly, also used to call me Marina Kahn, identifying me with an indigenist agent who had worked with them on developing a writing system for the Aweti language. Others gave me the invented name of Marinawalu, adding the suffix -*walu*, which is common to several Xinguano names. I later received the name of an Aweti grandmother, Jali, according to the traditional name-giving system. When I recently visited the village with my daughter, my Aweti mother gave her the name of Tsimaju.

I never set out to understand what could have made my friend give me the name of a mythical character. Could it be that she had perceived a connection between us? Or had she simply chosen a random name from the standard Aweti naming stock?[7] In addition, why did my Aweti friends insist on giving me other names besides the ones I already have? I take these questions as a starting point for some considerations about the form of relation presented by Aweti name-giving practices.

The Names of the Person

Every person in the Upper Xingu should have at least two names: boys are expected to receive a name from their mother's father, and another one from their father's father, while girls should receive names from their mother's mother and their father's mother. Ideally, people receive a name from their grandparents in their first months of life, or even when they are born, with neither a specific date nor a specific naming ceremony. These names are called by the Aweti *tekyt eput*, which I would tentatively translate as 'green names'.[8] Girls should change their names at menarche or during puberty seclusion. Boys ideally give up their childhood names at the ear-piercing ceremony, performed while they are still children, but often their ears are pierced at birth, usually by their own grandfather. In this case, they are not given any childhood names ('green' ones). People are not supposed to call someone by a name that has already been changed to another one, since there is a risk that something bad could happen to that person, such as being bitten by a snake or stumbling in the bushes.

The same family names go from village to village in the Upper Xingu through inter-ethnic marriages: while neither prescriptive nor preferential, such marriages are allowed and common. Although some of them are recognizably associated with some linguistic groups, broadly they are shared by all those whom the Aweti refer to as *mo'aza*—humans or, in a narrower sense, Upper Xinguano people. Therefore, several names whose meaning is known in one language do not have a meaning in another. There are also names that do not mean anything in any language—they are 'names only'. I have never noticed an interest in the meaning or any kind of extra-social origins of family names on the part of my interlocutors. Names of mythical characters, like the one I received from my Aweti friend, are rare even if they exist within the scope of possibilities of name-giving, as became clear when she named me.

In addition to family names, many people also have nicknames and white people's names,[9] but none of them are compulsory. The Aweti make a distinction between them and inherited names, which are recognized as 'true names' (*et ytoto*), rather than just 'ways of calling [someone]' (*tejojtat*). The absence of a familiar name is sometimes compensated for by the presence of a 'way of calling' that may or may not be a white person's name. Whereas many people have only family names and no nicknames, others have only nicknames but no white people's names. The transfer of the latter within a family seems to be a possibility, but it is not taken very seriously, and it would be unthinkable in the case of nicknames, which are usually ironic. White people's names can be self-assigned—and it would not be unusual for someone to decide to change such a name at any time—but nicknames are always given by others, as is the case in most parts of the world.

Since it is prohibited to pronounce the names of affines, including parents-in-law, sons-in-law, daughters-in-law, brothers-in-law, and sisters-in-law, the father of a boy can call his son only by his father's name, while a mother must call him by her own father's name, and so on. Distant and even close relatives usually know only one of the names of a person, but it is not uncommon that they do not know any of the family names and call that person only by a nickname or by his or her white person's name. Some of my Aweti friends explained to me that the prohibition of pronouncing names of affines may extend to any name associated with the person, including nicknames. Yet there are people who do not accept being called by a nickname, as they always prefer to have their family name pronounced. The use of one or another type of name is not restricted to specific contexts.

As they give their names to the grandchildren who are born, adults must acquire new names, often no longer received from their elders, but remembered from the name stock once possessed by their dead ancestors. The relationship between new and abandoned names is one of substitution rather than accumulation, but names already received by a person never cease to be 'theirs' in the sense that they are at their disposal for transfer. From this cluster of paternal and maternal names, it is possible to choose indiscriminately which will be transferred to which grandchild. Therefore, from the point of view of the person who gives names, it does not matter which ones came from the mother's side and which came from the father's side, since all will be equivalent at the time of giving names to their descendants. People avoid bestowing the same name to two people when they are living in the same village, but controversies about who would have greater or lesser legitimacy to use a name are not uncommon.

In order to name their grandchildren, people have to go beyond their own names and the names of their brothers, and even those of their immediate classificatory brothers. Names of cross-cousins are also commonly used, as well as names of distant cognates—people from other villages with whom they have little relation. In a sense, 'knowing' a family name is equivalent to 'having' a family name. But even in relation to the names of close relatives, there is a risk that someone will interpret the act of naming as a kind of theft. Since more family names are always needed, giving a forename or a sibling name to someone who lives in another village is a highly significant act. Names acquired far from home are often paid for with valuables, such as shell necklaces and pots, but a name-receiver must still be recognized as a cognate of the name-giver, coming from the second descending generation.

When all available names have been given to their older brothers and cousins, many children are born without a family name. Elders, in turn, also tend to be nameless after using and passing on all the names they could remember. Therefore, elders and children often have 'invented names' (*mimo'ege put*)—names that are not on the list of those coming from their ancestors. These invented names can be bestowed by relatives or friends. I once learned that two old Aweti, both already lacking family names, had given names to each other. One gave to the other the name Kaxinawá—an 'Indian name' (*waraju et*),[10] learned on some trip to the city, as he explained to me—while he received the name of a mythical character, Wyrakaty, from that person.

The fact that my partner and I received names from Aweti mythology, therefore, was not entirely unusual in the Aweti naming practices. It was not by chance, I believe, that I first had to behave like a granddaughter, being able to listen and understand her grandfather's stories to be worthy of being named. On the other hand, it is clear that at that time, or for those people, my partner and I did not participate in family relations that could assure us family names. At least we had friends who could name us, similar to what had happened to the elders who had run out of family names.

But this was just an isolated episode illustrating a more general fact. The Aweti were clearly amused at the possibility of addressing me by names other than my own. Ehezu, Marinawalu, Marina Khan—all these names had something in common: they brought me closer to the Aweti's world through historical, affective, and aesthetic connections. During my time with the Aweti, I began to understand that personal names (in all their varieties) serve to elicit specific qualities in people, thus producing people as a result of their relations. From this point of view, it would be strange to stay with just one name. This was made especially clear to me in conversations about chiefdom.

Some Elements for an Ethnographic Theory of Descent

The Aweti term *morekwat*, usually translated as chief, designates a kind of regional aristocracy in which the village chiefs ideally participate, but it may also allude to the exemplary behavior of any individual. In all these cases, *morekwat* is someone who perfectly exhibits, or should exhibit, the moral behavior that defines humanity/Xinguanity. The fact that Upper Xinguano chiefs are ideally succeeded by their first-born sons was taken by some authors to indicate the existence of a lineage system associated with class status in the Upper Xingu (see especially Heckenberger 2000, 2005; see also Dole 1966). This question, however, needs to be analyzed in light of a more thorough investigation into what exactly is transferred between grandparents, fathers, and children; how this transferral occurs; and how it relates to the constitution of chiefdom. Having this in mind, Guerreiro (2015: 141–172) discusses Kalapalo (Karib Xinguano) utterances about inherited chief status, concluding that a notion of substance transmission through conception that assures any kind of status is absent in Kalapalo ideas, although blood may be used as an idiom to connote the efforts to produce similarity between parents and sons. This production involves a series of techniques to build beautiful and capable bodies, always associated with a strong moral character. Although Guerreiro does not mention the transmission of names as part of this process, this was a point frequently emphasized to me by the Aweti when talking about the chief status. The transmission of names must be understood, though, as one among other forms of the 'construction of the person' (Seeger et al. 1979), a classical theme in Amazonian philosophies.

As we have seen, names of grandparents are assigned to grandchildren without any specified rule of transmission, although certain preferences are considered. Given the preference for marriage between close cross-cousins,[11] it is common for spouses to have the same grandparents and for a pair of brothers-in-law to have the same set of names to pass on to their grandchildren. It is therefore in a very vague sense that the transfer of names to descendants reflects or allows the existence of lineages among the Aweti. But how can we understand the fact that names are mobilized to justify chiefdom?

"This name belonged to a *mokut etsat*. That is why I did not give it to my son," a friend once explained to me about the naming of his sons. A *mokut etsat* is a man whose cause of death is a counter-spell, that is, a sorcerer.[12] It should be clear that my friend was not referring to a sorcerer among his relatives, but to a namesake relative of a famous Aweti sorcerer, the protagonist of an ancient story. Therefore, his considerations did not call into question a genealogical connection revealed by the name, but rather the qualities that it could associate with the name-receiver. Other conversations showed that this calculation also works in reverse. An Aweti friend once explained to me how a boy, who at a young age proved to be very intelligent and skillful in everything he did, was given the name of an ancient *morekwat*, especially chosen among the names of his grandfather. Upon receiving a chief's name, the person is persuaded to act as such. An Aweti elder told me that he had been promised the name of a great *morekwat* by his mother's father when he was a child. He noted that after having received that name, he could never lie or lose control.

In the family that hosted me, there was a boy whom everyone called Nopirí. I once asked them to explain the meaning of that nickname to me. They told me that since there were no names available on the mother's side when he was born, he did not receive any name. As he was growing up, his older sisters began to make fun of this situation, calling him *pobre* ('poor' in Portuguese). Since the Aweti are generally fond of playing word games, his family soon turned that adjective into a new name, Nopirí (he is now known as Epi). The term 'poor' seems to me to sum up well the condition of persons without a family name: they lack something that others have but that is not essential. As the Aweti considerations about the names of chiefs and sorcerers of the past show, a name has the power to add a certain value to a person, but it is perfectly possible to live without a name. For practical life, it is obvious that each person must have at least one name, be it a family name or a nickname.

In analyzing the relationship between clan names, nicknames, and non-indigenous names for the Tukano of northwestern Amazonia, Hugh-Jones (2006) argues that the transfer of names associated with spiritual qualities, exclusively owned by patrilineal clans, is counterbalanced by the acquisition of nicknames, which are always acquired through everyday interactions that make reference to corporal signs or remarkable personal history events. Instead of connecting persons to a group of descent as clan names do, Tukanoan nicknames individualize them within this group. While clan names establish ties of spiritual participation, nicknames fulfill an individuating function. Aweti nicknames are created according to a rationale similar to that mobilized by Tukanoan nicknames. My interlocutors' comments on the effect of certain family names on name-receivers, however, suggest that the transfer of family names among the Aweti often follows comparable principles, making it impossible for us to identify a clear distinction of effects, as seems to be the case for Tukano onomastics, between types of names in this ethnographic context.

A person is often nicknamed after the family name or the nickname of another person. There is an Aweti girl whom everyone calls by the name of a much older woman who currently resides in another village. When I asked why, someone explained to me that the girl has a peculiar way of placing her foot on the ground when she stops on the bicycle, a body shape resembling that of her name-giver. Another boy is called by the Aweti word that designates 'shoe' because he resembles a Kuikuro man (Carib Xinguano) whose name means 'shoe' in his language. In the village school, the teacher calls a student, his cross-cousin, by the name of a Kamayurá (Tupi Xinguano) girl whom she resembles. A young man from the village is called Foguinho (Little Fire) because they consider him similar to the homonymous character on a soap opera that everyone followed on television via generators in 2007. A girl was nicknamed Xavante (another indigenous ethnonym) when her mother mistakenly cut her bangs over her ears in a manner that resembles the typical haircut of that indigenous group. A young man became angry with his young wife, who could not set up a grill for smoking fish, and he instantly received the nickname of a former Aweti chief, known for being nervous about his wives. Another man who, as a teenager, could not wait to have his first sexual intercourse, having thus remained short in stature,[13] was nicknamed by his own father with the family name of a Suyá man known for his short height. My namesake Marina, who soon decided that she was my sister in the village, was named after Marina Villas-Boas, the wife of the government agent who managed the indigenous area at the time and the person into whose hands my namesake was born.

In contrast to the scarcity of family names, the ways of calling a person do not stop proliferating. Family names are distinguished from nicknames and white people's names as valuable goods, and they may even be bought or stolen, as I have said. Not for nothing, they are recognized as 'real' names (but the qualifier *ytoto* also designates a large quantity, 'many'); they are names in their full power. 'Real' names have a special effect that in no way applies to nicknames and non-indigenous names, whose value is much more referential. I have never heard of anyone who got angry for having the name of a white person recognized as such, or who has become akin to someone because of a nickname, although I can imagine the Aweti making such hypotheses jokingly. The logic is always the reverse—the nickname, or non-indigenous name, eventually encompasses a previously detected connection, and usually with humorous connotations. In addition, because they are non-transferable, nicknames and non-indigenous names activate relationships between only two generations. Hence, perhaps their 'poverty', from the Aweti point of view.

However, the point I want to make is that just like nicknames indicate historical, logical, or aesthetic connections between people, 'real' names are not indiscriminately transferred to descendants; instead, they are used to activate particular relationships. As nicknames, 'real' names not only connect people to groups of relatives, but also particularize them—or rather, they particularize as they connect people to certain relatives. Bestowing family names involves recognizing qualities that already exist and those that can be produced through the act of naming, leading people to explore similarities and proximity between namesakes, in a way comparable to what happens with nicknames. Just as the *morekwat* represents the ideal of humanity, or the 'real people', in a distinction of degree but not of nature with respect to ordinary people, 'real' names are distinguished from the other ways of calling a person to perform at the highest degree what every name does: establishing a relationship that, at best, can convey qualities to its new bearer.

The importance of having a chief name in order to be a chief does not have to do with showing the presence of the physical or animistic substance of chiefdom—for, I repeat, I have never heard anything like it. Rather, it points out the fact that one is invested and recognized by others as a 'given' chief, whose chief qualities can be replicated, expressed, and developed. In this sense, names actually make chiefs, producing not only moral but also physical qualities since, because they are more conscientious, chiefs are also those who follow the rules of pubertal seclusion more closely, and thus constitute stronger bodies.

Names as Devices of Counter-Identity

What does a name do? The inadequacy of the representation paradigm—by which the name is taken as a signifier of the name-bearer—is a recurrent theme in the investigation of non-modern (but also modern) onomastic regimes that bring to the fore the performative character of names (see Bodenhorn and Bruck 2006; see also all the contributions to this book). When questioning the automatic association between name and identity, Lévi-Strauss ([1962] 1989) already pointed in this direction: even in contexts in which naming is supposedly 'free', such as ours, naming combines the attribution of identity and the classification of the name-receiver, of the name-giver, or more probably of both. However, Lévi-Strauss's emphasis on the logical (classificatory) character of the established relations is not enough to account for the effectiveness of the Aweti names, as must be already clear.

In his analytic synthesis of lowland South American onomastic systems, Viveiros de Castro (1992) suggests that the Lévi-Straussian classificatory model could apply to those societies where the acquisition of names follows familial lines, but not the ones that value names taken from outside the social world. He takes the Ge of central Brazil as a paradigmatic instance of the first case and the Tupinambá of the sixteenth century as a clear example of the second, but is explicit about conceiving the two models as poles of a 'continuum' (ibid.: 143–155). More than developing a case typology, this distinction helps to clarify different logics involved in 'endonymic' and 'exonymic' practices, if we adopt the terms proposed by the author. As Viveiros de Castro puts it, endonymic systems based on the transfer of names between members of the same social group, usually among the living ones, frequently operate as sociological classifiers, organizing relations through naming. On the other hand, the exonymic practices adopted by the highly belligerent peoples inhabiting the Brazilian coast at the time of the European invasion—for whom the adoption of names of dead enemies was an essential motivation for war—would be less concerned with the positioning of the name-receiver in a network of relations than with his radical particularization.[14] But it is not just a matter of opposing collectivizing or individuating effects of being named. More significantly, according to Viveiros de Castro, endonymic and exonymic practices point to distinct regimes of subjectivation through naming.

Later analyses of endonymic systems in the Amazon confirm that the value of the distinction proposed by Viveiros de Castro is less classificatory than analytical, allowing forces or aspects of naming practices to be to distinguished in a series of contexts. Regarding the Tukano of the northwestern Amazonia, as already mentioned, Hugh-Jones (2006) argues that clan names transferred between agnatic relatives can only be understood alongside the giving of nicknames and non-indigenous names in terms of their complementary effects.[15] Comparing Ge onomastics, Coelho de Souza (2002: 280–281) notes, in turn, another type of combination, also expressed in terms of the composition of different aspects of the person. On the one hand, she argues, the name objectifies the relations that result in the constitution of the person as relative and fully human. On the other hand, having its origin in mythical ancestors and other extra-social sources, the name connects the person to the time of the myth and to the possibility of metamorphosis continually reinstated by the ritual, to reintroduce the differences necessary to the reproduction of the social world (ibid.: 571). While the transfer of names between relatives constitutes the person as an equal and as a member of a specific social group, inserting the person into a universe of intra-group relations, the relation between name and name-receiver could be defined as exonymic, in Viveiros de Castro's terms, so that the name operates as a principle of alteration.

Unlike the Ge and Tukano systems, the Aweti onomastic practices do not allow for the distinction of matrimonial groups or of groups associated with the exclusive possession of material and immaterial goods (see especially Coelho de Souza 2002; Hugh-Jones 2006; Lea 2012).[16] So what is involved in the transfer of names among relatives in the Upper Xingu? The interpretations of Hugh-Jones and Coelho de Souza suggest the possibility of understanding it in terms of different and combining dynamic forces. What seems to matter to the Aweti, in a more general sense, is the generational criteria—the perception that a person is the continuity of a universe of ascendants, of "our grandparents." Through names that are replicated in all the Upper Xingu villages and throughout generations, the Aweti world is configured as a geographically and temporally stable unit, without losing sight of local particularities. In addition, the pair of names from the maternal and paternal sides constitutes the person as the product of the joint action of two collectives,[17] clearly distinguished by the prohibition of naming their kin, which obliges the parents of a child to address it always by the name of his or her own 'side'.[18]

As far as the quality of the name is concerned, however, the value of family names also lies in the possibility of adding particular qualities to the name-receiver. The emphasis on the acquisition of names among cognates of the second ascending generation indicates that the transformative power in question lies in the history of the Upper Xinguanos themselves, the deeds of their ancestors. A chief is someone who confirms, repeats, and adds to the history of other chiefs after whom he is named. But nothing is forcibly inherited, and the right relations must be activated (or obliterated) through naming. Thus, a name always comes from both 'the inside' and 'the outside', producing a difference in the person who receives it.[19] The 'true' name not only connotes family continuity, but also promotes individuating qualities, in this sense differentiating the receiver from what it was before receiving it. Descent takes the form of alteration.[20]

This effect is emphasized by the fact that the Aweti and their Upper Xinguano neighbors are always changing their names, something that reveals a peculiar relation between a name and the named person. When people talk about their family names, they do not refer to them as their own names, but as "the name my mommy calls me" or "the name my daddy calls me." It is clear from this formulation that a name does not just *belong to* someone; its main characteristic is that it was *given by* someone. This seems to imply that no name can fix the identity of a person and, further, that a person is not supposed to be of a self-determined and determinable nature. Names do not subsume the person of the name-receiver: there is always the possibility of a subject being identified by other names, by other subjects. Thus, rather than emblems or even producers of identity, names seem to constitute counter-identity devices among the Aweti.

This effect of the Aweti name-giving practices addresses a recurrent theme in Amazonian ontologies—the idea that children need to be 'made' relatives through caregiving, because they are not yet considered human when they are born (see Gow 1997). The identity of kinship is not conveyed by conception but must be actively produced (Viveiros de Castro 2002: 447). The emphasis given by Amazonian peoples to bodily construction (Seeger et al. 1979) is directly linked to this problem, since the constructed bodies are identified as both relatives and humans. The act of naming is part of this process: names make proper humans, that is, relatives. My point here is to show that even when there is a transfer of names from grandparents to grandchildren, as in the case of the Upper Xinguano system, the relation that takes place in the naming act implies the production of the name-receiver as different not only from her or his relatives (who never possess the same sets of names) but even from her- or himself. Of course, this individuating process is always accompanied by the opposite effect of producing people in connection to other people.

Conclusion: Back to Ehezu

Noticing that Tukano languages use the same terms to refer to personal names, group languages, vital power, and things, Hugh-Jones (2006: 76, 77) argues that names not only signify but are the very essence of things for those north-western Amazonian peoples. His observation is also derived from the fact that Tukano clan names (along with certain ornaments and ritual knowledge) are understood as part of the vital principle that unites the members of the clan.[21] The Aweti relation with their personal names would not allow me to say that, for them, names are (and reveal) the essence of entities, if this means that the name and the named being should coincide fully. The profusion of 'real' names and ways of calling a person, without ensuring any kind of stable social or substantial identity, undermines the possibility of determining individual or collective essences. The Aweti comments on the effect of names on people show that, rather than the essences of things, personal names are things that can be added to individuals by giving them good or bad qualities. People and names affect each other: a name is imbued with the qualities of the person who possesses it; people are imbued with the qualities of the name they receive. Its effect is close to the one evoked by Roy Wagner (1972), through the notion of metaphor, used to interpret, among other things, the Daribi onomastic system as a procedure of individuation 'by addition'. The Daribi name does not represent an individuality; it creates the individuality by associating the person with a series of influences and marks—an animal species, a namesake, the circumstances of the gestation or the birth of the name-receiver, and so forth.

My argument has been organized around two independent problems: why I received specific names from my Aweti friends, and how to understand the constitution of Aweti chiefdom in terms of the transfer of family names. My analysis of the Aweti onomastic practices shows that it is only possible to speak in terms of a chief's lineage (or even of cognate groups) having in mind that names—alongside other techniques and knowledges applied to produce 'real' people, flowing along unorthodox channels of transfer—effectively produce chiefs by attributing particular qualities to whoever receives specific names.

These observations are useful to illuminate the first problem, because the effect of the names I have received can only be of the same type. I was produced as an Aweti person (or, rather, as 'the white of the Aweti') through these names. While my nicknames could be taken as a manifestation of humorous intimacy, the mythical name Ehezu—which is close, because it belongs to their familiar stories about the world, but also distant, because it bespeaks ancient beings, previous to the origin of the present humanity, and is loaded with a power strange to their present world—seems to give the right measure of the kind of person I can be to them. The name as a relation thus suggests (or reaffirms) that, for the Aweti, the name of the relation is difference.

Acknowledgments

I am grateful to Florencia Tola, Marcelo González Gálvez, and Giovanna Bacchiddu for the invitation to participate in the workshop "What Is a Relation?" and to all the participants, whose discussions were so inspiring. I am also indebted to Tânia Stolze Lima for her astute comments on the manuscript and to the editors of this book for their careful readings.

Marina Vanzolini is a Professor in the Department of Social Anthropology at the University of São Paulo. She has carried out fieldwork since 2004 with the Aweti from the Upper Xingu in Central Brazil and has published a book on Xinguano sorcery practices, *A flecha do ciúme: O parentesco e seu avesso segundo os Aweti do Alto Xingu* (2015). Her publications focus on sorcery and shamanism, kinship, and indigenous cosmopolitics. Her current research interests include indigenous conceptions of myth and language.

Notes

1. Strathern's overall conclusions about the values attributed to the generic term 'relation' seem to apply for Latin languages in which corresponding notions do not designate kin ties, yet extend to social and epistemological connections.

2. For an early ethnographic presentation, see Bateson (1958); for a structuralist reading on the matter, see Lévi-Strauss ([1962] 1989); and for a thorough investigation on the theme, see Bruck and Bodenhorn (2006).

3. See the extrapolation of this question, raised by the Araweté ethnography, in Viveiros de Castro's (1996) synthesis on Amerindian perspectivism, as well as Lima's (1996) formulation on the Yudjá case.

4. Most game meat is prohibited because it is considered dangerous for consumption by the indigenous peoples of the region. This restriction is constantly evoked by the Upper Xinguanos as a diacritical of their way of being. As for vegetables, although other species, domesticated or not, are regularly consumed, they do not compare to cassava in terms of the amount consumed and the time spent on production—with the exception of pequi, an edible tree fruit and an essential component of the Xinguano diet in the rainy season.

5. See Guerreiro (2015) for an excellent analysis of the ritual, known by the Brazilianized Tupi term *quarup*.

6. The Aweti, now numbering about 250 people, are divided into three villages with a predominantly Aweti population (two of which have a significant presence of Kamayurá affines), in addition to being dispersed as married individuals in neighboring villages. The study that follows is primarily derived from a 12-month fieldwork period conducted between 2006 and 2010, although my research had been initiated earlier and continues to the present day in more sporadic visits.

7. At the time that the naming occurred, I did not realize the obvious connection between this episode and the many cases in which Euro-Americans were interpreted by tribal peoples as related to mythical ancestors or were attributed mystical powers associated with the past. See Sahlins (1981) for a classical analysis of Captain Cook's tragedy in the eighteenth century, and also Levi-Strauss (1993) for a reading on the incorporation of the 'white man' as a character in a sixteenth-century Tupian myth. As must be clear in this chapter, the name choice in my case seems to follow a logic similar to that involved in other comparable historical events: as a foreigner coming from a far-off, technically powerful society, I was associated with powerful characters of the distant past through the name Ehezu. That this interpretation was not clear to me at the time can be partially explained by the fact that I had (and still have) not heard of similar attributions of indigenous names to anthropologists or other Westerners in the Upper Xingu region. Certainly this does not assure any uniqueness to my experience, as other instances were probably not reported. In what follows I try to understand the fact of receiving that name as part of the Aweti naming practices, illuminated by and illuminating of their notions about the person and the relation.

8. *Tekyt eput*: *te*, third-person possessive pronominal prefix; *-kyt*, green; *-e(t)*, name; *put*, -ex.

9. Literally, a *cara'iwa* name. The term *cara'iwa* is usually translated by the Aweti as 'white people', meaning non-indigenous peoples in general. Since nicknames, as presented below, can be anything, including non-indigenous names, what distinguishes a *cara'iwa* name is the fact that it is taken from the known stock of Brazilian names.

10. The term *waraju* usually refers to indigenous peoples whom the Aweti distinguish from themselves and other Upper Xinguano peoples. Eventually, the same notion may be used in reference to all indigenous peoples (including those from the Upper Xingu), in oppositon to non-indigenous ones. Kaxinawá is the ethnonym of a large indigenous group from Western Amazonia, living more than 1,800 miles away from the Upper Xingu.

11. This preference was mentioned by my interlocutors, but such a marriage is not always possible, due to the limitations in terms of population that make it difficult to find a suitable spouse among close relatives.

12. *Mokut etsat* refers to the technique of tying the skin of the thumb (*mokut*) of the dead, through which one is expected to reach the sorcerer who caused the death. The expression means (in a loose translation) 'someone who suffers through the skin of the former thumb'.

13. I was told that people cease to grow after their first sexual intercourse—hence the constant warnings of Aweti parents for their children to postpone this moment.

14. Although, of course, both outcomes cannot be totally distinguished, since this particularization was a necessary step for a man's inclusion in kinship and political orders among these Tupian groups (see especially Sztutman 2013).

15. See also Viveiros de Castro's comments in Hugh-Jones (2006: 94–95).

16. It is worth noting in this respect that, as the analyses of Hugh-Jones and Coelho de Souza make clear, if the Ge and Tukano onomastics order relations between groups and individuals, classification is an effect of the production of individuals by the attribution of qualities, a process that (also) takes place through names. As Hugh-Jones (2006: 76) explains, it is not the patrilineal descent that guarantees the transfer of unique names and other clan attributes to the Tukano. Rather, it is the sharing of names, language, ornaments, and sacred musical instruments, understood as spiritual substances, that determines the constitution of the patrilineal group. The Tukano name classifies only as an effect of the substantial relationship it establishes between people who share the same vital principle.

17. It 'objectifies' the person as the result of this action, as Coelho de Souza (2002) puts it, adopting a Strathernian vocabulary.

18. See Wagner (1967, 1977) on the effects of affinal behavior in terms of defining 'consanguineal' units.

19. Based on Hugh-Jones's comments on his distinction between endonymic and exonymic systems, Viveiros de Castro has rephrased his initial proposition, noting that even where there is an internal transfer of names, it is never given by parents and always requires a certain distance between name-receiver and name-giver. "Amazonian endonymy is always a limit of exonymy," Viveiros de Castro concludes (cited in Hugh-Jones 2006: 92).

20. See Bodenhorn (2006) for an analysis of a case in which the transfer of qualities through names is associated with a theory of reincarnation, unlike the Aweti case.
21. I have never heard from the Aweti the idea of a correspondence between name and soul, which is common in several Amazonian contexts such as the Guarani Mbyá case analyzed by Macedo and Sztutman (2014). I believe that the very notion of 'soul' as something possessed by an entity is strange to my Aweti friends' way of thinking (see Vanzolini 2014, 2015). In any case, for most of the indigenous peoples of the South American lowlands, rather than an identity principle, the soul seems to be a principle of alteration, which allows humans to communicate with spirits and animals by adopting their non-human perspectives (Lima 1996; Viveiros de Castro 1996).

References

Bateson, Gregory. 1958. *Naven*. Stanford, CA: Stanford University Press.

Bodenhorn, Barbara. 2006. "Calling into Being: Naming and Speaking Names on Alaska's North Slope." In Bruck and Bodenhorn 2006, 139–156.

Bodenhorn, Barbara, and Gabriele vom Bruck. 2006. "'Entangled in Histories': An Introduction to the Anthropology of Names and Naming." In Bruck and Bodenhorn 2006, 1–30.

Bruck, Gabriele vom, and Barbara Bodenhorn, eds. 2006. *The Anthropology of Names and Naming*. New York: Cambridge University Press.

Clastres, Pierre. (1974) 2003. *A sociedade contra o Estado: Pesquisas de antropologia política* [Society against the state: Essays in political anthropology]. São Paulo: Cosac Naify.

Coelho de Souza, Marcela. 2002. "O traço e o círculo: O conceito de parentesco entre os Jê e seus antropólogos" [The dash and the circle: The concept of kinship between the Jê and their anthropologists]. PhD diss., Federal University of Rio de Janeiro.

Dole, Gertrude E. 1966. "Anarchy without Chaos: Alternatives to Political Authority among the Kuikuru." In *Political Anthropology*, ed. Marc J. Swartz, Victor W. Turner, and Arthur Tuden, 73–88. Chicago: Aldine.

Gow, Peter. 1997. "O parentesco como consciência humana: O caso dos Piro" [Kinship as a human consciousness: The case of the Piro]. *Mana* 3 (2): 39–65.

Guerreiro, Antonio. 2015. *Ancestrais e suas sombras: Uma etnografia da chefia Kalapalo e seu ritual mortuário* [Ancestors and their shadows: Na ethnography of Kalapalo's leadership and its mortuary ritual]. Campinas: Editora Unicamp.

Heckenberger, Michael J. 2000. "Estrutura, história e transformação: A cultura xinguana" [Structure, history, and transformation: The Xingu culture]. In *Os povos do Alto Xingu: História e cultura* [The people of the Upper Xingu: History and culture], ed. Bruna Franchetto and Michael J. Heckenberger, 21–58. Rio de Janeiro: Federal University of Rio de Janeiro.

Heckenberger, Michael J. 2005. *The Ecology of Power: Culture, Place, and Person-hood in the Southern Amazon, AD 1000–2000*. New York: Routledge.

Hugh-Jones, Stephen. 2006. "The Substance of Northwest Amazonian Names." In Bruck and Bodenhorn 2006, 73–96.

Lea, Vanessa R. 2012. *Riquezas intangíveis de pessoas partíreis: Os Mebêngôkre (Kayapó) do Brasil Central* [Intangible wealth of partible people: The Mebêngôkre (Kayapó) of central Brazil]. São Paulo: EDUSP.

Lévi-Strauss, Claude. (1956) 2008. "As organizações dualistas existem?" [Do dualistic organizations exist?]. In *Antropologia Estrutural* [Structural anthropology], 193–234. São Paulo: Cosac Naify.

Lévi-Strauss, Claude. (1962) 1989. *O pensamento selvagem* [The savage mind]. Campinas: Papirus Editora.

Lévi-Strauss, Claude. 1993. *História de Lince* [The story of Lynx]. São Paulo: Companhia das Letras.

Lima, Tânia Stolze. 1996. "O dois e seu múltiplo: Reflexões sobre o perspectivismo em uma cosmologia tupi" [The two and its multiple: Reflections on perspectivism in a Tupi cosmology]. *Mana* 2 (2): 21–47.

Macedo, Valéria, and Renato Sztutman. 2014. "A parte de que se é parte: Notas sobre individuação e divinização (a partir dos Guarani)" [The part that you are part of: Notes on individuation and divinization (from the Guarani)]. *Cadernos de Campo* 23 (23): 287–302.

Overing, Joanna, and Alan Passes. 2000. "Introduction: Conviviality and the Opening Up of Amazonian Anthropology." In *The Anthropology of Love and Anger: The Aesthetics of Conviviality in Native Amazonia*, ed. Joanna Overing and Alan Passes, 1–30. London: Routledge.

Overing Kaplan, Joanna. 1977. "Orientation for Paper Topics" and "Comments." Presented at the symposium "Social Time and Social Space in Lowland South American Societies." *Actes du XLII Congrès International des Américanistes* 2: 9–10, 387–394.

Rivière, Peter. 1993. "The Amerindianization of Descent and Affinity." *L'Homme* 33 (126–128): 507–516.

Sahlins, Marshall. 1981. *Historical Metaphors and Mythical Realities: Structure in the Early History of the Sandwich Islands Kingdom*. Ann Arbor: University of Michigan Press.

Seeger, Anthony, Roberto da Matta, and Eduardo Viveiros de Castro. 1979. "A construção da pessoa nas sociedades indígenas brasileiras" [The construction of the person in Brazilian indigenous societies]. *Boletim do Museu Nacional* 32: 2–19.

Strathern, Marilyn. 1995. *The Relation: Issues in Complexity and Scale*. Cambridge: Prickly Pear Press.

Strathern, Marilyn. 2013. "Opening Up Relations." Paper presented at the "Indigenous Cosmopolitics" conference, Sawyer Seminar on the Comparative Study of Cultures, University of California, Davis.

Strathern, Marilyn. 2014. "Reading Relations Backwards." *Journal of the Royal Anthropological Institute* (n.s.) 20 (1): 3–19.

Strathern, Marilyn. 2016. "Revolvendo as raízes da antropologia: Algumas reflexões sobre 'relações.'" [Revolving the roots of anthropology: Some reflections on "relations"]. *Revista de Antropologia* 59 (1): 224–257.

Sztutman, Renato. 2013. *O profeta e o principal: A ação política ameríndia e seus personagens* [The prophet and the principal: Amerindian political action and its characters]. São Paulo: EDUSP.

Vanzolini, Marina. 2014. "Daquilo que não se sabe bem o que é: A indeterminação como poder nos mundos afroindígenas" [From what is not well known what it is: Indeterminacy as power in the Afro-indigenous worlds]. *Cadernos de Campo* 23: 271–285.

Vanzolini, Marina. 2015. *A flecha do ciúme: O parentesco e seu avesso segundo os Aweti do Alto Xingu* [The arrow of jealousy: Kinship and its reverse according to the Aweti of the Upper Xingu]. São Paulo: Terceiro Nome.

Viveiros de Castro, Eduardo. 1992. *From the Enemy's Point of View: Humanity and Divinity in an Amazonian Society*. Trans. Catherine V. Howard. Chicago: University of Chicago Press.

Viveiros de Castro, Eduardo. 1996. "Os pronomes cosmológicos e o perspectivismo ameríndio" [The cosmological pronouns and Amerindian perspectivism]. *Mana* 2 (2): 115–144.

Viveiros de Castro, Eduardo. 2002. "Atualização e contra-efetuação do virtual: O processo do parentesco" [Update and counter-effect of the virtual: The kinship process]. In *A inconstância da alma selvagem* [The inconstancy of the wild soul], 401–455. São Paulo: Cosac Naify.

Viveiros de Castro, Eduardo. 2004. "Perspectival Anthropology and the Method of Controlled Equivocation." *Tipití* 2 (1): 3–22.

Viveiros de Castro, Eduardo. 2009. "'The Gift and the Given: Three Nano-essays on Kinship and Magic." In *Kinship and Beyond: The Genealogical Model Reconsidered*, ed. Sandra Bamford and James Leach, 237–268. New York: Berghahn Books.

Wagner, Roy. 1967. *The Curse of Souw: Principles of Daribi Clan Definition and Alliance in New Guinea*. Chicago: University of Chicago Press.

Wagner, Roy. 1972. *Habu: The Innovation of Meaning in Daribi Religion*. Chicago: University of Chicago Press.

Wagner, Roy. 1977. "Analogic Kinship: A Daribi Example." *American Ethnologist* 4 (4): 623–642.

Chapter 6

RITUALIZING THE EVERYDAY
The Dangerous Imperative of Hospitality in Apiao, Chiloé

Giovanna Bacchiddu

The unreciprocated gift still makes the person who has accepted it inferior.

—Marcel Mauss, *The Gift*

On the island of Apiao[1] (Chiloé, Chile), social relations are rarely acted out in public. People largely ignore each other when meeting in public spaces: they greet each other hastily and do not speak, nor do they walk together if heading in the same direction. Between close and distant neighbors and relatives alike, no familiarity is expressed. And yet the same people who hardly acknowledge each other in public have a completely different attitude when meeting in each other's households, where they devote full attention to their interlocutors. This

Notes for this chapter begin on page 142.

chapter explores this apparent paradox, illustrating that the only way to build and articulate meaningful relationships between different Apiao people and with different entities is to take them into the private, domestic space. The household's kitchen is the social space *par excellence* where the most important social act—hospitality (food offering and receiving)—takes place.

What is the significance of the avoidance of sociality in public? Why is hospitality so paramount, and what can a close look at its rituality reveal about the way Amerindians experience relations? What is the place of asymmetry, and why is it necessary?

In Apiao, all individuals—transcending categories such as kin (consanguine/affine), enemies, or friends—are considered potentially hostile others who need to be tamed through the action of establishing alliances. As such, they have to be treated formally in contexts that allow ties to be made or confirmed, such as attending to them as guests whenever they come visiting.[2] The establishment of alliances creates networks that temporarily lack hostility, but it also enables mechanisms of unbalance and debts. The only people with whom it is not necessary to establish alliances and to treat formally are cohabiting consanguines—until the moment they move out. The other is always a potentially dangerous Other with whom negotiation is needed, and the proper setting for negotiation is the private, domestic space. This same system applies to the relations that people establish with powerful otherworldly beings.

The present discussion takes as a starting point two observations on Amerindian sociality: Fernando Santos-Granero's (2009: 6) view that people are embodied social relations, and Peter Rivière's (1984: 98) contention that society is no more than an aggregate of the relationships that constitute it. This chapter responds to the questions posed by the introduction to this book by offering an analysis of the way that Apiao people conceive of the bonds connecting people and different entities to one another and how these bonds are inextricably imbricated in a constant flow of reciprocal exchange, recreated simultaneously throughout the island's social world. I shall demonstrate how relations consist of engagements in an active exchange, where each participant takes turns offering and receiving, and how this paradigm, which includes connections between humans and supernatural entities, is the condition for the maintenance of a cosmological equilibrium. This will allow me to reflect on issues of asymmetrical relations and their indispensability in the Amerindian context.

As Marcel Mauss ([1954] 1990) argues, being part of a gift exchange system produces an asymmetry between the parties involved that can be adjusted by returning the gift, only to simultaneously produce another instance of asymmetry. This implicit asymmetry is notable because it seems to contrast with Apiao people's constant statement "Aquí somos todos parejos" (Here we are all the same)[3] and displays of sameness, coupled with efforts to attain lack of differentiation and homogeneity, an attitude that I have previously defined as "antagonism reversed" (Bacchiddu 2017a: 56). Asymmetry, however, is necessary to produce an alternation of distance and closeness, of dependence and autonomy that regulates relations. We will see how these aspects play out in the Apiao context, triggering a regular exercise of incorporation and expulsion of the other in the contingent, unstable dyads that are formed and dissolved all the time, whose protagonists are necessarily antagonists and, in Tânia Stolze Lima's terms (2000), are temporarily able to impose their point of view on the other.

Eduardo Viveiros de Castro (2001: 43n26) maintains that "'no relation without differentiation' is the first cardinal postulate of Amazonian ontology." When Apiao people declare sameness, they indicate a continuity of status, disposition toward the future, social obligations, and unity vis-à-vis the non-islanders. However, in order to meaningfully relate to each other, they must be different or differentiated; in other words, they have to be de-consanguinized. This is because there is no need to establish a relation with those who are the same as oneself, that is, the co-resident consanguines who do not need to ask each other anything. Indeed, the hospitality rules discussed in this chapter apply not only to all non-consanguines, but also to those consanguines who have left the household to live apart and build a family, for they have become others and must be treated as such. These rules also frame the relations with the most dangerous guests: the dead and the miraculous saints, who are taken into the social circle and dealt with exactly like all the others, inserted in the network of alliances, 'domesticated', brought home (Bacchiddu 2011, 2017a; Santos-Granero 2007: 7).

Meaningful socio-cosmological acts in Apiao are always mediated through hospitality and must take place within a framework of offering and receiving food and drink. During social visits and religious rituals alike, a specific code of conduct informs interaction, fixed speech formulas punctuate dialogue, and special body postures are adopted. The rituality of hospitality, constantly performed, has an implicit sacredness in both quotidian and religious events. Food and drinks must always be offered, accepted, and reciprocated in a powerful display of Maussian gift exchange rules. While sameness is constantly stressed in discourse, during visitations it appears momentarily downplayed and replaced with a contingent hierarchy, strategically employed. This is explicit in the offering of food, always rhetorically belittled by the host, and in the asking ritual, where host and guest perform a dialogue where one 'supplicates' the other with accentuated humbleness and redundant modesty. This strategy is manipulative (Ortner 1978) in that it aims to obtain something by elevating the interlocutor's position. The visiting mechanism allows people to alternate between the positions of guest and host, continually creating asymmetry and highlighting difference, the productive/generative force behind the constitution of relations (see the introduction to this book).

People periodically visit each other with the apparent purpose of asking for something or returning something that they had previously borrowed. During visits, both host and guest engage in a long ritual of offering and receiving, according to specific sequences of 'dialogic' acts that follow the same pattern, no matter the connection between the individuals involved. It is during these visits that relationships are tested, negotiated, confirmed, and perpetuated. Only co-residential consanguines are mutually exempt from this carefully regulated practice. When they move out, they immediately become generic others, who treat each other and are treated as non-consanguines.[4]

This brings us back to my earlier question about hospitality being so paramount and ritualized in this community and contrasting so patently with the lack of interaction observed in public settings. As Candea and da Col (2012) aptly point out, hospitality is a foundational anthropological concept that touches upon the discipline's conceptual staples, such as gift-giving, exchange, identity, alterity, and consubstantiality, among others. In this chapter I intend to focus on hospitality's dangers and its potentially problematic implications, and on how these get entangled with the above-mentioned analytical categories. According to Marcel Hénaff (2010: 79), "ceremonial gift-giving is not a state of peace; it is a controlled conflict." Hénaff underlines how gift exchange always occurs in a context of social antagonism and latent conflict, and is meant to mediate and control a potentially dangerous and confrontational relationship. In his classic analysis of Greek hospitality, Herzfeld (1987: 77) similarly points out how hospitality provides a means of expressing and reversing a pattern of domination at the same time.

Drawing on these authors' analyses of hospitality, reciprocity, and gift-giving practices, I will highlight how the convivial and apparently innocuous traditions of attending to guests and receiving hospitality disguise a potential conflict, constantly kept at bay through those same practices. Both host and guest are inserted in—and constrained by—an obligatory and strict sequence of reciprocal acts where power circulates from host to guest and vice versa, obliging them to momentarily surrender their declared sameness and engage in a game of practical and stylistic negotiation within a temporarily asymmetric relation. This can happen only in an intimate space like someone's household kitchen, a space that by defining hosts and guests allows the contingent asymmetry, in contrast with the undifferentiated public space, where all are 'the same' (*parejos*) and negotiating is pointless. What follows is an attempt to accurately describe the rituality of hospitality, highlighting its sacredness, obligation, and danger, as well as its cosmic repercussions. Hospitality as played out in Apiao offers us the possibility to view a model of relation as the perpetual movement of transformation (Lévi-Strauss 1995; Viveiros de Castro 2001), operated by constant efforts through which sameness becomes otherness, otherness is turned into sameness, and being proper individuals entails having the autonomy to interact with same and others alike, skillfully engaging in constant negotiation. Thus, the Apiao form of relation—which is possible only within a hospitality framework—parallels the process of kinship in Viveiros de Castro's (2001: 33) seminal writing as "the cosmological movement of transformation of affinity (alterity) into consanguinity (identity) and back again."

Atender a la gente: Hospitality

Fellow islanders may occasionally run into each other while going somewhere—at the beach while working on their boat or at seaweed collection; at school or at a funeral; on the platform while waiting to travel to town; on the boat to and from town; or in the town where they travel regularly, and so forth. None of these occasions calls for people to pay special attention to one another. In fact, they hardly share a word, besides a hurried greeting or a simple acknowledgment. At most, they shake hands, barely making eye contact. Everyone seems to mind their own business. If talking, they keep it brief and mostly whisper, aware that they might be overheard. When people need to talk, they always do so in private. The public space seems inappropriate or unfit for sharing or communicating. As I have previously explored (Bacchiddu 2017a), in this small community people avoid acting in public—or, rather, limit their public actions—in order to shield themselves from visibility that would make them socially vulnerable.[5] In my analysis, I argue that the visibility of one's actions exposes individuals to their peers' judgment, potentially causing frictions and conflicts (ibid.). The most appropriate space for interaction is someone's kitchen, where crucial conversations are held and important decisions are made. Only in a space where food and drinks circulate can the other—visitor or dead/saint—be truthfully and fully brought into a relation and domesticated, or made an ally. In this sense, the Apiao version of the classic analytic dichotomy between public and domestic becomes 'in someone's household kitchen' versus 'anywhere else'. The real opposition occurs between what goes on inside houses and what occurs outside of them (ibid.).

Despite its common occurrence, visiting is a serious and fraught practice, since it implies crossing boundaries, defining roles, and highlighting otherness. But no matter the potential dangers involved, visiting and relating are indispensable for the living. There is always an express purpose for visiting, as it is uncommon for people to leave their houses for mere sociality, even among close relatives. Typically holding a stick for self-defense, guests announce their presence by whistling from outside the premises, which are enclosed by wooden fences or barbed wire. Households are protected by dogs that always bark vigorously at visitors and may even attack them. When the hosts spot visitors or hear the dogs barking at the presence of a stranger, they whisper the newcomer's name to each other, wondering about the reason for the visit. Then they quickly tidy up. Meanwhile, the host goes out, calms the dogs, and invites the visitors to come in with the formula "Más adelante" (lit., 'come more inside'), implying that by gaining the household precincts, the visitors have already been 'inside'. Upon entering, the guests will always say "Permiso" or "Permisito" (Excuse me), and "Buenos días" (Good morning) or "Buenas noches" (Good evening).

Host and guests greet each other formally by shaking hands. Hand shaking, done by offering a well stretched-out arm, is the common greeting gesture, even between siblings and between parents and children. Non-residential close kin/ consanguines are treated formally like all the other visitors. This important detail shows that alliances occur between people who are 'different'. When consanguines leave their original household to form a family, they become generic others to be attended, who come to ask favors and to whom favors can be asked.

The visitors are always allowed into the house, unless they need to be attended to outside for a quick matter and do not enter. But this is not considered ideal, and most people, whenever visiting, tend to stay for a while. They are invited to sit on the bench by the stove, or the best chairs are wiped with a cloth and offered to them. They sit during the whole visit without taking off any of their several layers of clothes despite the obvious difference in temperature between inside and outside; as a result, they often sweat copiously. If children accompany them, they will stay put for the entire time without uttering a word.

The host quickly slices fresh bread and pours fresh *mate* (a herbal tea) into the gourd, positioning her/himself as '*mate* giver'. Sitting by the stove, the sugar container in her/his lap, a teapot at hand, the host serves *mate* in a circle to the visitors and to whoever is present. After drinking the *mate* through a metallic straw, the guests return the gourd to the host, who tops it up with a spoonful of sugar and enough hot water, and passes it again to the guests or to whoever is sitting next to him, and so on. The *mate* gourd circulates from host to guests and vice versa, following a spatial sequence. Water is always ready for *mate*, since habitually there are one or more teapots on the stovetop. If there is no bread, a woman quickly prepares some dough and fries round-shaped tortillas to feed the guests. Sometimes cold cooked meat is offered with the bread. All the food is put on a chair placed in front of the visitors so they can help themselves, as from a small, private table.

Generally, male and female adults and children are treated alike, with the same amount of food and drink being offered to both. When alcohol is offered, children are served exactly as the adults, and their parents encourage them to accept the offer, although it is understandable that a child might not consume as much as an adult. All visitors are treated equally, but some special guests (relatives who left the island, teachers, old and respected neighbors, *compadres*, godchildren, affluent people, missionaries, and travelers, if previously known) are served cooked food several times while in the house. Both male and female hosts attend to the visitors. If no woman is at home, the man offers bread and *mate*. He does not cook, and he is in charge of serving alcohol. If there is *chicha* (locally produced apple cider) in the house, it is always offered in quantity; the host keeps an eye on the guests' glasses and fills them up as soon as they are empty. No visitor is ever asked if she or he would like something to eat or drink, and no visitor would ever refuse food or drink. The mere fact of visiting implies the offering and consumption of food and drink, irrespective of the time of day.

I once accompanied a young man who was collecting donations for a local religious festival. We visited more than 20 households in two days and were always attended in the same way. We were offered food and drinks in each household we visited, and at lunchtime we were offered a meal. We ended up having lunch some four or five times, not being able to refuse because "Eso no se hace" (You don't do that) or "Eso es muy feo" (That is very ugly). Only toward the end of the day, really tired and having eaten more than enough, were we allowed to be excused and could avoid sitting for yet another meal. However, this was possible only at close acquaintances' households, and even then we had to sit sipping *mate* at least for a while.

During a visit, whatever activity was taking place is interrupted, and the attention of the household members is devoted solely to the guest. The whole domestic microcosm is put on hold, with all tasks postponed until order is restored. While drinking *mate*, host and guest either engage in a short, generic conversation or remain silent. Sometimes silence reigns for a long time before the visitor breaks it, explaining the reason for his presence in the house. The host would never inquire about it: it would be utterly rude to do so. To state the motivation for the visit at the outset would indicate unwillingness to accept hospitality: only after having consumed the food and a good amount of *mate* will the guest express his demands. This is usually done in a humble manner, with a deferential and submissive attitude (Bacchiddu 2010). The visitor might come to borrow some food or a tool, to offer meat for sale before slaughtering a cow, or to ask for help in the form of a day of work. Whatever the reason for the visit, neither host nor guest can avoid the task of offering and receiving food and drink.

Reparar: Refusing the Offer

Refusing offers in the context of hospitality is simply unthinkable. Only when those involved are close to each other can guests give good reasons not to take any food, but they would still have to accept *mate*. Generally, they would be scolded loudly by the hostess, who would angrily ask them, raising her voice: "Me estás reparando la comida, qué?" (Are you disdaining my cooked food, what?). *Reparar* in the local Spanish indicates the attitude of judgmentally assessing the quality of the hosts' belongings and considering their offer of food to be not good or below expectations. While this is almost to be expected from an outsider (Bacchiddu 2012)—which is why Apiao people deal reluctantly with outsiders in their own households, unless they know them well enough and trust them—should this happen between fellow islanders, it would be a warning bell of some serious conflict. I was often advised to always accept whatever I was being offered. In case I was not eager to eat or drink, I should always take at least some. Despite not being a smoker, I had to accept cigarettes if they were distributed and keep them in my pocket, because it would be considered insulting and disrespectful to refuse them.

The visiting etiquette I have just described is practiced on a daily basis. It also applies to guests received throughout religious *novenas*—ritual celebrations held in honor of the dead or of a local miraculous saint that take place frequently on the island. These are repeated daily for sequences of nine consecutive days and are marked by a strict code of behavior. *Novenas* are always held in someone's household and replicate the patterns of hospitality on a wider scale, gathering groups of guests numbering 50 or more. On such occasions, the *mate* is replaced by abundant platefuls of cooked and uncooked food and several rounds of drinks. All the guests are treated equally and act in the same way, silently consuming all that is offered. The framework of hospitality in *novenas* replicates the everyday context: an offering host and receiving guests. What changes is only the scale. The implications of these rituals are stronger—and more dangerous—since food and drinks circulate in the name of the entity for which the meeting was summoned. In this sacred context, attending poorly or disdaining the offer would be doubly offensive, both toward the host and toward the deceased or the saint in honor of whom the offerings are made. Such a breach carries inevitable cosmic consequences, as the laws of hospitality and reciprocity dictate that rules must be followed in order to avoid retaliation brought forth by the cosmic imbalance that such actions activate (Bacchiddu 2011, 2017b).[6]

Guests never give thanks while receiving: the rule for *mate* drinking states that they will say thanks (*gracias*) only when they do not want anymore *mate*, that is, upon returning the gourd to the host for the last time. However, the etiquette requires that the guests, while leaving, give thanks for whatever they received, mentioning each item: "Thanks for the *mate* and the bread/lunch/ *chicha*." The importance of acknowledging and thanking assumes a sacred connotation on special occasions, and fixed formulas are used to thank someone appropriately. The failure to do so implies conflict and social disruption.

As mentioned above, until the guests give thanks, signaling that they do not want any more *mate*, the host must keep serving them. In this peculiar situation, the control apparently belongs only to the host, who is in charge of attending to the guests. The visitors seem in a vulnerable position: upon entering someone else's home, they are trespassing on someone else's property, encircled by fences and protected by dogs. Getting into the kitchen—the only heated space of the household—and partaking of a private, domestic space and its food and drinks, the guests apparently occupy a lower position in the hierarchy: they are formally polite, have a deferential attitude, and always display humbleness, especially if they need to obtain something. Their voice, facial expressions, body postures, and word choices express deferential submission and full dependence on the host's benevolence to have their requests granted (Bacchiddu 2010). However, despite appearances, the control of the situation rests in the hands of the guests. Here a reversal of the pattern of domination emerges, as mentioned by Herzfeld (1987). A clear indication of this is that through their presence guests bind the host family to themselves inescapably, forcing them to interrupt any other activity and focus their attention on them, indirectly obliging them to attend to their guests until the moment they utter the reason for the visit or offer thanks for the *mate*. Until this happens, the host must keep offering *mate*—patiently and in silence—no matter how long she or he has been serving it or how many people have been served. Trapped in the position of *mate* giver, at the mercy of the guest, the host becomes 'the victim', in Herzfeld's words.[7]

However, what I wish to demonstrate is that control, as well as a contingent higher position, is ping-ponged between host and guests throughout the entire visiting interaction. In other words, hierarchy is not substantial but perspectival (Lima 2000). Powerful non-human entities (the dead, the saint) are part of the exchange network, and people establish alliances with them, initiating a relation through a commitment to systematically offer food and drinks to the community (*promesas*). *Novenas* are organized to reciprocate gifts requested from a powerful entity and obtained; in return, people offer the gift of generous hospitality to the collectivity-turned-guests. *Novenas* are counter-gifts that materialize the outcome of a successful relation, borne out of a process of negotiation (Bacchiddu 2011). In attending *novenas*, community members accept the hospitality, knowing that their position as guests is contingent and unstable: soon they will host their own *novena*, whose success will depend on guests' attendance. The power implicit in the position of host and guest is a contingent force that is passed round—just like the *mate* gourd. Non-human others are domesticated, brought home, and inserted into the reciprocity circle (see Santos-Granero 2007: 7), thus allowing islanders to temporarily overcome hierarchy. However, this circle is continuously recreated through the alternation of the position of power that being host or guest implies.

The Imperative of Reciprocity

The implicit tenet of Apiao's entire social and religious life is a principle of reciprocity. A regular give-and-take rules over all active relations, based on a dense network of scrupulously balanced reciprocities. Relations are regulated by how each party renews the terms of the relationship in each encounter, when alliances are confronted with a different challenge and tested. If the expectations are fulfilled, the relationship continues; if they are unfulfilled, or 'betrayed',[8] the relationship henceforth will change, reflecting the extent of the negligence. Gifts, food, visits, offerings, help, and miracles are given in the measure and quality in which they were received and acknowledged in previous circumstances. Relationships are confirmed and perpetuated by regular flows of giving and receiving; they are interrupted or modified by irregular flows of giving and receiving. If a saint ignores requests, he is not due anything, as he has refused to enter into a relation. If he grants requests, he must be paid back according to the promise made when proposing the alliance.

What circulates could be material objects, like food or tools, or appropriate 'good behavior', such as kindness, generosity, solidarity. This flow represents an implicit pact established or renewed between dyads in order to avert potential conflict (Hénaff 2010) and serious retaliation from powerful others (Bacchiddu 2011, 2017b). The exchange and payment of debts should always be symmetrical. The following example shows a regular flow of symmetrical reciprocity. My host family attended to Laurita, a respected elderly neighbor, with bread and *mate* as usual. When she left, however, they always gave her the food she did not consume to take home with her: "llévese su pancito!" (Take your bread with you!) was the common goodbye. When I asked why Laurita—unlike other visitors—was always given bread, they explained that she always did the same for them whenever they visited her: "Así se hace" (This is the way it has to be done). If someone does something for you in a certain way, it must be reciprocated identically. As an example of asymmetry, after a guest had left, a woman scolded her husband for having attended to him with *chicha*. "Why did you give him *chicha*? He never gives *chicha* to anybody. That's why his *chicha* lasts for the whole winter!" In serving *chicha*, the man accomplished his duty as a host, but given the reciprocity imperative, he had been more generous than he ought to have been: offers given must always match offers received.

In the context of interaction with the dead/the saint, it is acceptable to put oneself in an indebted position by committing to offer a certain amount and attending to it scrupulously. One can exceed the promise but not fall short of it, as the consequences could put the renegade in a dangerous position or even a life-threatening situation (Bacchiddu 2011, 2017b).

Suplicar: Ritualizing the Everyday

Our neighbor Sara came to my host family's household and, as etiquette requires, sat down for a good while before uttering the reason for her visit.

Eventually, she addressed a plea to my landlady, who was also her *comadre*.[9] Her facial expression revealed intense distress and severe preoccupation: "Vengo con un sufrimiento muy grande, comadre. Nos prestarán su horno pa' cocer pan pa' la novena?" (I come with a big affliction, *comadre*. Will you lend us your oven to bake bread for the *novena?*). Sara used the expression *un sufrimiento muy grande* to signal that she was coming to ask a big favor. Her words implied much more than they meant, providing an example of what linguist Kerbrat-Orecchioni (2004: 32) defines as verbal production that modifies the interlocutive context, allowing words to materialize into an action. Sara was not asking my landlady simply to use her oven, but to bake the bread for the entire *novena*, since she owned the special oven necessary for this task and had the knowledge to use it. Such a request—perfectly familiar and recognizable to my landlady—was an appeal for help,[10] and, like all requests in Apiao, it was uttered in the formal, ritual way that the circumstance required, using fixed formulas. Sara's formal request for help is an action called *suplicar* (to formally ask someone to help with some work).

The expression *suplicar* (to implore), instead of the common *pedir* (to ask), points to an almost desperate plea and highlights the sacredness of the request. People 'implore' others for religious occasions, such as funerals, *novenas*, or work parties, when the collaboration of several people is needed. Typically, this involves the launch of a boat, pig slaughtering and processing, *chicha* making, and planting and harvesting. These occasions are considered sacred in nature; the need for help is justified and should never be refused. Whoever needs cooperation visits some chosen individuals, who belong to an established network of alliances, and formally requests their collaboration. Women are often asked to help with cooking, and they spend the whole day cooking in the house of the requester, who directs them by indicating their tasks.

The sacred aspect surrounding hospitality is enhanced by the action and meaning of *suplicar*, apparent in Sara's choice of words (ritual expressions, fixed formulas) and attitude. Upon leaving, her parting words were "Tengan paciencia, comadre" (Be patient, *comadre*),[11] a further petition of recognition and a form of acknowledging the binding pact that had just been established. This request is an instance of a repeated exchange, replicated through time, between two individuals and their households, and between other Apiao individuals who alternatively occupy the position of guest and host. As Viveiros de Castro (2004: 477) reminds us, every exchange act is a response to a previous exchange act: it is impossible to find an absolute beginning to these concatenations. These relations reveal how autonomous individuals are at the same time fully dependent on others to fulfill their social and cosmic roles (see the introduction to this book). Their space, resources, and will are made available (or not) to help/be helped according to the contingent situation, continuously throughout their lives.

Hospitality is the framework in which favors are asked and granted, and where people ritually ask for cooperation. All parties involved know that once asked, they cannot refuse, and in this sense asking is manipulative. In her classic discussion of hospitality rules and gift-giving transactions, Sherry Ortner (1978) argues that food is an extremely powerful tool, since one who offers food is entitled to ask favors of one who receives it. While in Apiao this is reversed (the guest being the one asking), the ethnography confirms Ortner's insight that food/drinks offerings are generally instrumental and socially manipulative: "At the core of any hospitality event, there is a material transaction: A host gives food to his guest. Feeding is culturally considered to be an act of great power, and although in a large wedding or funeral party, for example, the host has no immediately manipulative intent, most of the other usages of the hospitality framework are explicitly manipulative" (ibid.: 68).

In Apiao, asking—despite the overstated humility in the actual performance of the request—is not to compel, but to put someone in the position of not being able to refuse. This applies not only to what is asked, but also to what is offered, or the imperative of accepting and giving thanks for each item received. In this sense, food offerings—as with requests, sacred or less sacred—impose a positive reaction. The manipulative guest is in control, at least temporarily.

The humble attitude while making a request, a peculiar stylistic frame of momentarily muddling up sameness (i.e., similarity of condition and intent) and turning it into otherness, is a typical approach in Apiao. In the context of hospitality, understatement is used as a rhetorical device to summon the interlocutor's attention. While offering abundant food, the host might say "Here are some little potatoes for you" (*Aquí tiene papitas*) or "Help yourself to a little piece of bread" (*Sírvanse pancito*), always adding "Just excuse [me]" (*Disculpe nomás*), belittling the food offered in order to give the receiver the impression of being of higher status, achieved by belittling oneself and humbly apologizing. This same device, which Herzfeld (1987: 80) appropriately defines as "the rhetoric of exaggeration by inversion," is noticeable in the ritual fixed formulas. The goal is to practice a strategic inversion that temporarily gives the guest a higher status, but what the host is really aiming at is to underline her own condition of generosity/humbleness/resilience to the audience, while giving the guest the impression of having accepted a subordinate position.

Candea and da Col (2012: S11) highlight how "hospitality, like the illusionist's craft, operates according to the 'distraction principle': the attention of the audience is cleverly misdirected" for a specific purpose, in a subtle power play. This too is a form of control—a "technology of control" (ibid.: S3). The control bounces back and forth between host and guest in dialogic form through these strategic formal devices. For the exchange to happen, sameness must be muddled up, albeit contingently and temporarily. Those people who think of themselves as 'all the same' have to turn that sameness into difference so that relations can occur, thus becoming others to each other—indispensable others, as such.

The *suplica* invitation is always performed humbly, using linguistic expressions belonging to a fixed repertoire that aims at highlighting the lower status of the requester and elevating to a higher position the one who is asked. Those who ask humiliate themselves, as if surrendering themselves into their hosts' hands, relinquishing their dignity for the sake of the sacred request. However, as Steven Rubenstein (2007: 379) reminds us, the term "sacred ... signals that something is both valued and feared." In this ritual, a certain amount of power is passed on in a give-and-take that invests people with alternating roles and different amounts of control to handle.

The guests supplicate the hosts, surrendering the power to make or break a relationship, and yet they are in control—until the host accepts the challenge, which always involves an effort of some sort. Once they accept the request, they are back in control, aware of being needed. Through the *suplica*, the requester acknowledges the host's ability to accomplish special tasks and celebrates that skill: to be asked is an honor, a flattering signal of appreciation. But, crucially, with the ritual act of asking, one is starting (or, more correctly, restarting) a cycle of circular reciprocity, automatically indebting oneself to a future instance of being asked to reciprocate (Pitt-Rivers 1968; Viveiros de Castro 2004). Likewise, people establish relations with the saint/dead, requesting favors of them and agreeing to return the favor if their request is fulfilled, bringing these entities into the reciprocity circle, domesticating them.

It should by now be evident that such careful, distinct transactions cannot happen in an undifferentiated public space, but need an enclosed area where the embroidery of negotiation can be slowly crafted. Facial and vocal expressions, body postures, fixed formulas, food and drinks offered and received—all these details would be lost outside the household. As soon as the guests leave, freeing the host from the obligation to attend to them, they again turn into generic, undifferentiated others, who are hardly acknowledged in public.

Betrayal: The Denial of Help and the Breaking of the Circle

What happens when the hosts act on the power that is momentarily passed on to them and choose to decline collaboration? Given the sacredness of the *suplica*, denying reciprocity indicates a dangerous handling of power, a serious matter that can eventually lead to acute conflict and the severance of relations. The following case of unrequited reciprocity regards an individual who, having benefited from being a host, subsequently declined returning the favor when he refused to be a guest. The logic of exchange is bent, creating a fracture.

Francisco bought and repaired an old boat to use for diving for clams and sea urchins, his main source of income. Repairs on the boat required months of work, which took place on the beach. Once the boat was fixed, Francisco organized a work party for the launch: *la bota*. This is a tough job requiring several men, who are compensated with abundant food and drink at the celebration following *la bota*, and are given ritual gifts of meat and bread to take home.

The night before the launch, Francisco chose each guest for the work party for a precise reason: Carlos because he had helped at various times; Juan because he had offered wood for the boat; Pablo because he had helped repair the boat; and Pedro because "we're neighbors, *compadres*,[12] colleagues, and he called me when he launched his boat." Finally, Elena was invited because she had sold Francisco the lamb for the barbecue. He visited them at their homes and asked them formally and ritually, with a *suplica*. Everybody responded positively except Pedro: he gave some excuse and said that he would not go. This refusal angered Francisco and his wife. The fact that they were *compadres*, neighbors, and fellow workers only made matters worse. Against all expectations and common sense, Pedro did not fulfill his reciprocal duty, the *vuelta 'e mano* (lit., 'to give a hand back', or return the favor). Months earlier he had formally requested Francisco's help for his own *bota*. "I left my work to help him then, and now that I ask him to help me, he refuses. He did not return the favor! It was his turn to help!" Francisco said passionately. Unable to understand at the time, I naively asked if he was short of workers, to which Francisco energetically replied: "I have workers in excess [*esos sobran*]! I invited him not out of necessity but out of affection, because this is a private event, for a few chosen guests!" He was really upset, as was his wife, who reminded him reproachfully that he had fulfilled (*cumplir*) his duty as a *compadre*, accepting the *suplica*, working all day and then receiving food and drink, until he became so inebriated that eventually he could not walk home properly. When his wife arrived from town loaded with their monthly provisions, he was unable to carry the heavy load home. Francisco's wife remarked that he had neglected his own family to be a good *compadre*, and now he was "betrayed."

The case of the boat launch presents a duality of circumstances: the ritual call (*suplica*) and the invitation to the social event intrinsically implied in the launch, where plenty of food and alcohol are served and distributed for the guests to take home. The gifts are intended as payback in exchange for labor, as happens at every work party (*minga*). It is a duty to accept the invitation, but it is also an honor to be invited. At the launch there is always a small crowd of curious and occasional helpers on the beach. They are offered some alcohol, but they are not invited to the house, unlike those who are formally requested, who enjoy an interesting mix of privilege and duty. This shows once again the inappropriateness of the public space in the management of significant relations: it is only at one's home that others can be properly attended to, only at home that one can deploy the hospitality apparatus and thus demonstrate the willingness to engage in a relation.

The avoidance of sociality in public indicates an acknowledgment of the status of undifferentiated sameness—in Apiao terms, being *parejos*. On the one hand, such status provides safety as homogeneity minimizes rivalries based in antagonism or competition. On the other hand, for relations to happen, people must temporarily exit sameness and become others, and this can happen only in a dialogic sequence involving interlocutors who alternatively take the role of host and guest. Shifting the axis of action to the household, the avoidance enables people to play an active part in (precarious) alliances. Through hospitality, difference emerges; in allowing difference, hospitality enables relations.

As Lima (2000: 48) has observed, asymmetry, as "the capacity of a subject … to impose its point of view on another," is not substantial, but is a "reversible relation" that cannot be determined *a priori* precisely because it depends on a contingent reality, on whatever is happening in that very moment and how it is experienced by those who live it. Although the Apiao context is not strictly perspectivist, this concept strongly resonates with the ethnography and is extremely useful for reflecting on the nature of relations in indigenous South America. It helps us to understand asymmetry as a dialogic exchange between people who temporarily control their interlocutor's point of view. 'Betraying' the responsibility entailed by that position of privilege—refusing the request, denying help, ignoring the invitation—indicates the abuse of the power that the guest, in his apparently humble, lower position, entrusts to the host. That power is meant to circulate, to bounce from one interlocutor to the other, because everyone knows that their position of host or guest is contingent. By holding on to that volatile power, a host is breaking the reciprocity circle, denying the alliance he or she was supposed to renew. This amounts to a serious breach in a small, insular context with a limited social pool, where alliances are vital for the community's well-being. As I have discussed elsewhere (Bacchiddu 2012, 2010, 2017a, 2017b), negotiation is the most important resource that Apiao people have to establish, and to renew, relationships with fellow islanders and powerful others, including townspeople, the dead, and miraculous saints. Negotiation is the toolbox of strategic resources; it enables the community to engage with alterity and carefully balance the difficulty of attending to their own needs while maintaining alliances and keeping their interlocutors happy.

According to Pitt-Rivers (1968), the stranger/guest (and, by extension, one's interlocutor) is by default possibly dangerous: he is "potentially anything … he is above all not to be trusted" (ibid.: 16) and always represents a threat to the established rules. Pitt-Rivers argues that the potential danger inherent in the visitors justifies the hostility felt toward them. I would like to draw attention to the powerful concept of 'potentiality', pointed out by both Pitt-Rivers and Hénaff. The danger of the guests lies precisely in their unpredictability: they could be good and hand back the power to their interlocutor after having kept it for a while, or they could betray their host, refusing to return that power.

The literature on Amerindian sociality recognizes the problematic potential of relations within the traditional social categories of consanguines, affines, and strangers. Such problematic elements include onerous obligations, feuding, aggression, retaliation, and revenge. Santos-Granero (2007) argues that establishing bonds of friendship with human and non-human entities is a way to keep close ambiguous, potentially dangerous others, while at the same time obtaining benefits such as safety, prestige, care, and a better quality of life. The thrust behind the formation of these bonds is fear. Friendship—a connection substantially different from kinship and affinity—is an antidote to potential fear, predation, and mutual destruction (ibid.; see also Descola 1996: 156–164). Danger is averted through formalized, highly ritualistic bonds that are usually voluntary, unlike the obligatory nature of kin/affinal relations, characterized by mandatory duties.

Significantly, Apiao sociality cuts across these categories: kin, affines, and strangers, all belong to the same category of undistinguished others. All individuals are at the same time equal to each other (*parejos*) and others to each other, depending on their relative location to their interlocutors, which is perspectival. If they meet in a public setting, they are *parejos*, and no obligations tie them to one another—just like co-habiting consanguines. If they meet in a domestic space, their sameness turns into otherness, calling for an unfolding of stylistic, practical, and cosmic rules, which dictate that the host offers and the guest receives. These relations are not voluntarily contracted friendships, and yet they serve the same purpose: to keep potentially dangerous others at bay. This productively transforms sameness, the default status, into otherness, thus releasing the generative capacity of relations triggered by the incorporation of constitutive otherness (see the introduction to this book).

The other is first and foremost a guest. There is no other possible way to conceive of relations in Apiao: consanguines, relatives, neighbors, and *compadres* are all treated and attended to like strangers—and dangerous strangers at that.[13] The articulation of the attention offered and received will determine the subsequent relationship, which could, accordingly, be confirmed, brought to a halt, or interrupted altogether. Each new opportunity to deal with an interlocutor—especially in ritual contexts—affects the relationship between the parties. If the law of reciprocity is not respected, the relationship will be invariably damaged. This is not a moral imperative: rather, it is the appropriate form of managing ties at the local and cosmic level.

The Least Dangerous Situation: Reciprocity in a Public Setting

The following episode illustrates an exception to the general rule of exchange being meaningful only if conducted in someone's kitchen. In this case, a continuous flow of exchange among *parejos*, or 'sames', in a public setting represents perhaps the safest instance of reciprocity, where the power is passed from host to guest in a matter of seconds and the potential for harm is greatly reduced.

The local celebration of Chilean Independence Day, on 18 September, is the most important lay social event of the year. On the occasion that I attended, the football team building became a discotheque, and some people were dancing to loud *cueca* music, while others were sitting and watching. Most of the participants—young men—were standing in circles, chatting and laughing, and everyone was carrying a bottle with either wine or *chicha*. Each man was constantly offering his bottle to his neighbor, who accepted it, drank once or twice from it, returned the bottle, and offered his own to someone else, who in turn took it, drank once or twice, and returned it. Each man did this with each person in the circle, offering his bottle to someone who accepted and returned, and vice versa.

Throughout the entire party there was a constant flow of bottles being passed from hand to hand, from person to person. This constant offering and receiving of identical items, owned at the same time by different people, is a meaningful symbol of reciprocity as a normative social rule. At the same time, by exchanging bottles in a continuous flow, Apiao men were acting out their sameness, offering what they had and accepting what they were given in return. They were synthesizing their social life in a single act, crystallizing it in an ideal form, free of potential danger. The party's location, a public space, was neutral, thereby freeing all participants from hospitality obligations and asymmetry: all were alternatively host and guest by simply passing/receiving a bottle. Goods (the drinks that were passed around) were there to be passed to someone else, rather than to be consumed by those who had bought them. The party was an uninterrupted sharing feast. This situation is in many ways similar to the one Lévi-Strauss (1969) describes in the episode about the two restaurant guests pouring wine into one another's glass. The content is exactly the same, but the gesture of reciprocity marks the willingness to entertain a relationship: "The two bottles are identical in volume, and their contents similar in quality. Each person in this revealing scene has, in the final analysis, received no more than if he had consumed his own wine. From an economic viewpoint, no one has gained and no one has lost. But the point is that there is much more in the exchange itself than in the things exchanged" (ibid.: 59).

Rivière (1984: 71) contends that "strangeness is not an absolute but a relative quality; there are degrees of otherness. Likewise, there is no fixed dichotomy between 'us' and 'them', but rather a sliding scale with the distinction being drawn according to context." Apiao people constantly stress their sameness in occupation, purpose, and lifestyle. And yet, the very foundation of their sociality is predicated upon a temporary suspension of the proclaimed sameness, which takes place each time the ritual of hospitality occurs. In hospitality, the power shifts from guest to host and back in a reciprocal game that highlights the intrinsic potential danger in social relations that depend on the management of power in ritually charged situations. The obligatory ritual displayed in hospitality both hides and reveals the latent hostility that binds and separates people in a constant and compulsory give-and-take. In this performance, repeated daily in each Apiao household, people play at temporarily imposing their point of view on the other, knowing full well that it will not last long.

Acknowledgments

Financial support from the CIIR center (CONICYT/FONDAP/15110006) is gratefully acknowledged. Parts of this chapter were written while holding a Visiting Fellowship at CALAS, Maria Sybilla Merian Center for Advanced Latin American Studies, Universidad de Guadalajara, Mexico, whose hospitality and support are also gratefully acknowledged. I thank all the participants in the workshop "What Is a Relation? Ethnographic Perspectives from Indigenous South America" for their thought-provoking comments on a previous draft of this chapter, as well as participants in a seminar held at CALAS. Peter Gow, Filippo Zerilli, two anonymous reviewers, and Martin Holbraad have provided insightful observations, allowing me to enrich my analysis considerably. My deepest gratitude goes to my Apiao friends, who have been welcoming me into their homes for nearly two decades.

Giovanna Bacchiddu is an Associate Professor of Anthropology at the Pontificia Universidad Católica de Chile. She has been researching social life in a small, insular community of Chiloé for two decades. She has written on religion, kinship, sociality, and education. She has also conducted research on international adoption.

Notes

1. Apiao (Chiloé, in southern Chile) is a small rural island of approximately 700 inhabitants of indigenous origin who live off agriculture, small animal farming, and shell/seaweed collecting.
2. The notion of hospitality is locally indicated by the expression *atender a la gente*.
3. When making this statement, Apiao people use the word *parejo* (the same, similar) rather than *igual* (equal, alike) to stress sameness and homogeneity.
4. I realized this when I witnessed a ritual gift exchange between a woman and her daughter who had moved out only a few months before. When I inquired about the reason for the strong rituality between two intimate family members, I was told: "Ella ya es familia a parte" (She now belongs to another family). I also witnessed a formal interaction in another situation when an elderly mother visited her daughter in order to borrow a kilo of sugar.
5. The avoidance discussed here is different from the prescribed name avoidance analyzed by Stasch (2011), which refers to specific taboos between categories of people—prohibitions that eventually intensify relatedness through its negation. In Apiao, the avoidance does not respond to a prohibition but rather underlines the pointlessness of relating in an unfit setting.
6. When Apiao people suffer misfortunes they generally question whether they have failed to honor a pact or repay a debt to a powerful other (see also Bacchiddu 2011, 2017b).
7. Although Herzfeld (1987) denotes the guest as a 'victim' of the hosts' requests, uttered in the context of generous hospitality, he also argues that social obligations compel each party to reciprocal generosity and sharing of something they can easily recover/replenish. He also observes that in Greek the word *yarenis* is a "reciprocal term meaning 'host/guest'" (ibid.: 78), a point made by Pitt-Rivers (1968: 21) for the French word *hôte*.
8. People often speak in terms of betrayal when referring to individuals who changed their attitude, thus betraying reciprocity (*traicionero/a*).
9. The two women were linked by *compadrazgo* (ritual co-parenthood) ties.
10. In fact, Sara had requested a huge task. It would take my landlady three days to turn 40 kilos of wheat into bread. She was going to be helped by two other women; however, she was going to be in charge of the making and baking of the bread.
11. The Spanish spoken in Apiao often requires addressing individuals in the plural form.
12. Again, the two men were linked by *compadrazgo* ties.
13. It is important to mention that in this geographical area witchcraft beliefs play a strong part in sociality and that much of the management of distrust, power control, and negotiation with alterity is due to witchcraft-related preoccupations. This phenomenon has historical roots: at the end of the nineteenth century, the state implemented a legal process against suspected witches that led to a massive, violent repression of the local indigenous population. Unfortunately, limited space prevents me from elaborating on this important subject.

Apiao people still face discrimination from other Chileans for being indigenous peasant islanders, replicating a pattern of stigmatization enhanced by geographical isolation and socio-economic marginality (Bacchiddu 2017c).

References

Bacchiddu, Giovanna. 2010. "Getting Tamed to Silent Rules: Experiencing 'The Other' in Apiao, Southern Chile." In *Mutuality and Empathy: Self and Other in the Ethnographic Encounter*, ed. Anne S. Grønseth and Dona L. Davis, 21–34. Wantage: Sean Kingston Publishing.

Bacchiddu, Giovanna. 2011. "Holding the Saint in One's Arms: Miracles and Exchange in Apiao, Southern Chile." In *Encounters of Body and Soul in Contemporary Religious Practices: Anthropological Reflections*, ed. Anna Fedele and Roy Llera Blanes, 23–42. New York: Berghahn Books.

Bacchiddu, Giovanna. 2012. "'Doing Things Properly': Religious Aspects in Everyday Sociality in Apiao, Chiloé." In *Ordinary Lives and Grand Schemes: An Anthropology of Everyday Religion*, ed. Samuli Schielke and Liza Debevec, 66–81. New York: Berghahn Books.

Bacchiddu, Giovanna. 2017a. "The Danger of Knowledge: Exercising Sameness, Bound to Differentiation." In *The Ethics of Knowledge Creation: Transactions, Relations and Persons*, ed. Lisette Josephides and Anne S. Grønseth, 49–75. New York: Berghahn Books.

Bacchiddu, Giovanna. 2017b. "Fear and Prayers: Negotiating with the Dead in Apiao, Chiloé (Chile)." In *Death in the Early Twenty-First Century: Authority, Innovation, and Mortuary Rites*, ed. Sébastien P. Boret, Susan O. Long, and Sergei Kan, 31–62. New York: Palgrave Macmillan.

Bacchiddu, Giovanna. 2017c. "Updating the Map of Desires: Mobile Phones, Satellite Dishes and Abundance as Facets of Modernity in Apiao, Chiloé, Southern Chile." *Suomen Antropologi* 42 (1): 45–66.

Candea, Matei, and Giovanni da Col. 2012. "The Return to Hospitality." *Journal of the Royal Anthropological Institute* (n.s.) 18 (S1): S1–S19. doi:10.1111/j.1467-9655.2012.01757.x.

Descola, Philippe. 1996. *The Spears of Twilight: Life and Death in the Amazon Jungle*. Trans. Janet Lloyd. New York: New Press.

Hénaff, Marcel. 2010. "I/You: Reciprocity, Gift-Giving, and the Third Party." *META: Research in Hermeneutics, Phenomenology, and Practical Philosophy* 2 (1): 57–83. http://www.metajournal.org//articles_pdf/57-83-henaff-meta3-tehno.pdf.

Herzfeld, Michael. 1987. "'As in Your Own House': Hospitality, Ethnography, and the Stereotype of Mediterranean Society." In *Honor and Shame and the Unity of the Mediterranean*, ed. David D. Gilmore, 75–89. Washington, DC: American Anthropological Association.

Kerbrat-Orecchioni, Catherine. 2004. "Que peut-on 'faire' avec du dire?" [What can we "do" with saying?]. *Cahiers de Linguistique Française* 26: 27–43. http://clf.unige.ch/files/4614/4102/7605/02-Kerbrat_nclf26.pdf.

Lévi-Strauss, Claude. 1969. *The Elementary Structures of Kinship*. Trans. James H. Bell and John R. von Strumer. London: Eyre and Spottiswoode.

Lévi-Strauss, Claude. 1995. *The Story of Lynx*. Trans. Catherine Tihanyi. Chicago: University of Chicago Press.

Lima, Tânia Stolze. 2000. "Towards an Ethnographic Theory of the Nature/Culture Distinction in Juruna Cosmology." *Revista Brasileira de Ciências Sociais*, Special Issue 1: 43–52. http://dx.doi.org/10.1590/S0102-69092000000500004.

Mauss, Marcel. (1954) 1990. *The Gift: The Form and Reason for Exchange in Archaic Societies*. Trans. W. D. Halls. London: Routledge.

Ortner, Sherry B. 1978. *Sherpas through Their Rituals*. Cambridge: Cambridge University Press.

Pitt-Rivers, Julian. 1968. "The Stranger, the Guest, and the Hostile Host: Introduction to the Study of the Laws of Hospitality." In *Contributions to Mediterranean Sociology: Mediterranean Rural Communities and Social Change*, ed. John G. Peristiany, 13–30. Paris: Mouton.

Rivière, Peter. 1984. *Individual and Society in Guiana: A Comparative Study of Amerindian Social Organisation*. Cambridge: Cambridge University Press.

Rubenstein, Steven L. 2007. "Circulation, Accumulation, and the Power of Shuar Shrunken Heads." *Cultural Anthropology* 22 (3): 357–399. doi:10.1525/can.2007.22.3.357.

Santos-Granero, Fernando. 2007. "Of Fear and Friendship: Amazonian Sociality beyond Kinship and Affinity." *Journal of the Royal Anthropological Institute* (n.s.) 13 (1): 1–18. doi:10.1111/j.1467-9655.2007.00410.x.

Santos-Granero, Fernando. 2009. "Introduction: Amerindian Constructional Views of the World." In *The Occult Life of Things: Native Amazonian Theories of Materiality and Personhood*, ed. Fernando Santos-Granero, 1–29. Tucson: University of Arizona Press.

Stasch, Rupert. 2011. "Word Avoidance as a Relation-Making Act: A Paradigm for Analysis of Name Utterance Taboos." *Anthropological Quarterly* 84 (1): 101–120. doi:10.1353/anq.2011.0005.

Viveiros de Castro, Eduardo. 2001. "GUT Feelings about Amazonia: Potential Affinity and the Construction of Sociality." In *Beyond the Visible and the Material: The Amerindianization of Society in the Work of Peter Rivière*, ed. Laura M. Rival and Neil L. Whitehead, 19–44. Oxford: Oxford University Press.

Viveiros de Castro, Eduardo. 2004. "Exchanging Perspectives: The Transformation of Objects into Subjects in Amerindian Ontologies." *Common Knowledge* 10 (3): 463–484. doi:10.1215/0961754X-10-3-463.

AFTERWORD
Relations and Relatives

Aparecida Vilaça

The aim of this book is to comprehend, via the study of specific ethnographic cases, some of the multitude of ways through which relations are conceived and lived in South American native communities, indigenous as well as peasant and pastoralist. Three of the six chapters focus on the indigenous world, located in the Chaco (Tola/Qom) and Amazonia (Vanzolini/Aweti, Lagrou/Huni Kuin), two concern Andean peasant and pastoralist communities (Pazzarelli/ Huachichocana, Bonelli/Pehuenche), and one discusses a peasant community on a small island in southern Chile (Bacchiddu/Apiao). It thus amounts to a welcome comparative exercise that, as the editors observe in their introduction, seeks to identify the continuities between Andean socio-cosmological systems and those of the South American lowlands, frequently treated in the ethnological literature as distinct universes.

Reflecting the transformation in the concept of the relation over the course of anthropology's history (Strathern 2014, 2016, 2018)—which ceased to be employed to think about the connections between pre-given entities and instead became interpreted as a constitutive part of them—the persons and objects described here are complex, interchangeable, and unstable beings, affected by relations of the most diverse kinds.

The anthropological concepts in the book that inspire reflections on relations, and inevitably on persons, derive from Melanesian ethnologies, such as fractality and dividualism (Strathern 1988; Wagner 1975), and Amazonian ethnologies, including potential affinity, perspectivism, and dualism in disequilibrium (Lévi-Strauss 1995; Lima 1999; Viveiros de Castro 1993, 1996, 1998). Given that over at least the last two decades an intense theoretical collaboration has been developing between specialists from the two regions, we could say that the regional concepts today find themselves mixed, having been deployed in the elaboration of conceptions of personhood and relationality applicable in the virtual ethnographic area baptized by Hugh-Jones (2001) as 'Melazonia'. Consequently, it may be observed that, although inter–South American comparison is one of this book's objectives, the path traced is primarily toward the Amazonian (or 'Melazonian') pole of this supposed regional continuum. The effect of this approach is that concepts central to the Andean ethnological literature, such as hierarchy, asymmetry, and domination, are approached back to front, since the emphasis is given to the egalitarian effect that the instability and alternation of relational positions produce in apparently asymmetric configurations.

Having thus determined the conceptual spectrum that informs the universe of the inhabitants of the different ethnographic areas analyzed, the introduction's authors go further in attempting to synthesize the relational dynamics described in this book. Clearly inspired by the works of Joanna Overing (1985, 1986), they conclude that the regional specificity could be described in terms of a dynamic between autonomy and dependency. As the authors put it, while the 'other' is necessary to the constitution of the person (a dependency on the outside), autonomy also constitutes a central value, such that this 'other' must be either incorporated and controlled ("the taming of relations") or avoided and excluded. In sum, as the authors see it, this volume illustrates ethnographically different modes of an always unstable equilibrium between the need for the other and the differentiation of the other.

Although the body is cited as a privileged space for these operations in most of the chapters, it is only in Bonelli's text on the Pehuenche that we find a detailed ethnographic presentation of the native conception of the body. In highlighting the importance of the visible aspect of the person for the production of relations, mediated by the gaze and by physical contact, the author sets the Pehuenche ethnography in dialogue with the Amazonian discussions of the body, and in particular with the central place that vision occupies in perspectivist ontologies.

Inspired by Strathern, Vanzolini shows how the onomastic system of the Aweti, a Tupi group of the Upper Xingu, produces similar persons (to the name-giving ascendants) and distinct persons simultaneously, given that the same person receives the names of different ascendants. The central argument, however, does not refer to this play between difference and similarity in relation to others, but to a continuous self-differentiation through each new name the person receives over a lifetime. Names, Vanzolini asserts, produce effects not only on the relational context in which the named person is inserted, that is, on his or her situation within the group, but on the person him- or herself, who becomes transformed by the effect of the name.

Lagrou explores the arts of the Huni Kuin, a Pano-speaking group of Western Amazonia, especially their designs and the songs related to them. I note that the question of asymmetries, so central to Andean discussions, is directly explored only in Lagrou's and Bacchiddu's chapters. Among the Amazonian Huni Kuin, asymmetries emerge in complex painting designs that recall the shape of a Klein bottle in which outside and inside become confused. This graphically depicted oscillation is associated by Lagrou with a central relational aspect of the Amazonian universe: the alternation of the supposedly asymmetric positions bring symmetry to the foreground once again, as occurs with the positions of predator and prey in the context of hunting activities. The result is a constant shifting between symmetric and asymmetric forms, producing a zone of ambiguity, an in-between, that indigenous peoples choose to inhabit.

In the case of the peasants of indigenous origin inhabiting the Chilean island of Apiao, studied by Bacchiddu, the symmetric character of differences is objectified in the alternation of the host and guest positions in the everyday rituals of formal visits and hospitality. In a community that perceives itself as homogeneous, a ritually constructed momentary asymmetry functions to establish new relations through the circulation of goods. The parasitic status assumed by the guests in these complex verbal, alimentary, and corporal interactions is reminiscent of the relations of an Amazonian indigenous group, the Paumari (Arawa), with white people, as described by Bonilla (2009). Making themselves needy, the Paumari force the whites to respond by giving, just like house visitors among the Apiao, inverting the relation of domination by turning their predators into their prey—the same kind of inversion elicited by the complex mazes of the Huni Kuin designs.

This idea of complex and sinuous forms brings us to Pazzarelli's chapter on the pastoralists of Huachichocana in the Argentinean Andes. Through his observation of the ritual slaughter of sheep and goats and the construction of pens, the author identifies the emphasis given to topological shapes to the detriment of flat and angular geometric forms. Sheep intestines are associated with the curves of the pens, whose sinuosity allows a complex interplay of perspectives between people, predatory animals, and spirits. By inverting the aspect of the dead animals through specific folds and displays, the local inhabitants are able to trick other beings, potential predators, transforming the dead body into a living entity and vice versa. The forms here, like the Huni Kuin designs and, to some extent, the Aweti names, produce specific effects by eliciting the desired perspectives—in other words, they function as manipulators of the 'other's' gaze.

In her analysis of the Qom (Guaycurú/Argentinean Gran Chaco), Tola examines the question of the relation through the idea of a "relational excess" deemed harmful, a cause of sickness and death via sorcery, which needs to be ruptured by refusing to continue the revenge cycle set off by a particular death. The author calls this interruption "anti-revenge," at the same time that she associates sorcery with incest since it is more common between genealogically proximate couples after they separate. In sum, it amounts to an exercise in achieving the right amount of distance, a widespread theme in South American mythology (Lévi-Strauss 1964, 1968). Revenge—or more precisely, its possibility—also makes evident the internally multiple aspect of the Qom person in line with the other models described here. In an inversion of the Amazonian model of warfare where the dead enemy becomes part of the killer's person, among the Qom it is the sorcerer who becomes part of the body of his victim soon after death, which enables him to be found and killed by the latter's kin.

While the complex inter- and intra-societal and inter- and intra-personal relational fabrics are finely delineated by the contributors through rich ethnographic illustrations, they say little about the relations between indigenous peoples and colonizers, even though in the introduction the editors state their concern to address this topic and discuss it at length. Thus, for example, although Tola mentions in passing the remark of a Qom friend about the difficulty he felt, as an evangelical, in taking revenge, no further comment is made about this subject. What effect does Christianization have on 'anti-revenge'? Vanzolini mentions "white people's names" used by the Aweti, situating them as another kind of nickname and in contraposition to the "'real' names" transmitted by the ascendants. But she does not explore the proliferation of these names due to the government bureaucracy in which Brazilian indigenous peoples are today immersed, requiring them to possess documents in order to access social benefits. Do indigenous names or white people's names appear on Aweti identity cards? And how does the fixing of names in perennial and immutable documents affect the relational dynamic traditionally produced by the constant exchanges of names over the course of a life? Does the Christianization of the Huni Kuin (or at least a portion of the population, as we know) have an impact on their ayahuasca-based visionary practices? Although these questions are not central to the book's overall line of argument, they comprise, I believe, important paths to be mapped out to provide readers with a more nuanced panorama of the problems explored within its pages.

To conclude, I wish to contribute a brief example of this perspective. In her chapter, Vanzolini calls attention to an important characteristic of the Aweti and certainly of many Amazonian peoples: unlike most Euro-American peoples, they have no word for 'relation'. What are usually named are specific relations or the terms of these relations—brother-in-law, father-in-law, brother, father, enemy—although generic terms for kin/relatives are commonplace, designating persons with whom one has close relations, especially co-residents.

Vanzolini, in her chapter, reminds us that Viveiros de Castro (2004), theorizing about the founding place of affinity in the Amerindian world, claims that if a generic term for 'relation' exists there, it would be 'brother-in-law' (or 'father-in-law', 'son-in-law', 'mother-in-law'), which contains within itself the principle of difference between the related terms. As Lévi-Strauss (1995) taught us, brothers-in-law are two men with distinct perspectives of the same woman: sister to one of them, wife to the other. Brothers-in-law and affines in general (at least those not consanguinized by proximity and living together) are mediators between generalized enmity and the consanguinity of kinship, not in the sense of a bridge connecting two terms, but as themselves containers of the potential complexity of the two opposite positions.

Viveiros de Castro (2004) contrasts this principle of generic difference embodied in the term 'brother-in-law' to the Euro-American/Christian emphasis on identity and similarity, which entails that for Euro-Americans the given and founding relation is that of siblingship. Among them, the generic term for 'relation' would be 'brother/sister', someone equal to myself, someone who sees my sister as a sister too. Recounting an anecdotal event that took place in Acre, when a well-known musician wanted to use the indigenous term *txai* (brother-in-law) for the cover of his new album, believing that it was the term for 'brother' (since this was the term the indigenous people he was visiting used to address him), Viveiros de Castro coined the notion of an 'equivocal translation'. In other words, 'brother' was not a mistaken translation for the indigenous term *txai*, since it too designated a generic relationship. Only for the indigenous people, the place of the brother-in-law was occupied by the Euro-American 'brother', causing the musician's confusion.

For around two decades now, a specific relational term in Portuguese has become part of the indigenous universe as a whole: *parente* (kin/relative). This term is used exclusively in the inter-ethnic context, serving as a vocative and a term of reference for any other indigenous person, defined in opposition to non-indigenous. This is how previously mutually unacquainted indigenous people refer to each other in assemblies and other meetings mediated (or not) by whites: "As my *parente* just said ..." or "How are you, *parente*?" White people present in the same contexts are called either by their own names, or the name of the institution they represent, or simply "non-indigenous people" or "whites." As far as I know, the term *parente* is never used with the connotation it possesses for Euro-Americans—that is, a genealogically related person or kin, properly speaking. For the latter, consanguine kin terms in the native language or in Portuguese are used, even in the context of assemblies—parents, siblings, grandparents, but never *parente* (relative). So what does this apparent equivocation imply?

Clearly, the use of the term *parente* in inter-ethnic contexts, especially in those mediated by white people, produces a positive political effect on the composition, for the outside, of an indigenous collectivity, which acquires cohesion and legitimacy by being constituted in opposition to the non-indigenous population. *Parente* transfers to the indigenous world the relation that Euro-Americans make between blood and kinship through the scientificist view that all indigenous peoples have the same biological origin and thus share a generalized kinship.

It is as though the term *parente* had been adopted as an equivalent to 'brother' and therefore was seen as the ideal generic relationship based on similarity. However, the fact that it is used exclusively in inter-ethnic contexts, necessarily excluding real kin from its scope, suggests the possibility of another translation, precisely the one proposed by Viveiros de Castro (2004) as a generic term for the relation in Amazonia, that is, 'brother-in-law'.

I think the term *parente* is so successful because it manages to encompass the terms 'brother-in-law' and 'brother' in a single word—not a halfway term but a term with a double meaning, oscillating and dependent on perspective. From the indigenous viewpoint, *parente* has the connotation of 'brother-in-law', with all its charge of alterity and rivalry, since it names only those who are different. From the non-indigenous perspective, therefore, *parente*, as used by indigenous people during speeches in the assemblies, means 'brother'. *Parente* is one of those "twisted words" that Townsley (1993: 460; see also Carneiro da Cunha 1998: 12–13) identifies in the shamanism of the Yaminawa (Pano, Acre). These are words from normal language applied to quite distinct objects: a fish may be called collared peccary, for example. It is the manner shamans have found of resolving the dilemma of enunciating distinct perspectives in the same narrative. Like the Huni Kuin designs, the Aweti names, and the folds made in the dead bodies of the Huachichocana animals, the term *parente* thus induces a play of perspectives, leading white people to see indigenous cohesion while simultaneously emphasizing internal differences.

Aparecida Vilaça is a Professor of Social Anthropology at the Museu Nacional, Universidade Federal do Rio de Janeiro. She is the author of *Praying and Preying: Christianity in Indegenous Amazonia* (2016), *Strange Enemies: Indigenous Agency and Scenes of Encounters in Amazonia* (2010), and *Quem somos nós. Os Wari' encontram os brancos* (2006), among other influential books and journal articles.

References

Bonilla, Oiara. 2009. "The Skin of History: Paumari Perspectives on Conversion and Transformation." In *Native Christians: Modes and Effects of Christianity among Indigenous Peoples of the Americas*, ed. Aparecida Vilaça and Robin M. Wright, 127–145. Aldershot: Ashgate.

Carneiro da Cunha, Manuela. 1998. "Pontos de vista sobre a floresta amazônica: Xamanismo e tradução" [Views on the Amazon forest: Shamanism and translation]. *Mana* 4 (1): 7–22.

Hugh-Jones, Stephen. 2001. "The Gender of Some Amazonian Gifts: An Experiment with an Experiment." In *Gender in Amazonia and Melanesia: An Exploration of the Comparative Method*, ed. Thomas Gregor and Donald Tuzin, 245–278. Berkeley: University of California Press.

Lévi-Strauss, Claude. 1964. *Mythologiques: Le cru et le cuit* [*Mythologiques*: The raw and the cooked]. Paris: Plon.

Lévi-Strauss, Claude. 1968. *Mythologiques: L'origine des manières de table* [*Mythologiques*: The origin of table manners]. Paris: Plon.

Lévi-Strauss, Claude. 1995. *The Story of Lynx*. Trans. by Catherine Tihanyi. Chicago: University of Chicago Press.

Lima, Tânia Stolze. 1999. "The Two and Its Many: Reflections on Perspectivism in a Tupi Cosmology." *Ethnos* 64 (1): 107–131. Originally published in Spanish in 1996.

Overing, Joanna. 1985. "There Is No End of Evil: The Guilty Innocents and Their Fallible God." In *The Anthropology of Evil*, ed. David Parkin, 244–278. Oxford: Basil Blackwell.

Overing, Joanna. 1986. "Images of Cannibalism, Death and Domination in a 'Non Violent' Society." *Journal de la Société des Américanistes* 72: 133–156.

Strathern, Marilyn. 1988. *The Gender of the Gift: Problems with Women and Problems with Society in Melanesia*. Berkeley: University of California Press.

Strathern, Marilyn. 2014. "Reading Relations Backwards." *Journal of the Royal Anthropological Institute* (n.s.) 20 (1): 3–19.

Strathern, Marilyn. 2016. "Revolvendo as raízes da antropologia: Algumas reflexões sobre 'relações'" [Revolving the roots of anthropology: Some reflections on 'relations']. *Revista de Antropolologia* 59 (1): 224–257

Strathern, Marilyn. 2018. "Relations." In *Cambridge Encyclopedia of Anthropology*. https://www.anthroencyclopedia.com/entry/relations.

Townsley, Graham. 1993. "Song Paths: The Ways and Means of Yaminahua Shamanic Knowledge." *L'Homme* 33 (126–128): 449–468.

Viveiros de Castro, Eduardo. 1993. "Alguns aspectos da afinidade no dravidianato amazônico" [Some aspects of affinity in Amazonian Dravidianism] In *Amazônia: Etnologia e história indígena* [Amazon: Ethnology and indigenous history], ed. Manuela Carneiro da Cunha and Eduardo Viveiros de Castro, 149–210. São Paulo: Núcleo de História Indígena e do Indigenismo da USP/FAPESP.

Viveiros de Castro, Eduardo. 1996. "Os pronomes cosmológicos e o perspectivismo ameríndio" [The cosmological pronouns and Amerindian perspectivism]. *Mana* 2 (2): 115–143.

Viveiros de Castro, Eduardo. 1998. "Cosmological Deixis and Amerindian Perspectivism." *Journal of the Royal Anthropological Institute* 4 (3): 469–488.

Viveiros de Castro, Eduardo. 2004. "Perspectival Anthropology and the Method of Controlled Equivocation." *Tipití* 2 (1): 3–22.

Wagner, Roy. 1975. *The Invention of Culture*. Englewood Cliffs, NJ: Prentice-Hall.

CODA
Reflecting Back

Marilyn Strathern

This volume presents an opportunity to bring together older and newer strands of work on relations.[1] The first fell back on an analytical notion of aesthetics to convey certain kinds of persuasive appearances: Melanesian ethnography emphasized how much it mattered that relations took an appropriate form (recognizing the support of ancestors, for example). The second is a recent critique of relations as an explicit Euro-American concept in one of its vernacular contexts, namely, English usage. Here, the kinds of Amerindianist interests engaged by the special issue of this journal[2]—and as gleaned from certain translations into English—lead me to locate an aesthetic effect in the penumbra of connotations and associations that endow relations (English-speaking) with an aura or mood. What anthropologists ordinarily dismiss when they construct their analytical vocabularies becomes interesting.

In placing relations at the heart of a Melanesian synthesis (Strathern 1988), I was of course criticizing a pair of Euro-American concepts (individual, society) with another concept (relations) equally abstract. Looking back on the argument I am struck now by the methodological, or more appositely exposi-tional, role that aesthetics played in it. Aesthetic effects emerged simultaneously as a register of certain local forms (of being, acting) and as a register of the expositional intentions of the anthropological writer. Perhaps this is a peculiarity of the concept: no 'effect' has been described if the writer fails to convey it, at least in part. From this vantage point I offer a few comments on the aesthetics of relations.

Amerindian and Melanesian Reflections ...

Melanesians do not name—have no term for—relations (Crook 1997: 28), and the same has been remarked in an Amazonian context (Vanzolini, this volume); the anthropologist infers them. Nonetheless, Melanesian sensibilities over appearances, events, and happenings that take conventional and thus recognizable shape can become an analytical resource for demonstrating various ways in which people seemingly make relations known to one another. In my case (Strathern 1988: 187), a plethora of further abstractions betrayed the technical clumsiness of describing what the anthropologist had to make apparent. Perhaps my appealing to an aesthetic register, drawing attention to the appropriateness of specific forms, was something like an attempt to open up to controlled equivocation (for which I then had no name!) the otherwise unremarked analytical terms that followed, such as exchange, gardening, creation, clan, and so forth, all with relations implied.

More generally, thinking about the forms that relations take offers a kind of internal translation for the anthropologist of what is already partially apprehended by other means, and will apply in myriad ways across shifting configurations (Di Giminiani and González Gálvez 2018: 200–201; Lagrou, this volume). Apropos the Peruvian Urarina, Walker lists several relations (my term) by which he recognizes a general refusal of equivalence in people's dealings with one another, such as the convention of assuming the illegibility of others' intentions or volatility in disputation: "My friend one day is my enemy the next" (2020: 154). He suggests that such 'refusal' is grounded in an expanded notion of the common, what people feel grounds them, which embraces all manner of difference.[3] Consonantly, Costa and Fausto (2019) argue that anthropologists should be wary of those relations they might recognize too easily. It matters, for instance, to which relational field one assimilates the interspecific relations of Amazonian pet-keeping, since this becomes a question of which conceptual company they (the relations) find themselves in. For Costa and Fausto, pet-keeping is no more a variety of domestication than pet-masters are proprietorial sovereigns. The forms introduced through such reworkings turn on judgments of conceptual appropriateness. How appropriateness is registered, whether in people's sense of well-being, or in the persuasiveness of an analytical configuration, could be reckoned a response of an aesthetic kind.

That said, relations already particularized by their context or usage are one thing; is there a place for an aesthetic response to relation(s)[4] as an abstraction or generic, as the term is also deployed in English? I had not thought of the question earlier, but conceivably the Melanesian pairing of interrelated entities (symmetrically or otherwise) that figures the necessity of relating (Moutu 2013: 202; Strathern 1988: 188) could be imagined this way. More to the point, consider Lagrou's recent rendering of Amerindian relational aesthetics as it is woven, by the Huni Kuin, into design and song (this volume). From this Lagrou abstracts a more general condition of relating, the "in betweenness" of all beings, which activates the ever-multiplying potential for a being to embody an other (being) that would otherwise embody it.[5] For the Mapuche, Di Giminiani and González Gálvez (2018: 200) delineate "an ideal type of relation" that they understand as "incomplete or unfinished objectivation," while for living beings "to be in a relation" is in Paumari terms "to be captured" (Bonilla 2016: 126). Then, of course, Vanzolini (this volume) reminds us of Viveiros de Castro's (2004) perception that in Amazonian worlds a common form of relation is the figure translated as 'brother-in-law' or 'cross-cousin', which, in Vilaça's words (this volume), contains within itself "the principle of difference between the related terms." While embodiment of difference may be true of affinity in general, the specificity of the brother-in-law seems of particular aesthetic moment in the original (anthropological) account. It brings everything together in a single image—and generates an ethnographic/analytical counterpart.

What springs out as a counterpart to brother-in-law is brother, for "brotherhood is ... the general [Western] form of the relation" (Viveiros de Castro 2004: 18).[6] And then the world turns on its axis, since the latter kinds of brothers are presumed to be similar, minimally insofar as their commonality is bound by their same relation to a third party. Embedded in the Euro-Christian vernacular as it is, does drawing on such a term (brother) for an anthropological concept (relation) also create an aesthetic effect?

... and ...

Comparisons with Euro-American usage run through this handful of Amerindianist accounts. Needless to say, the issue is the language of description. But what do we do with the fact that Euro-Americans do indeed have a name or term for relation(s)[7] and, more generally, with the fact that analytical usage is characterized by abstraction? What conceptual call is there, in the course of writing or comprehension, for aesthetic effects then?

In the absence of specific local terms, describing one's interlocutors' sense of the appropriateness of certain forms of existence can give a shape to, or bring to a point, anthropological formulations otherwise diffused through the familiarity of theoretical consensus or everyday language. Relation as brother-in-law: one has to stop and think. Conversely, in the presence of a concept whose terms are already shaped and pointed by being named (say), the anthropologist might be surprised by aesthetic effects elsewhere. This is not to say that an abstract concept cannot have form (and I give an instance below), but rather to suggest that there might be some mileage in considering much that scholars ordinarily regard as a detraction from the denotative force of agreed-upon terms. I refer to the vernacular penumbra of connotation, to values, colorings, and such like, whether they cling to certain expressions or shift and change with this or that situation. So in the case of the Euro-American 'brother' for 'relation', we might say that the brotherly figure belongs to a whole company of images, not only figuring a common basis to relations but also, for example, giving an aura of positive affect to the notion of similarity. Connotations are always arguable away and easily dismissed from formal discourse. Given that, it may take something like the demonstration of an aesthetic effect—rendering a vernacular aesthetic of analytical interest—to bring them (the connotations) to the fore in the shaping work that they do.

With vernacular English usage of relations as my Euro-American example, I turn to some of the connotations of similarity. First, though, a shape for abstraction.

... Euro-American Ones

An imaginative endeavor to give visual shape to conceptual relations is presented by Holbraad (2020) through the diagram. While Holbraad draws attention to numerous modulations of relations, visualization is exemplary of an aesthetic response, in this case to concepts that manifest as abstractions. The concept is worked through another abstract configuration, or rather the configuration of an abstract form. Diagram gives abstraction a shape.[8]

Holbraad (2020: 4) explicitly addresses anthropology's ongoing need for conceptual invention: anthropological sensibility is above all "a kind of intellectual aesthetic" that gives ethnographic phenomena particular conceptual shapes, with transfiguring consequences. I would comment on how diagrams achieve this effect through singling out different elements, such as those that compose a relation, which can then be depicted as moving with respect to one another. Thus, Holbraad shows how anthropological understandings of Mauss's gift (specifically of the relationships entailed in reciprocity) metamorphose away from a concept of things passing between persons to one of persons magnifying themselves with respect to one another. In effect, persons and things change their ideational positions, demonstrated through diagrams imagined as a series that sequentially rearranges the 'betweenness' of these elements. This rearrangement of elements suggests that relation can be aestheticized, in the abstract, as a working model with parts.

I leave this imaginative space in order to turn to non-visual modes of apprehension as they work in the English vernacular, and to sensibilities that are rather a matter of mood or affect. It is obvious that relations will pick up numerous ever-changing connotations from the particular circumstances of usage. At the same time, values or attributes may attach to the very concept itself, creating a default mood, so to speak, which can compromise more neutral usage.[9] Thus, relations are commonly taken as benign or interesting before being seen as malign or of no interest.

A cluster of such attributes helps shape a positive aura surrounding relations themselves, English-speaking. In serving to bring entities together,[10] they offer a sense of closeness, of sameness or similarity, of commonality or comparability. These attributes may be further personified with respect to interpersonal relations,[11] evoking expectations of amiability, sociability, fellowship, or companionship. If this is beginning to sound altogether too friendly, recall Viveiros de Castro's (2015: 110) observation that seeing the world radiate out "from a socially positive intimacy to a socially negative distance" corresponds to a Western egocentric model of social life "where the prototype of the relation is self-identity," the inmost point. Relation with oneself founds every relation with another, notably in the case of the friend (after Aristotle) as an 'other self': "an other but an other as a 'moment' of the self" (ibid.: 185). In Western philosophy, this figure of the friend has been elucidated as a foundational otherness intrinsic to conceptualization and thought as such. In common English parlance, friendship carries a certain tenor of sociability, especially that promoted by a "society of similars" or the "equivalence of individuals" (Walker 2020: 149). Friendship is of interest in this context insofar as just such a tenor often seems to jump onto the back of relations.

"Friendship is the chief joy of human life," and the esteem and affection of one's friends constitutes the "chief part of human happiness," chimed David Hume and Adam Smith in the mid-eighteenth century (Rasmussen 2017: 5). This pair of Enlightenment philosophers each considered the other his best friend.[12] I have written elsewhere on the conviviality and agreeableness that Hume in particular breathed into his theorization of relations, which turned on how ideas come together through association. This was at a time when men congregated in associations of all kinds on the self-acknowledged basis of common interest and like-mindedness, not least as a ground for engaging in disputation. One notorious moment of divergence between Hume and Smith turns out to be as apposite and informative today as then (see Weston 2018).

What was at issue, and I follow Rasmussen's (2017: 90–91) account, was the concept of "sympathy" in the then expansive sense of "fellow feeling" as a fundamental human capacity. Both Hume and Smith agreed on its importance.

In being affected by the manner in which another appears cheerful or down-cast, Hume compared sympathy conveying feelings between people to "vibrating strings" conveying motion from one to another, an emotional contagion. By contrast, Smith argued that one cannot enter into other people's feelings without imaginatively placing oneself in their shoes, thereby being projected into an appreciation of their circumstances and perceiving what oneself would feel.[13] Hume's insistence[14] that whether sympathy is agreeable or disagreeable must depend on the kind of sentiment in question elicited a clarification from Smith. Irrespective of the nature of what is conveyed, Smith avowed, "we can take pleasure in the *harmony* of sentiments" (Rasmussen's gloss of Smith 2017: 111; my emphasis). Mutual sympathy is intrinsically pleasing in that "we naturally enjoy the feeling of sentimental concord" (ibid.: 110). In other words, it was the way feelings chime with one another, the relation itself, that was agreeable. 'Relation' is my interpolation here. Nonetheless, when his thoughts were elsewhere, Hume ([1739–1740] 2000) could also have talked of "the love of relations" (his phrase) as a matter of harmony. Insofar as people "associate together," evincing the sympathy "which always arises betwixt similar characters," and remark on the "resemblance betwixt themselves and others," the resemblance "operates after the manner of a relation, by producing a connexion of ideas" (ibid.: 229).[15]

In the pursuit of their argument, and in the way they draw on the English vernacular, the philosophers are creating an appreciation of relations through what I would call an aesthetic mood. The reiteration of what is similar and in concordance in terms of how pleasant company is and of the friendliness of close association between coevals produces a scatter of effects. Relations of affect and the affect of relations ricochet off each other. Present-day English-speakers may not go so far as to say, in Smith's language, that it is delightful and agreeable, but they would find most appropriate the concord implied in referring to entities being brought together, whether similar at the outset or rendered similar—comparable—in conjunction. Concord involves a premise of similarity, a vernacular description of relations, no less. Any tension between abstract formulation and specific usage falls away, if only momentarily. In its place is the conviction of (a persuasive) form.

Back

Turning to these historical formulations, just as an ethnographer might be informed by past events (e.g., Fausto and Heckenberger 2007), is of course offered today with intervening conceptual inventions in mind. I remark the obvious. Both Amerindian and Melanesian anthropology have benefited from alternative currents in Euro-American thinking that have refused the premise of similarity. Yet, with respect to anthropology's analytical languages, there still remains a significant dimension to the business of criticism. Those who speak and write in English do not altogether easily escape the tenacious connotations that the notion of relation, scurrying here and there in the interweaving of diverse arguments and theories, carries on its back.

Marilyn Strathern is Emeritus Professor of Social Anthropology at the University of Cambridge. She is the author of *Relations: An Anthropological Exposition* (2020), *Partial Connections* ([1991] 2004), and *The Gender of the Gift* (1988), among many other notable books and articles.

Editors' note: This piece was originally published in *Maloca: Revista de Estudos Indígenas*, volume 3 (2020) as part of a dossier entitled "A Estética e os Ameríndios," under a CC BY-NC-SA 4-0 license. We would like to thank Lucas da Costa Maciel, *Maloca*'s editorial team, and Prof. Marilyn Strathern for giving us the opportunity to include it in the present volume.

Notes

1. I am most grateful to *Maloca*'s Editorial Committee for suggesting I write a short piece for their special issue, and to the editor Lucas da Costa Maciel for giving me some sense of its ambition and scope. That journal's two readers must be thanked for their very stimulating comments. My further acknowledgment is to the International Balzan Foundation for funding a research venture at the Centre for Pacific Studies, University of St Andrews, engaging with both Melanesian and Amazonian materials, and under its auspice to Virginia Amaral, Simon Kenema, and Priscila Santos da Costa for their comments.
2. Editors' note: The journal that is referenced here is *Maloca: Revista de Estudos Indígenas*, volume 3 (2020).
3. Conversely put, relating through difference does not have to employ measurements of similarity and dissimilarity.
4. It is an expositional awkwardness in English that the plural form of relation also refers to relations in general and thus to a singular concept.
5. As in, see by being seen, ingest by being ingested. Given Lagrou's reference to "self-becoming by means of other-becoming" (this volume)—when compared with the elder-younger brother pair reported by Moutu (2013)—what she calls 'in betweenness' seems to refer to an ever-becoming state of being. This is to be distinguished from the "betweenness" that renders "the relation as a link between two self-contained units" (Di Giminiani and González Gálvez 2018: 202), which is its dominant usage in English (see Strathern 2020).

6. The real-time sequence by which Viveiros de Castro (2004: 16–17) arrived at the 'appropriateness' of an equivocal translation of brother-in-law as brothers is rehearsed in Vilaça's afterword to this volume. The comments of one reader on this piece make me realize the extent to which these formulations about 'brothers(-in-law)' depend terminologically, if not conceptually, on possibilities in English as opposed to Portuguese.

7. And the name is meant to be identifying. See Vanzolini's critical discussion apropos personal names in this volume.

8. Importantly in Holbraad's (2020: 21; emphasis omitted) account, insofar as the search is for conceptual relations "that the analyst has to imagine in order to describe … phenomena," abstraction does not—as he puts it—move away from life but toward it.

9. This is particularly so in interpersonal relations. In ordinary English, antagonistic relations between people may be imagined as an absence of relation, while attending to relations may be considered 'sentimental' or 'soft'. What follows comes from a longer work (Strathern 2020), where the here unexplored interdigitation of interpersonal and epistemic relations is discussed more fully.

10. I follow the vernacular emphasis on relations as first and foremost between discrete entities, criticized and bypassed in scholarly usage as Di Giminiani and González Gálvez (2018: 202) point out (see note 5). The amiable tenor of 'sociability' (see below) is among the reasons anthropologists have sought out the less laden term 'sociality' for more general purposes.

11. Leaving aside English idiosyncrasies with respect to kin relations. I hardly need add that this kind of sentimentalization of relations can generate highly exclusionary senses of belonging.

12. In correspondence they singularly addressed each other "My dearest friend," an epithet neither of them used with other correspondents (Rasmussen 2017: 4). I am grateful to Kath Weston for mentioning this book.

13. Walker (2020: 149) notes that a specific feature of the society of similars lies in the way "each individual … can imagine him- or herself in the condition of every other individual." We may take this as an aspect of the more general condition of Euro-Christian brotherhood, whereby brothers occupy the same point of view on an exterior world (Viveiros de Castro 2004: 18) or, as Vilaça (this volume) puts it, each sees the other's sister as a sister.

14. Smith regarded himself as having improved on Hume's account of sympathy. Hume subsequently entered into correspondence with Smith on the topic.

15. And the connection may be further invested with feeling. Thus Hume continues: "And as … a love or affection arises from the resemblance, we may learn that a sympathy with others is agreeable only by giving emotion to the spirits, since and easy sympathy and correspondent emotions are alone common to [the terms for/sense of] *relation, acquaintance, and resemblance*" ([1739–1740] 2000: 229; original italics).

References

Bonilla, Oiara. 2016. "Parasitism and Subjection: Modes of Paumari Predation." In *Ownership and Nurture: Studies in Native Amazonian Property Relations*, ed. Marc Brightman, Carlos Fausto, and Vanesa Grotti, 110–132. New York: Berghahn Books.

Costa, Luiz, and Carlos Fausto. 2019. "The Enemy, the Unwilling Guest and the Jaguar Host: An Amazonian Story." *L'Homme* 231–232: 195–226. https://doi.org/10.4000/lhomme.35579.

Crook, Tony. 2007. *Exchanging Skin: Anthropological Knowledge, Secrecy and Bolivip, Papua New Guinea*. Oxford: Oxford University Press for The British Academy.

Di Giminiani, Piergiorgio, and Marcelo González Gálvez. 2018. "Who Owns the Water? The Relation as Unfinished Objectification in the Mapuche Lived World." *Anthropological Forum* 28 (3): 199–216.

Fausto, Carlos, and Michael Heckenberger, eds. 2007. *Time and Memory in Indigenous Amazonia: Anthropological Perspectives*. Gainesville: University Press of Florida.

Holbraad, Martin. 2020. "The Shapes of Relations: Anthropology as Conceptual Morphology." *Philosophy of the Social Sciences* 50 (6): 495–522. https://doi.org/10.1177/0048393120917917.

Hume, David. [1739–1740] 2000. *A Treatise of Human Nature*. Ed. David Fate Norton and Mary J. Norton. Oxford: Oxford University Press.

Moutu, Andrew. 2013. *Names Are Thicker Than Blood: Kinship and Ownership amongst the Iatmul*. Oxford: Oxford University Press for The British Academy.

Rasmussen, Dennis C. 2017. *The Infidel and the Professor: David Hume, Adam Smith, and the Friendship That Shaped Modern Thought*. Princeton, NJ: Princeton University Press.

Strathern, Marilyn. 1988. *The Gender of the Gift: Problems with Women and Problems with Society in Melanesia*. Berkeley: California University Press.

Strathern, Marilyn. 2020. *Relations: An Anthropological Account*. Durham, NC: Duke University Press.

Viveiros de Castro, Eduardo. 2004. "Perspectival anthropology and the method of controlled equivocation." *Tipití: Journal of the Society for the Anthropology of Lowland South America* 2 (1): 3–22.

Viveiros de Castro, Eduardo. 2015. *The Relative Native: Essays on Indigenous Conceptual Worlds*. Trans. Martin Holbraad, David Rodgers, and Julia Sauma. Chicago: HAU Books.

Walker, Harry. 2020. "Equality without Equivalence: An Anthropology of the Common." *Journal of the Royal Anthropological Institute* 26 (1): 146–166.

Weston, Kath. 2018. "The Ethnographer's Magic as Sympathetic Magic." *Social Anthropology/Anthropologie Sociale* 26 (1): 15–29.

EPILOGUE
Cemeteries as Metaphors of Who We Are

Claudio Millacura Salas
Translated by Tyanna Slobe

> Temuco ciudad
> debajo de ti
> están durmiendo
> mis antepasados
> —Leonel Lienlaf, *La Luz Cae Vertical*[1]

Indigenous peoples understand temporality differently from the Western world.[2] The most common tense in Amerindian languages is the past. Due to this linguistic fact, we could say that the only thing that indigenous people (myself included) know is the past. And since it is the only thing we know, every time the past is endangered, questioned, pressured, destroyed, it is us who are being questioned, pressured, destroyed. There are no differences. By making this claim, I want to take advantage of the historical moment we are in, and not just to push the limits of the country "as far as possible."[3] And that country, Chile, is ending. I am talking about the historical moment that began with the uprisings of 18 October 2019. Today, this country finds itself deliberating for the first time in its history as a republic a constitution that represents everyone, with the diversity of perspectives that this territory called Chile contains, and not only those who have exercised power for over 200 years.[4]

With the social upheaval and the constitutional process, we are witnessing the inauguration of a country in an unprecedented fashion. A country that thinks in a different way. And this different way, then, introduces the possibility of conceptualizing ourselves in a different way, leaving behind certain conditions that did not allow us better comprehension, not only of where we live—where we come from—but fundamentally of who we are. So we are in an inaugural moment. And in this moment, I would like to move beyond some classifications, some divisions that also have the function of classifying nature, that which surrounds us. Here I am reclaiming my indigenous condition and note the particularities of every indigenous community: we do not make distinctions between nature and ourselves. Once again, we are the same. And if nature is questioned, pressured, damaged, what is questioned, pressured, damaged is us. Therefore, if we take a perspective that treats nature only as cultural heritage (*patrimonializadora de la naturaleza*),[5] we fall into this pattern of separating nature from people, and we ultimately make the mistake of believing that people are above nature. Any patrimonialization of nature needs to be conceptualized by the people who inhabit that nature. Because they are one and the same. And this ultimately means that we must not only safeguard nature, but also seek to safeguard the people who inhabit that nature.

If from an urban perspective, we once again commit the error of believing that the city thinks differently from those who inhabit it, then we are led to believe that buildings, streets, and plazas are what need to be protected. And the error is that what needs to be protected are the people who inhabit that city. Having said that, what I want to propose here is that we begin to understand that we are the heritage. Not only those of us who are here, but also those who are absent. Our dead, who are there, who accompany us, who despite having left remain, because they and we are the same. We are their result. Without them we are not here. Beyond the commemorative plaques, the architectural landmarks, the monuments, what the cemeteries contain is us. And why do I say 'us'? Because we indigenous people know that the difference between the living and the dead does not exist.[6]

The invitation now is to review how some of the indigenous peoples who inhabit this territory called Chile understand the relationship between nature, life, and its continuity—death.

• • •

On Tuesday, 24 December 2013, the body was found, floating in the waters of Ralco Dam. She who had been its strongest opponent due to the grave damage that it would cause to her native territory apparently stops fighting and surrenders to her ancestors to begin the journey to other lands, other dimensions:[7]

> The body of the mythical Pehuenche *dirigente* [political representative], Nicolasa Quintremán Calpán, appeared this morning floating in the water of the artificial lake Ralco. According to initial reports, the Pehuenche *dirigente*, who had problems with her vision, accidentally fell into the dam's basin. (Osses 2013)

The same press release points out a piece of information that should lead us to deeper reflection:

> Nicolasa Quintremán Calpán, 74, along with her sister Berta were strong opponents of the Ralco hydroelectric plant project in Alto Bío Bío, staging numerous demonstrations and voicing to anyone who would listen that "not even death" would remove them from their land. And so it was.

Further down, the report indicates that "María Curriao, *dirigente* from Alto Bío Bío, appealed to ancestral wisdom to understand what happened, adding that it's a pity to know that one of the historic women of Alto had succumbed to the same waters that she opposed so much" (ibid.). We learn from the same source that once the *Carabineros* (Chilean police force) completed the investigation, with the authorization of the prosecutor on duty, Nicolasa Quintremán's body was transferred to the medical legal institute for a rigorous autopsy in the town of Los Ángeles,[8] although they anticipated that the cause of the "accidental death" would be the fall and asphyxia.

To find out more about Nicolasa Quintremán's struggle, we draw on an article in *El País*, a newspaper from Spain, the origin of the company in charge of the construction of the Ralco hydroelectric plant.[9] In order to contextualize information about Nicolasa's death almost two months after it occurred, the report states the following:

> Ralco, meaning 'water dish' in the Pehuenche language, is the name with which Endesa baptized the large hydroelectric dam that they constructed near the communities of Queupuca Ralco and Ralco Lepoy, in the upper reaches of the Bío Bío river, 120 kilometers southeast of Los Ángeles, an area with a rainy and cold climate, where four thousand people of the Pehuenche Mapuche ethnic group lived … In 1997 they began excavation work of 9.2 meters in diameter and 7 kilometers in length, an area that was completely coated in concrete. In December 2000, Endesa began to divert the waters of the Bío Bío river, whose hydrographic basin of approximately 24,000 square kilometers runs about 400 kilometers from its source in the Galletué lagoon to its mouth at the sea. Thus, it channeled the river through a 500-meter-long and 13.5-meter-wide tunnel. (Cuentas 2014)

Resorting to a type of description that focuses on the political history behind Nicolasa's death, as many others who covered the sad news have done, is not by chance. In fact, historiography never is. Let's go back. Why? Here is the answer:

This is the context that then-president of Endesa Rodolfo Martín Villa declared to the media: "Chile is enviable in terms of its rule of law, it has good politicians, governors, and administrators, and it is trustworthy for anyone who wants to make investments there." Meanwhile, Nicolasa Quintremán came before the Chilean Congress to express: "To make Ralco is to kill the river, and its people along with it." (Cuentas 2014)

Without a doubt, Nicolasa Quintremán was right. However, if we focus only on this point, we will ignore other possible paths of historiography. I might embarrass Walter Benjamin a bit for not following his recommendations to discriminate between big and small protagonists, since nothing that happened can be ignored, forgotten (see Seoane 2018). It is not my intention to make the German philosopher, thinker, and historian uncomfortable—quite the opposite.

The 2004 documentary film *Apaga y Vámonos*, by Manel Mayol, showed the difficulties faced by the indigenous communities that protested the construction of the dam, who were deemed "terrorists" for subverting the order. It also suggests a possible reason why the directors of this megaproject were not very sensitive to the demands of the Pehuenche. The film highlights the background of Endesa's then-president. He was the national head of the Falangist student union, civil governor of Barcelona during Francisco Franco's military dictatorship, deputy of the Popular Party during the presidency of José María Aznar, and director of the commission for the Prestige oil spill. (Cuentas 2014)[10]

With the help of this media source, we learn of the various problems that the project had to face, among them verdicts of the Inter-American Court of Human Rights, not one, but five, against the Chilean government. It is difficult to explain why the following quote is more important than the previous ones, or the ones that were omitted and silenced. I can only suggest that they all show us the devastating consequences of the construction of said dam. The quote that I present below frames the story of this document:

In May of 2004 the flood occurred in the ancestral cemetery of Quepuca Ralco, where the remains of 56 people were found. Endesa knew of the situation with that cemetery and the consequences that carrying out the project would pose. Even so, the company decided to continue. (Cuentas 2014)

Having presented the historiographical context, we return to Nicolasa Quintremán, who asserts: "I don't have a reason to leave. Dead I will leave my lands, but not alive" (ibid.). Death therefore is not the end of life. *El Am* (Foerster 1993: 64–65), a term that is difficult to translate which refers to the spirit or energy that accompanies the body, will then continue with its journey.

On 23 July 2017, the listeners of a national radio station, Radio Cooperativa (2017), and readers of its webpage heard the news that several families from the island of Rapa Nui had begun burying their dead in their yards due to the saturation of the municipal cemetery of Hanga Roa, the main town of the island:[11]

> The cemetery is almost at capacity, and this has required a return to old traditions, which are incompatible with health regulations. The death of the *Nua* [matriarch] Ana Lola Tuki Teave at 91 years old last weekend was the occasion. On Monday her family buried her on the grounds of her house, in the middle of the town of Hanga Roa, where Ana raised 18 children and founded the Tuko Tuki clan. (Silva 2017)

The local leader Mai Teao remarked that due to the collapse of the cemetery, they have made efforts to enter more dead into said land, but it is complicated because they are always running up against other bodies. For its part, the Ministry of Health, through the Ministerial Secretariat of Health, warns Rapa Nui people that what they are doing goes against Article 135 of the health code:

> Article 135. The burial of corpses or human remains may only be buried in legally authorized cemeteries. However, the Director General of Health may authorize temporary or perpetual burial of cadavers in places that are not cemeteries, according to conditions established in each case. (Ministry of Health 1967)

In facing this situation, Tarita Alarcón—governor of the province of Easter Island between 2018 and 2021—reminded authorities that that theirs was not the only case and stated that "island personalities should be offered the same exceptions as those on the continent, who in some cases are buried in churches" (Radio Cooperativa 2017). Since the argument was strong, the right-wing senator and island representative Francisco Chahuan[12] assured that it was necessary to reconcile ancestral customs with the law in special cases, such as this one.

> As part of the traditions that have been conserved through the passage of time, there is the Rapa Nui funeral. This celebration, in the past, consisted in various mortuary rites that were carried out in a rigorous form according to the tradition, which said that the corpse should be wrapped in reed mats and moved by stretcher to an open-air space near the coast, where they would raise mounds of stones called *pipi horeko* to indicate the sacredness of the enclosure. (Castillo et al. 2011: 27–28)

Due to the influence of the Catholic Church, today in Rapa Nui the dead tend to be veiled in their homes, where they are accompanied by family and friends. It is normal to perform Catholic prayers and songs in the Rapa Nui language. The next day, the coffin is carried to the church in a procession. Following the funeral mass, the coffin is taken by caravan to the cemetery. Once in place, they proceed to the burial of the coffin, where it is covered with earth and natural flowers left by attendees. After a week, it is customary for close relatives to host a Rapa Nui *curanto*, a meal collectively cooked and offered to large crowds. Prayers and songs in honor of the deceased are performed for a month. The invitation, then, is to pay attention to how all the dead on the island look toward the sea. It cannot be another way. Moreover, the island is a grand space where living and departed cohabitate, under the watchful eye of "moai tangata, moia pa'a pa'a y moai vi'e" (Seelenfreund 2001: 31), the traditional sculpture figures of Rapa Nui.

Now let us review work carried out by Marcelo Maureira and colleagues on the funeral rites in northern Chile among the Aymara, Quechua, and Atacameño people.[13] Their conclusions state:

> The understanding of death among Andean communities in Chile presupposes this event as a culmination of a stage within the life cycle. The body and soul will separate to move to a new plane, without thinking of death as an end, but as a process of continuity of life based on the transition of the soul ... The soul of the deceased can move around in one's own earthly space together with the living, or stay within the spiritual world. No matter what kind of space the soul is in, the living maintain great attention to it, so that living and dead co-exist in an interrelation that can develop itself continuously through the birth and death of new generations within the community ... Therefore, death is much more than an event that indicates an end. The souls indicate the beginning of a new cycle of life, initiating a path that they do not walk alone, but they are accompanied by the entire community. (Maureira et al. 2018: 179)

In this same publication we can find the following story reported orally by the Aymara teacher Marcos Jiménez Mamani in 2016:

> Who are the *achachilas* [tutelary spirits]? The grandparents who passed away. When a grandparent dies, they become *achachilas* and they go to the hills, to the *malkus* [spirits of mountains], that is why when one asks for this ceremony of the *wilancha* or of the *pawa*, one always says: "We ask permission from the *achachilas*, or from the ancestors, or from the hills, protective *malkus*." This way everything is clearly marked. (Maureira et al. 2018: 159)[14]

Under the watchful eye of the *malkus*, the hills, the *achachilas*, we live until the moment of our departure, as Aymara poet Pedro Humire (1990) reminds us:

> Maybe then you can tell me
> That love that you keep for me.[15]

Those who visit, have visited, or will visit the south of this territory called Chile are able to observe how in those territories that have been saved from the great timber plantations of cash crop trees, such as the historically imported *Eucalyptus globulus*, what predominates the landscape is the native forest. It is not difficult to empathize with the Belgian engineer Gustave Verniory. In his travel diary, while working in 1889 on the construction of the railway line from Victoria to Tolten within the recently "incorporated" Araucanía, he writes about that "jungle" that flooded everything:

> From far away it looks like a compact mass of dark green; there is not the slightest transition between the pampas and the forest; one literally collides with this block of green. The trail entrance opened 15 days ago only looks like a black hole over the green backdrop ... I ask myself if I am dreaming, if it is really me who finds himself among this fabulous vegetation. (Verniory 1975: 115–116)

Today this landscape is different, or maybe it is us who are different because we are not moved by the absence of those grand trees with dazzling leaves, which, intelligently, unlike their European relatives, did not change their leaves with the arrival of autumn.

In writing about trees, volcanoes, and lakes in the Mapuche region, Skewes and Guerra (2016: 63) tell us: "In the Andean Mapuche world, from a contemporary materialist perspective, the *descansos* [small memorials held to commemorate a dead person] reveal the role of the trees, together with the lakes and volcanoes, in shaping a landscape that, in its generative processes, integrates human, non-human, and spiritual beings equally." The identification between trees and *che* ('person' in the Mapuche language Mapuzungun) is what allows, in Catholic terms, the transubstantiation. The mystery of faith that allows us to understand the transformation of bread and wine into the body and blood of Christ during the Eucharist is replaced in the Mapuche perspective on death by the *anülmapun*, a ceremony held to show respect to spiritual forces inhabiting a territory. As suggested by José Quidel Lincoleo (2016: 717), *anülmapun* is "a key term that shows us the intense relationship between the *che* and the *mapu* [land, world, territory]. Rite of reproachment, knowledge, negotiation, and payment to establish a group, *reyñma* [family], with the existing *geh mapu* [spirit masters of people]."

Quidel's definition complements Pichinao's (2015) and his colleagues' commentaries on the equilibrium between different *mogen* (forms of life) that inhabit the *mapu*. Along with Skewes and Guerra, I think that the *descansos*, the *mallku*, *ahu* spirits, and *ngen* spirit masters, among others, appear on our horizon of knowledge when we can open ourselves—or 'displace ourselves', as Skewes and Guerra (2016) suggest—toward the relationship between life and death and its relationship with nature, or rather, with the other lives that pass through the territory we inhabit. This last point is an invitation to break from the prominence of a type of thinking to the detriment of indigenous thought and, clearly, of indigenous people themselves. One of those connections that deserves to be investigated is the relationship between the Mapuche and the great trees, known in Mapuzungun as *koyan*, and classified as *Nothofagus obliqua*, the Patagonian oak. This relationship does not deserve to be studied to increase the unequal relationship of knowledge between Mapuche and non-Mapuche, but to aspire to other forms of comprehension that will allow us to heal the disastrous relationship that this territory called Chile maintains with its land and its inhabitants—both those who are present and those who are absent.

To conclude, let me refer once again to poetry. The verse by Mapuche poet Bernardo Colipán Filgueira (2011) perfectly captures my reflections on indigenous relations with death and the past:

> If one day they steal your breath
> I will blow my spirit
> inside of you

Throughout my life I have taught that memory, as opposed to historiography, is the antidote to oblivion. But the meaning of this memory includes the living and the dead, the present and the absent, and, without a doubt, all the territory and the life forms that pass through it. Or, to be consistent with the reflection shared here, it is *Itrofil Mogen*, a term in Mapuzungun indicating that all life forms are thought to be equally valuable and part of the same *mapu*.

Going back to poetry, it was a poet, Leonel Lienlaf, who taught me that the most urgent fight of indigenous communities is for their cemeteries, because whoever chooses where to bury their dead are owners of their territory. I would only add that they are owners together with their ancestors, nature, the cosmos. Beautiful metaphor. Pure poetry: life, death.

Claudio Millacura Salas is the Academic Coordinator of the Cátedra Indígena at Universidad de Chile, and an Assistant Professor in the Department of Anthropology at the same university. He has worked in different academic positions in the Americas, Europe, and Oceania. Most of his published work addresses issues related to intercultural education and ethno-history, which are also his main research interests.

Notes

1. Temuco city/underneath you/my ancestors/are sleeping.
2. This epilogue is an excerpt from Claudio Millacura's contribution to the seminar "Patrimonio, su dinamismo y los cambios sociales," held on 28 May 2021, Recoleta Municipality, Cultura es Recoleta. See https://www.youtube.com/watch?v = J2HxyTA6Z6M.

3. This expression was used by President Patricio Aylwin Azócar (1990–1994) to justify the need to not pressure the transition to democracy after the military dictatorship (1973–1990).

4. In the referendum of 25 October 2020, a grand majority, nearly 82 percent, voted in favor of drafting a new constitution to replace the previous version, which was implemented without public scrutiny in 1980 during the dictatorship of Augusto Pinochet. Currently, a constitutional convention elected with indigenous representatives, gender parity, and many representatives from civil society organizations are drafting the new constitution.

5. The term *patrimonializador* in Spanish refers to the controversial transformation of practices and ideas as cultural heritage. While the endowment of heritage status can offer new possibilities for public valorization, it can also work to strip indigenous ideas and practices of their experiential, ethical, and political meanings.

6. See Ratti and Giordano (2018) for a summary of this statement.

7. See Bugallo et al. (2016) for more on this point.

8. City and municipality located in the southern region of Bío Bío, also known as Region IX. Los Ángeles served as a military fort that during the Chilean invasion, misnamed at the time as the "pacification of the Arucanía" (in the nineteenth century), played a strategic role in the process of incorporating Mapuche territories into Chile. For more information, see Contreras (1943).

9. The corporation responsible for the construction of Ralco was Endesa Chile, a subsidiary of a company of the same name, of Spanish origin. Ralco is currently owned by the Italian Enel.

10. Falange is a term referring to the only two political parties allowed during Franco's fascist rule in Spain (1939–1975). Falangist ideology was founded on a corporativist principle inspired by Italian fascism and a trust in conservative Catholic ideals. The Prestige oil spill in 2002, which took place in the northern region of Galicia, was one the largest environmental disasters in the recent history of Spain.

11. Previously known as Easter Island, Rapa Nui was incorporated as a colony to the Chilean territory in 1888.

12. Politician from the National Renovation Party, and senator for the 6th constituency, Valparaíso Region, between 2018 and 2026. Rapa Nui is part of this electoral district.

13. The lands occupied by these three indigenous groups are in the territories that we know today as Argentina, Bolivia, Chile, and Peru.

14. *Wilancha* is a ritual where llamas are sacrificed for good will. *Pawa* is an incantation carried out around a table with symbolic offerings to Andean spirits and deities.

15. This is an excerpt from the poem "A las manos de una joven indígena" (At the hands of a young indigenous woman) written by Aymara poet Humire (1990).

References

Bugallo, Lucila, and Mario Vilca. 2016. *Wak'as, diablos y muertos: Alteridades significantes en el mundo andino* [Wak'as, devils, and dead: Significant alterities in the Andean world]. San Salvador de Jujuy: Universidad Nacional de Jujuy-EDIUNJU-IFEA.

Castillo, Elizabeth, Andrea Leiva, Macarena Marticorena, Mariela Meza, and Mónica Novoa. 2001. "Investigación de Algunas Tradiciones de Isla de Pascua Para un Encuentro Cultural: 'Acercando Rapa Nui a la Educación Preescolar'" [Research on some Easter Island traditions for a cultural encounter: "Bringing Rapa Nui closer to preschool education"]. Undergraduate thesis, Pontificia Universidad Católica de Valparaíso.

Colipán Filgueira, Bernardo. 2011. "Foja de Poesía No. 313." *Círculo de Poesía*. https://circulodepoesia.com/2011/09/foja-de-poesia-no-313-bernardo-colipan/.

Contreras, Domingo. 1943. *La ciudad de Santa María de Los Ángeles: Estudio histórico* [The city of Santa María de Los Ángeles: A historic study]. 2 vols. Santiago: Editorial Zigzag.

Cuentas, Sara. 2014. "Nicolasa Quintremán y el territorio sagrado del Bío Bío" [Nicolasa Quintremán and the sacred territory of Bío Bío]. *El País*, 20 February. https://elpais.com/elpais/2014/02/20/planeta_futuro/1392913018_924314.html.

Foerster, Rolf. 1993. *Introducción a la Religiosidad Mapuche* [Introduction to Mapuche religiosity]. Santiago: Editorial Universitaria.

Humire, Pedro. 1990. "Poesía Aymará: A las manos de una joven indígena" [Aymara poetry: At the hands of a young indigenous woman]. *Fortín Mapocho*, 16 December. http://www.bibliotecanacionaldigital.gob.cl/bnd/628/w3-article-556173.html.

Lienlaf, Leonel. 2018. *La Luz Cae Vertical* [Light falls vertical]. Santiago de Chile: Lumen.

Maureira, Marcelo, Sophia Cornibert, and Waldo Olavarría. 2018. "Los vivos se desviven por los muertos: Expresiones fúnebres entre los aymaras, quechuas y atacameños en el Norte de Chile" [The living care about the dead: Funerary expressions among Aymara, Quechua, and Atacameño peoples from northern Chile]. *Revista Rumbos TS* 17: 153–183.

Ministry of Health (Republic of Chile). 1967. "Código Sanitario. D.F.L. No. 725/67." Diario Oficial, 31 January. https://www.bcn.cl/leychile/navegar?idNorma = 5595.

Osses, Sergio. 2013. "Encuentran muerta a dirigente pehuenche Nicolasa Quintremán en aguas del lago Ralco" [Pehuenche leader Nicolasa Quintremán found dead in the waters of Lake Ranco]. *Biobiochile.cl*, 24 December. https://www.biobiochile.cl/noticias/2013/12/24/dirigente-pehuenche-nicolasa-quintreman-aparece-muerta-en-aguas-del-lago-ralco.shtml.

Pichinao, Jimena. 2015. "Ontología mapuche y catástrofes telúricas" [Mapuche ontology and telluric catastrophes]. In *Comunidades de América Latina: Perspectivas Etnográficas de Violencia y Territorio desde lo Indígena* [Communities of Latin America: Ethnographic perspectives on violence and territory from an indigenous point of view], ed. Lurgio Gávilan and Vicente Torres, 181–189. Cusco: Ceques Editores.

Quidel Lincoleo, José. 2016. "El quiebre ontológico a partir del contacto mapuche hispano" [The ontological break produced by the Spanish-Mapuche contact]. *Chungará* 48 (4): 713–719.

Radio Cooperativa. 2017. "Isla de Pascua: Familias optan por entierros en predios propios por saturación de cementerio" [Easter Island: Families opt for burial in their own property due to saturation of the cemetery]. 23 July. https://www.cooperativa.cl/noticias/pais/rapa-nui/isla-de-pascua-familias-optan-por-entierros-en-predios-propios-por/2017-07-23/120016.html.

Ratti, Camilo, and Pablo Giordano. 2018. "En el mundo andino, la vida y la muerte son dos caras de la misma moneda" [In the Andean world, life and death are two sides of the same coin]. Alfilo. https://ffyh.unc.edu.ar/alfilo/en-el-mundo-andino-la-vida-y-la-muerte-son-dos-caras-de-la-misma-moneda/.

Seelenfreund, Andrea. 2001. "Isla de Pascua: Arte escultórico, poderes de los antepasados" [Easter Island: Sculptural art, powers of the ancestors]. *Alas y Raíces* 3: 26–32. https://repositorio.uft.cl/xmlui/handle/20.500.12254/1079.

Seoane, Andrés. 2018. "Walter Benjamín, el filósofo que venció al olvido" [Walter Bejamin, the philosopher who defeated oblivion]. *El Cultural*, 25 January. https://elcultural.com/walter-benjamin-el-filosofo-que-vencio-al-olvido.

Silva, Tamara. 2017. "En Isla de Pascua comenzaron a enterrar a los muertos en patio de las casas: Cementerio está colapsado" [On Easter Island they began to bury the dead in their courtyards: Cemetery is collapsed] *Soychile.cl*, 23 July. https://www.soychile.cl/Valparaiso/Sociedad/2017/07/23/477352/En-Isla-de-Pascua-comenzaron-a-enterrar-a-los-muertos-en-patio-de-las-casas-cementerio-esta-colapsado.aspx.

Skewes, Juan Carlos, and Debbie Guerra. 2016. "Sobre árboles, volcanes y lagos: Algunos giros ontológicos para comprender la geografía mapuche cordillerana del sur de Chile" [On trees, volcanoes, and lakes: Some ontological turns to understand the Mapuche geography of southern Chile]. *Intersecciones en Antropología* 17 (1): 63–76. https://www.redalyc.org/articulo.oa?id=179547329005.

Verniory, Gustave. 1975. *Diez años en Araucanía, 1889–1899* [Ten years in Araucanía, 1889–1899]. Santiago: Ediciones de la Universidad de Chile.

INDEX

aesthetic(s), 26, 153, 155
  'Amerindian relational', 26, 41n3, 155
  battlefield of Huni, 39
  connections between people, 111, 114
  Huni Kuin art of relating, 29
  on its transcultural applicability, 40n2
  modulation of perspectives, 60
  relational, 42
  treatment of meats and leathers, 54
affinity, 41n7, 79n2, 128, 155
  founding place in Amerindian world,
    149
  'potential', 68–69, 78, 146
  symmetrical, 28
alliance(s), 125–126, 129, 132–134, 138
Alto Bío Bío, 69–74, 76, 164
Alto Purus River, 29
alterity, 87, 127–128, 138
  "deadly alterity," 100n7
  economy of, 27
  identity and, 86
  negotiation with, 142n13
  and rivalry, 150
Amazon, 27, 42n15, 115
  northwest (region), 105
  northwest people, 105, 117
Amazonia, 68, 74
  Amerindian, 27–28
  Western, 26, 37, 120, 147
Amazonian ethnologies, 146
  indigenous philosophies, 107, 112
  indigenous societies, 95, 106, 147–148
  model of warfare, 148
  ontologies, 117, 126
  perspectivism, 60

  pet-keeping, 154
  Western Rainforest, 40
Amerindian cosmologies, 6, 10, 79
  dualisms, 107
  ethnology, 'ontological turn', 27
  logic of perspectivist inversions, 29
  notion of kinship, 69
  ontology, 34, 41n2, 126
  people(s), 26, 80n6, 88
  personhood, 39
  relational aesthetics, 41n3
  sociality, 27, 125, 139
  theory of relations, 63
  war, 96
anaconda-becoming, process of, 29, 32
Andean societies, 8
  animism, 49
  communities in Chile, 167
  difference of perspectives, 62
  ethnological literature, 146
  modulation of perspectivism, 61
  peasant, 141
  shepherds, 47
Andes, the, 60, 62
  Argentinean, 48, 147
animal-becoming, 32
  -butchering, 48
  -shepherd bundle, 61
  -skinning process, 53
animú, 50, 52, 54–55, 60, 62
Apiao, island of, 124–127, 135, 142n1
Apiao people, 125–126, 131, 134, 138,
    141, 143, 147
Araucania, 168
Argentina, 47, 49

Argentinean Chaco, 83–84.
  Andean Highlands, 3, 5
  See also Gran Chaco
Arnold, Denise, Y., 52, 59–61
art of singing, 32
asymmetry, 41n4, 125–127, 133, 138, 140, 146–147
Augusta, Fray Félix José de, 74
autonomy, 69–70, 72, 74–78, 86, 126, 128, 134, 146
ayahuasca, 27, 31, 39.
  -based visionary practice, 148
  See also *huni*
Aymara highlands, 52
Aymara people, 167
  achachilas, 168
Aweti, 104–118, 119n6
  personal names, 106

Bío Bío river, 164
body-collective, 29
body/bodies, permeability of, 90
Bonning, Ewald, 80n8
Brazil, central, 6, 12, 104–105, 115
Brazilian coast, 115
Buenos Aires, 83, 98
butchering, 52, 57, 62
  ethnography of, 59
  sequence, 50–51
  topologies of, 49, 53, 60

Candea, Matei, 127, 135
Caniguan, Jaqueline, 74
Cashinahua, 40n1
cemetery/cemeteries, 165–166, 169
chedungun (Pehuenche language), 71
chiefdom(s), 27
  Aweti, 118
  Upper Xinguano groups, 106, 111–112, 114
Chile, 162–163, 165
  northern Chile, 167
  southern Chile, 68, 72, 75, 78
Chiloé, 124
Clastres, Pierre, 27
Coelho de Souza, Marcela, 115–116 120n16
Col, Giovanni da, 127, 135
Colipán Filgueira, Bernardo, 169
community, multi-lingual, 106
commensality, 11

consubstantiality, processes of, 86, 89, 91, 95, 97–98, 127
copla(s), 56, 63, 64n7
  ronda de, 56–57, 59
corporeal support, 74–75, 77, 79n3
corral (animal corral), 47, 50
  de lana, 55
  folding and wrapping operations, 49, 53, 55
  forms and forces, 48, 55, 62
  gut *corral*, 51–52, 57–58
Costa, Luiz, 154
Course, Magnus, 73, 75–77, 79n2
cross-cousin, 107, 110, 112–113, 155.
  See also relation(s), 'brother-in-law'

Daribi onomastic system, 118
death, 76, 84, 87, 89–90, 93, 163, 165
  'alaxaic ('death madness'), 94–95, 97–98
  consubstantiality and, 90
  as a gradual murder, 88
  Mapuche, 80n6
  and past, 165–169
  as a process of continuity of life, 167
Dennett, Daniel, 33
descent, native theory of, 106–107, 111, 116
Descola, Philippe, 7, 27, 41n4, 139
design
  agency of, 38
  Huni Kuin, 26
  labyrinth, 30, 37
  production in painting and weaving, 36
  xunu, 38
difference, 118, 136
dirigente (political representative), 164
dividual(s), 3
dividualism, 146
domesticate, to, 136
domination, 127, 132, 146
  alternation of, 147
Dransart, Penny, 64n6
dualism, 34, 39, 48
duality, 70, 74
  am-corporeal support, 74
  autonomy and dependence on others, 13
  relational, 72, 74–75, 78
  seeing and singing, 33

Eastern Island, 166
El País (newspaper), 164
"enchanted animals," 72
enemy, 87, 94, 96–98
engaging with animals, modes of, 8
   animism, 7–8, 27, 49
   hunting, 8, 147
   mutuality, 8, 14, 39
   pastoralism, 5, 8, 49, 145
enmity, 28, 61, 92, 149
exchange, logic of, 137. *See also* gift
   exchange system

Fausto, Carlos, 28, 80n4, 154
Formosa (province), 83, 99n3
fractality, 145
friendship, 139, 157
funerary practices, 69, 74, 76. *See also*
   ritual, funeral

gaze, the, 37–38, 55, 60, 63
   mutuality of, 39
   as a relational process, 54
Gê peoples (central Brazilian), 105,
   115–116
Gell, Alfred, 33, 37, 43n16
gift exchange system, 125–126
   counter-gift, 132
   symmetrical reciprocity, 133
Gran Chaco (region), 83, 86, 100n7
   Chaco enemies, 96
   Chaco war, 87
   Chaco warrior, 97
greeting practice(s), 69, 73–75, 77
Guaycurú group(s), 83
Guerra, Debbie, 168
Guerreiro, Antonio, 111–112

Hanga Roa, 166
Hénaff, Marcel, 127, 139
heritage, 163
Herzfeld, Michael, 135
hierarchy, perspectival, 132
Holbraad, Martin, 156
hospitality, 124–128
   manipulative, 135
   obligatory ritual, 140
Huachichocana, 47–49, 53, 60, 62–63
Hugh-Jones, Stephen, 112, 115, 117,
   120n16, 146
huni, 29, 31

Huni Kuin, 26, 28–29, 33–34, 37, 40n1,
   42nn14–15, 147–148, 150, 155
txana ibu, 28
huni song(s), 31
   healing, 39
   seeing and singing duality, 33

image-beings, 33
individuation (of persons), 86, 90, 94,
   97–98, 117
Ingold, Tim, 37, 43n16
interconnectedness, 85
inversion, dynamic of, 39

Jujuy Province, 49

Kalapalo, 111
kalül, 74–75. *See also* corporeal support
Kanamari, 28
Kelly, José, 93
Kerbrat-Orecchioni, Katherine, 134
kindred, cognatic, 91, 93
Küchler, Susanne, 42n15

Laishi, 91
Lévi-Strauss, Claude
   Amerindian dualisms, 107
   analogy of a hinge, 69
   brothers-in-law, 149
   'dualism in perpetual disequilibrium',
      34, 146
   egalitarian political system in lowland
      South America, 27
   'Klein bottle' configuration, 30
   model affinity and relations with
      strangers, 68
   on name and identity, 115
   on two restaurant guests exchange,
      140
Lienlaf, Lionel, 169
Lima, Tânia Stolze, 27, 41n4, 126, 138
Locke, John, 70
Los Ángeles, town of, 164, 170n8

Mapuche people, 73, 79n2
   and great trees relationship, 168–169
Mapuche-Spanish dictionary, 74
master, the concept of, 27–29. *See also*
   domination
Maureira, Marcelo, 167

Mauss, Marcel, 125
Mayol, Manuel, 165
Melanesia, 3, 37, 42n15, 63, 64n3
merographic connection(s), 49, 59–63
Mesoamerica, 27, 63, 64n9
myth, 116
    Amerindian myth of the origin of the
        moon, 30, 42n10
    Dua Busen, 31
    Ehezu, 108, 118

name(s), 104–105, 117
    of dead enemies, 115
    as devices of counter-identity, 114, 116
    as a principle of alteration, 116
    as a relation, 118
    self-differentiation, 146
    transfer of, 112, 115–116, 118
    'true names' (*et ytoto*), 109, 114
name-giving practice, 108, 111, 116
naming, prohibition of, 110, 116
narrator(s), 108
negotiation, 128, 136, 137

onomastics, indigenous, 105
Ortner, Sherry, 135
other-becoming, process of, 31–32, 39,
    135–136
    'in betweenness', 34, 39, 159
otherness, 26, 69, 75, 127, 135
    dependence on, 72, 78, 86, 126, 134,
      146
Overing, Joanna, 4, 9–11, 41n5, 146

Panoan-speaking people, 28, 40n1
parente, 149–150
Passes, Alan, 10–11
patrimonialization, 163
pattern, 5, 26, 28–31
    apotropaic, 37
    geometric, 42n15
    labyrinth, 38
    peasant, 145
Pehuenche, 69–71, 76–78, 146, 164
perception, sensorial, 70–76, 78
    double, 71
    mutual, 74–75, 77–78
person
    che, 69–70, 73–74, 77, 79n2, 168
    huni, 29
    shiyaxawa, 84

personhood, 146
    in Amazonia, 42
    Amerindian, 39
    fractal, 29, 33, 42n15
    Pehuenche, 70
    Qom understanding of, 12
    shared, 73
perspectivism, 27, 39, 41nn3–4, 49,
    60–62, 146
Pitarch, Pedro, 60, 64n9
Pitt-Rivers, Julian, 138–139
Platt, Tristan, 48
predation, 27, 63, 86, 139
    Amerindian philosophy of, 87
    ontological, 60, 87
predator, 94, 96–97
proximity, excess of, 92–93
Puna (region), 49

Qom, 83, 93–94, 98, 99n2
    kinship system, 86, 92
    Möbius strip, 95, 97
    rural communities, 87, 99n3
    war, 95–96, 98
Quechua, 167
Quidel Lincoleo, José, 168

Ralco Dam (hydroelectric plant project),
    163–164
Ralco (lake), 164
Rapa Nui island of, 166
Rasmussen, Dennis, 157
reciprocity, 77, 127, 131
    betrayal, 136–137
    a cycle of circular, 136
    symmetrical, 133
regionalism, 3
relatedness, 68, 85, 94–95
relational excess, 84–85, 89–90, 93–94,
    96–98
relation(s)
    'brother-in-law', 107, 156.
    with enemies, 86
    fractal, 28
    host and guest, 127–132
    human/non-human, 27, 84, 96, 125,
      132
    killer-enemy, 96
    kin, 91–92, 94
    master-pet, 28
    as a means for knowledge, 105

mutually dependent, 59, 61, 105
network of, 86, 96, 98, 115
organs are, 51
predatory, 28, 49, 62
redundant relations of similarity, 61
symmetrical and asymmetrical, 27–29
topological, 61
transformative, 69
See also *parente*
resemblance(s), 37, 42n11, 47, 54–55,
    58–59, 61–62, 158, 160n15
morphological, 52
types of, 49–50
revenge, 50, 54, 83–94, 96–98
anti-, 83, 86, 94–96, 98
attacker(s), 89, 91–92, 95–96, 100n9
avenger(s), 86, 92, 96–98
contra, 92, 98, 100n9
as a duty, 88
Rio de Janeiro, 40
ritual
anülmapun, 168
`burial, 76, 166
fertility, 80n7
funeral, 77, 106, 134, 166
ingestion of the vine *huni*, 29
intake of ayahuasca, 27
huni songs, 29, 33
novenas, 131
offering and receiving, 127
señaladas (marking ceremonies), 49,
    55, 64n4
Rivière, Peter, 106, 125, 140
Rubenstein, Steven L., 136

sameness, 125–127, 135, 163
turn into difference, 136, 139
Santos-Granero, Fernando, 28, 41n5, 125,
    139
scheme, relational, 72
seña(s), 47, 50, 57–58, 61–62. *See also*
    resemblance(s)
shaman, 28, 84–85, 98
Pi'oxonaq, 87
Yube, 29
shepherd-hosts, 57
Skewes, Juan Carlos, 168
'slavery', 28
society, egalitarian, 27, 106
sorcerer, 95, 98, 112
conaxanaxae, 89

no-longer-relative-, 95
sorcery, 83, 85, 87, 89, 93–94, 96
attacks, 84, 87–88, 91, 97
badmouthing, 90
denanaxa'n, 93
envy, 88
incest and, 90
'logic of contagion', 90
murder, 86, 90, 96, 98
shamanic, 86
soul
body (*yuda yuxin*), 33
eye (*bedu yuxin*), 33
South America, 68, 84
indigenous, 3, 79n2, 86, 105, 138, 145
lowland(s), 27, 105, 121, 145
lowland societies, 86, 105, 121n21, 145
Southern Andes, 47, 51–52, 61
spirit
am (*ina mongen*), 70–71, 73, 75–77,
    80n8, 165
double-am, 74
evil, 74–75, 77
invisible double, 71–72, 75
ngen, 72, 80n5
Strathern, Marilyn, 15, 153
artifacts/patterns in Oceania, 42n15
individuals as units of a bigger sys-
    tem, 1
merographic connection, 59–60
Qom person as a network, 85
relation manifested through form, 37
on the term 'relation' in the English
    language, 104, 107
'work of seeing', 59
suerte (luck), 51–52, 60–62
familial, 54
suplicar (to implore), 134, 136
Sztutman, Renato, 41n5

taming, 62, 96, 125
of relations, 10–11, 105
'untamed relationality', 76
Taussig, Michael, 34
Toba, 85, 99n2. *See also* Qom
transformation, processes of, 32, 91, 95, 127
Tukano, 112, 115–117, 120n16
Tukanoan people, 39, 41n9
Tupi, 100nn7–8
-Guarani people, 106
-speaking group, 104, 108

Tumbaya (department), 49
Tupinambá, 115

Upper Xingu (region), 105–108, 116
Upper Xinguano people, 108, 119n4
uprising, 162

Verniory, Gustav, 168
vine, 29, 31–33, 35–37
visiting, 128
    etiquette, 131, 133
Viveiros de Castro, Eduardo, 68
    affinity and consanguinity distinction,
        11
    on the Araweté case, 96–97, 100n7
    'equivocations', 107
    indigenous onomastics, 105–106, 115

Wagner, Roy, 117
    "fractal person," idea of, 2
witch(es), 75, 88–89
    bewitched, 84
witchcraft
    attacks, 90, 99n4
    beliefs, 142n13
witranalwe, 69, 74–77

Xingu River, 104

Yanomami, 32
Yapita, Juan de Dios, 52, 59–61
Yube, 29–30, 32–36, 38–39, 41
    Ainbu, 36
    Xeni, 32
Yudjá, 27, 37, 41n4, 119n3

CPSIA information can be obtained
at www.ICGtesting.com
Printed in the USA
LVHW082044060522
718035LV00012B/372